Thoreau the Land Surveyor

UNIVERSITY PRESS OF FLORIDA

Florida A&M University, Tallahassee

Florida Atlantic University, Boca Raton

Florida Gulf Coast University, Ft. Myers

Florida International University, Miami

Florida State University, Tallahassee

New College of Florida, Sarasota

University of Central Florida, Orlando

University of Florida, Gainesville

University of North Florida, Jacksonville

University of South Florida, Tampa

University of West Florida, Pensacola

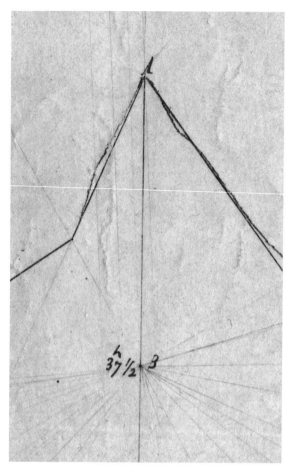

DETAIL, PRELIMINARY DRAFT OF WALDEN POND
SURVEY. In the winter of 1846, Henry Thoreau began
the composition of *Walden*, not with the drafting of sentences but with the drafting of a landscape. The line from
point A at the southern extremity of the pond was the
first measurement in his Walden survey. Point B is where
he stood with a tripod-mounted surveying compass on
the pond's frozen surface. Radiating outward from point
B are lines of bearing, labeled A through Z at the far
edges of the full-size document. The genesis of *Walden*
was a materialization of the earth's magnetic field, a
merger of mathematic and linguistic symbols transcribed
in physical contact with the pond itself and authored as
much by the compass needle as by Thoreau.

PATRICK CHURA

THOREAU THE LAND SURVEYOR

UNIVERSITY PRESS OF FLORIDA

Gainesville · Tallahassee · Tampa · Boca Raton
Pensacola · Orlando · Miami · Jacksonville
Ft. Myers · Sarasota

First cloth printing, 2010
First paperback printing, 2011

Library of Congress Cataloging-in-Publication Data
Chura, Patrick, 1964–
Thoreau the land surveyor/Patrick Chura.
p. cm.
Includes bibliographical references and index.
ISBN 978-0-8130-3493-5 (cloth: alk. paper)
ISBN 978-0-8130-4147-6 (pbk.: alk. paper)
1. Thoreau, Henry David, 1817–1862—Knowledge—Surveying.
2. Authors, American—19th century—Biography. 3. Surveyors—United States—Biography. 4. Surveying—United States—History—19th century. I. Title.
PS3053.C47 2010   818.3099—dc22
[B]   2010007782

The University Press of Florida is the scholarly publishing agency for the State University System of Florida, comprising Florida A&M University, Florida Atlantic University, Florida Gulf Coast University, Florida International University, Florida State University, New College of Florida, University of Central Florida, University of Florida, University of North Florida, University of South Florida, and University of West Florida.

University Press of Florida
15 Northwest 15th Street
Gainesville, FL 32611-2079
http://www.upf.com

Contents

Illustrations

Preface

Thoreau once told a surveying client that the essence of his job was finding what predecessors had left behind. All his life, as he explained to Abel Brooks in 1857, he had been "making bounds, or rather finding them, remaking what has been unmade."[1] This book remakes some of Thoreau's boundaries—not the many physical property lines he created while surveying but intangible markers, remnants of his life and character that have been lost or neglected. In part, it is a book about the recovery of history, a difficult but exhilarating process.

It began with a desire to know more about nineteenth-century surveying itself—about what Thoreau actually did to earn money from 1849 to 1861. In the chapters that follow, I reconstruct essential processes of his work in the field and explore their meaning. This nontraditional critical approach was taken in preparation for the book's other and more conventional aspect: a contextualized study of Thoreau's journals, letters, field notes and published works for what they reveal about his use of land surveying as both a method of environmental inquiry and a primary source of income over the last dozen or so years of his life.

Since my father was a land surveyor and I, like my three brothers, accompanied him on many surveying outings in the 1970s and 80s, I had a strong sense of what Thoreau's fieldwork involved. My father, now retired, was a good surveyor and civil engineer, but his theodolite was not much more technologically advanced than Thoreau's compass. His steel measuring tapes were not much different from the sixty-six-foot iron-and-steel Gunter's chain Thoreau used. The orange-and-white-striped range pole and philly rod I carried while helping my dad lay out parking lots and strip malls in the suburbs of Saint Louis thirty years ago were not essentially different from the "graduated staff" made of a birch sapling Thoreau used to sound the Concord River and conduct leveling experiments around Walden Pond.

My dad's career accounts for my initial interest in Thoreau's surveying, but there were others steps taken to prepare for this project. In the summer of 2006, I received a research grant from the University of Akron to spend some time in Concord with the Thoreau Survey Collection of the Concord Free Public Library. I worked primarily with the material in Thoreau's field notebook. The resulting article, "Economic and Environmental Perspectives in the Surveying 'Field-Notes' of Henry David Thoreau," parts of which are reproduced here, appeared in the *Concord Saunterer: A Journal of Thoreau Studies* in 2007.

To get some training with nineteenth-century tools and field methods, I took a course in historical surveying offered by the University of Akron Surveying and Mapping Department. We practiced in a dusty field near the campus tennis courts, using a replica brass compass and Gunter's chain. Our homework each week was to take the field notes we had made, "cast up" the data, and draft plane surveys of various shapes and levels of difficulty. Professors Gary Schuller and Mike Besch were generous with their knowledge, answering my many questions about antebellum surveying in general and Thoreau's work in particular. My six classmates, from whom I also learned much, were members of the university's historical surveying team.

With equipment on loan from the university and valuable help from Andy Kis, a recently returned veteran of the Iraq War who is now a land surveyor, I retraced, with compass and chain, some of Thoreau's old lines in Concord over several cold wet days in March 2008. After obtaining the necessary access permissions, Andy and I resurveyed an area that was meaningful to Thoreau at the western edge of Walden Pond. At Orchard House, we located and ran a 1,540-foot line Thoreau had surveyed on Bronson Alcott's property in 1857. Thoreau had indicated that he left a hickory stake and mound of fieldstones at the northwest corner of the property. Though the parcel is now subdivided into house lots, the old corner is still accessible. Near its location on an isolated wooded hillside we found more than a score of football-sized stones, scattered over a few square yards but clearly once arranged in a grouping. The next day, pacing distances on a draft survey Thoreau had made in an area south of

Walden, we came across a large oak, old enough to have been there in the 1850s, that had obviously been blazed—marked by a surveyor's axe—and still bore a prominent scar. We could not be absolutely certain that either one of these landscape alterations was Thoreau's work. But the trip was less about discovering monumentation than about walking briefly in Thoreau's footsteps and carrying out procedures that had shaped his consciousness.

The pond was only partially frozen that March, so we could not take our compass onto its surface as Thoreau had in the winter of 1846. We were nevertheless able to recreate several of the readings of bearing he took for his famous plan of Walden Pond. Using equipment very similar to his, we set up at the cabin site, positioning the legs of the tripod at the cabin threshold, and took bearings to the center of the pond and to the railroad tracks, reconstructing measurements at the core of the Walden survey. Though our sight lines were somewhat obstructed owing to the presence of more trees around the pond than there had been in the 1840s, our bearings were within a few degrees of Thoreau's. I recall copying down the angle made by the cabin, the center of the pond and the railroad—by our reckoning it was thirty-eight degrees—and standing for a moment behind the compass, transfixed by the view and by a feeling that the day had been meaningful.

Afterward, carrying the chain, compass box, tripod, auto level and range poles back along the wooded trail in the late-afternoon twilight, we encountered an elderly saunterer in a long gray overcoat, walking stick in hand, who observed us in passing. Perhaps he wondered if we were harbingers of some new encroachment on the woods, for he paused a few steps beyond us and politely called back, asking about our equipment. When I told him our story, he seemed quite pleased and exclaimed, "Oh, that's very interesting!" He understood, I think, that we were amateurs— as Thoreau himself had been when he measured the pond—and were there for reasons he could appreciate.

In July of 2008, I used a copy of Thoreau's preliminary sketch of Walden Pond first to reformulate the Walden field notes and then to redraw the map itself. These simple tasks became a thought-provoking, at times moving experience. When, in reproducing the beautifully radiating lines of the survey, the lines began to intersect and the pond began to take visible shape, I derived a sense of accomplishment that became a strong incentive to this project. To learn more about something Thoreau cared deeply about was important to me, but I was also thrilled to be recovering an unusual type of lost information. Poring over an enlarged copy I had made of the draft survey, I considered that I was reading a new Thoreau text.

In the process, certain things were revealed. I had been aware that Thoreau was a meticulous worker and thinker, but I was now more deeply impressed with the time-consuming nature of his drafting and how much life and mental energy his more than 165 land surveys had demanded of him. Reproducing the field notes had taken about twelve hours and drawing the Walden map another full day, during which I became completely engrossed in the tasks and lost all track of time. Doing what Thoreau did brought home the realization that the work required a type of focus, concentration and patience that is rare in this age of short attention spans. My immersion in numbers and geometry broke down my comfortable, self-limiting reliance on letters and language, awakening me to the possibility that mathematics had liberated Thoreau's thinking as well.

Several times during the writing of this book, I've been reminded of our encounter with the elderly gentleman in the Walden woods by reading about similar encounters in Thoreau's journal. Once while Thoreau was working in the Concord countryside, "an Italian with a hand organ" stopped to marvel at the surveyor's compass. Thoreau likened the man's inquisitiveness to the children who were "curious about *his* machine."[2] As the incident shows, the compass is an instrument capable of stirring fascination. Part of my argument here is that in Thoreau's hands it was not only a simple device for doing work, but a machine in the modern sense—a complex mechanism for modifying and transforming power.

While he was surveying the Kettell farm in April 1858, a woman approached Thoreau and said of his compass, "This is what regulates the moon and stars."[3] In his journal, Thoreau transcribed Mrs. Polly Houghton's interesting remark without comment. If he had been pressed for an interpretation, however, he might very well have acknowledged a form of truth in her observation. As this book will show, surveying tools often did serve Thoreau as a means of "regulating" his universe—of monitoring its characteristics, probing its truths and translating its laws.

On still another occasion, Abel Brooks, the nearly deaf landowner to whom Thoreau had explained his lifelong purpose of remaking boundaries, was fascinated by the compass but apparently less perceptive than Mrs. Houghton: "He did not in the least understand my instrument," Thoreau observed, "but had full faith that it knew the way straight through the thickest wood to missing bounds."[4] This book, though hopefully more discerning than the hard-of-hearing client, rests on a comparable faith that the compass points the way, leading to the discovery of significant lost bounds and lost measures in the life of Henry Thoreau.

Acknowledgments

For both surveyors and writers, it's hard to work alone. I could not have completed this project without much help and support.

For sharing their knowledge of historic surveying, I owe a debt of gratitude to Gary Schuller and Mike Besch of the University of Akron Surveying and Mapping Department. I am especially grateful to Andy Kis for giving up his spring break in March 2008 to survey with me in the fields and woods of Concord. At several stages of this project I also benefited from the professional advice of Barry Savage.

I would like to thank the Faculty Research Committee at the University of Akron for the grant that took me to Concord in 2006 to begin this research. During several trips to Concord I had valuable help from Leslie Perrin Wilson and Connie Manoli-Skocay of the Concord Free Public Library. Thanks also to Jan Turnquist at Orchard House, Denise Morrissey at the Walden Woods State Reservation, David Wood and Erin McGough at the Concord Museum, and Matthew Barrett at the Town of Concord Public Works Department.

Laura Dassow Walls provided expert editing of my original article on this topic and encouragement as the book developed. Richard Schneider and Sandra Harbert Petrulious responded thoughtfully to my work in progress. At University Press of Florida, Amy Gorelick deserves special mention for keeping this project on track, along with Jacqueline Kinghorn Brown and Ainslie Gilligan for their help in bringing it to completion. I am grateful as well to Hillary Nunn for her astute comments on the manuscript. Thanks also to my former teaching colleagues and the excellent students at DeSmet Jesuit High School in St. Louis, for many insights about literature and history.

While my brothers and I were growing up, there were many days when we cursed surveying, but this book wouldn't have happened if my dad, Thomas Chura, hadn't gotten us out of bed and made us help him with his fieldwork on many Saturdays. From him we learned to look for the lot corner until it was found.

For three years, my wife, Jolanta, and my children, Nicholas and Annika, listened patiently to my stories about Thoreau. To them most of all I am deeply grateful for the innumerable ways they shared in this work.

Thoreau the Land Surveyor

1

The Surveyor and the State

I feel that with regard to Nature I live a sort of border life, on the confines of a world into which I make
occasional and transient forays only, and my patriotism and allegiance to the state into whose territories I seem to retreat are those of a moss-trooper.

—Thoreau, "Walking"

BEFORE CAPTAIN JOHN SMITH was saved by Pocahantas, he was
saved by a surveyor's compass. Smith's *General History of Virginia, New
England, and the Summer Isles* tells of his being taken prisoner in 1607 by
the Algonquin king Opechankanaugh, the younger half brother of feder-
ation chief Powhatan. Expecting to be killed but attempting to make the
Natives "friendly . . . if possible" toward him, Smith presented his captors
with "a round ivory double compass dial" that had been used in his map-
making explorations of the Virginia coast. He describes the Indians "gaz-
ing in wonder at the playing of the needle," and their amazement when
he "demonstrated by that globe-like jewel the roundness of the earth and
skies." Just before Smith's intended execution, the Native king, who had
been carefully examining the instrument, held the compass aloft and
prompted his warriors to lay down their weapons. Smith was subse-

quently led to a meeting with Powhatan in the village of Orapaks, the site of the maiden Pocahantas's celebrated intervention on his behalf.[1]

The Pocahantas legend is a more romantic story than the compass anecdote, but the fact that a surveying instrument played a role in John Smith's survival carries greater cultural significance. Land surveying has long been a tool of empire, linked not coincidentally with the development and hegemony of white European society over Native peoples in the New World. One of the first to recognize this in the colonial period was English surveyor John Love, whose 1688 treatise *Geodaesia: or, The Art of Surveying and Measuring of Land Made Easie* became the standard surveying text in the English-speaking world. In his introduction to *Geodaesia*, Love traced dramatic analogies between the ability to measure land and the development of dominant, imperial civilizations. "In Egypt," he notes, "every rustick could measure his own land." In the Roman worldview, a man who "had not so much geometry in him as to know how to measure his field" was deemed "incapable of commanding a legion." *Geodaesia* extolled not only the political power surveying supported, but the qualities of character produced by the profession: "Besides the many profits this art brings to man, it is a study so pleasant, and affords such wholesome and innocent exercise, that we seldom find a man that has once entered himself into the study of geometry, or geodaesia, can ever wholly lay it aside." As an example of its practical uses, Love reminded readers that "the sounding of a river or a harbour, is a matter of great import, not only to seamen but all such as seamen live by." Of the surveyor's art, Love concluded that "none but unadvised men ever did, or do now speak evil of it."[2]

In ways Love could not have foreseen, the political development of the United States would owe a great deal to concepts and technologies of measurement. The geographical circumstances, cultural traits and legal traditions of colonial America—with limitless expanses to explore and clearly designated boundaries essential to land ownership—made surveying an indispensable technology. Along with any attempt at permanent settlement of the continent, and sometimes preceding it, came surveyors. It has been claimed that Native Americans referred to the surveyor's compass as the "land stealer";[3] whether this is legend or fact, Native Americans learned quickly that the presence of the white man with the compass—and the wooden stakes, stone monuments and tree blazes he left behind—foretold cataclysmic changes for their civilization. Historian Andro Linklater observes that the struggle for North America "everywhere depended on being able to measure and describe the land more precisely than the indigenous peoples could."[4] In the history of American continental conquest, cultures that measured accurately had distinct advantages over those that did not.

Once land was formally located and officially acquired, the multiple purposes of establishing individual ownership, taxable value and legal jurisdiction were embodied in the person of the land surveyor. The surveyor not only carried considerable state-invested power but swore an oath that affirmed his honesty, the accuracy of his measures, and his loyalty to the state's protocols of property definition and distribution. As a public trustee, the surveyor was an agent of state authority in areas where it had yet to be established and a crucial tool for maintaining the rule of law in a uniquely American system of law under which, for better or worse, property rights were the foundation and mainspring.

Schoolchildren are taught that George Washington's first career was land surveying. Perhaps teachers also mention that surveying instruction was frequently a part of a gentleman's education in the eighteenth and early nineteenth centuries. But the role surveying played in the accumulation of property that made Washington one of the country's largest landowners—and probably the wealthiest man in the United States at the time of the Constitutional Convention—is less well known. Washington began the study of surveying at the age of fifteen. In 1749, decades before he took the presidential oath, the seventeen-year-old took the oath of public office as surveyor of the newly formed Virginia county of Culpeper. Working for affluent private clients including the powerful Lord Fairfax, the energetic young man often exchanged his labor for the chance to lay claim to choice land tracts. In only about three years of active professional surveying, the future president made at least 190 surveys, earned cash income of about four hundred pounds, and became the owner of over a thousand acres of good land in the Shenandoah valley.[5] Washington is evidence of the potential of early American surveyors to tap into the prime source of wealth on the American continent and become "junior partners in the great land speculations of the day."[6]

Washington's surveying is significant here to the extent that it demonstrates the premeditated collaboration between the surveying profession and the colonial aristocracy in the maintenance of a hierarchical social order. The class-based privileges that surveyors enjoyed in Washington's day provided access to real estate, the most stable form of economic power in a property-based society. The running of lines across uncharted wilderness nurtured Washington's sense of universal order but also inculcated a deep respect for the rights of ownership.[7] Acknowledging the symbiosis between property rights and measuring skills, Washington touted the practical value of his surveying vocation: "Nothing can be more essentially necessary to any person possessed of a large landed estate, the bounds of some part or other of which is always in controversy."[8] Considering how well he benefited from the establishment and enforcement of boundaries, it is not surprising that Washington held rather conservative views on land tenancy and western settlement. Unlike Thomas Jefferson, Washington foresaw in the American West not a freeholder's empire, but the spread of traditional systems of labor relations, land tenure and race-class hierarchy.[9]

The same year Henry David Thoreau took up residence in his cabin on Ralph Waldo Emerson's land at Walden Pond, James Fenimore Cooper wrote a novel that did for the profession of land surveying what Melville's *Moby-Dick* did for whaling. If there is such a term, Cooper's 1845 *The Chainbearer* might be called a surveying romance. The novel is in no way the equal of Melville's in terms of philosophical depth, but it does a good deal of cultural work by illuminating the significance of land surveying in both early American social history and the politics of the mid-nineteenth century. As the novel opens, the figure of George Washington is used as a heroic model for the profession. "His Excellency," as the novel's title character refers to him, "was not only the best, but the honestest surveyor mankind had ever enjoyed." Cooper's working-class "Chainbearer," an aging Dutch surveyor, takes intense pride and "great exultation" in claiming Washington as a fellow professional who confirms the nobility of the calling: "It would be the happiest day of my life," Chainbearer reflects, "could I only carry chain while he surveyed."[10]

The protagonist of *The Chainbearer* is Mordaunt Littlepage, a Princeton-educated gentleman owner of a patrimonial estate in upper New York just after the Revolutionary War. Along with a conventional romantic-love plot, Cooper sets up an opposition between the ownership rights of the New York Dutch gentry, symbolized by Littlepage, and the situation of their land-poor tenant farmers who actually live and work on the estates. The latter are represented in the figure of Aaron Timberman, or Thousandacres, a squatter who illegally helps himself to the profitable timber resources on the land originally granted to Littlepage's ancestors. Politically, Timberman echoes a version of Lockean natural rights in a state of nature, asserting, "I respect possession, which ought to be the only lawful title to property, in a free country." Far from illegitimate as a concept, this idea found powerful expression in the post–Revolutionary War United States. Timberman's view that land belonged to those who "improved" it attained for many Americans the status of a professed creed, as did the desire, also expressed by Timberman, "to gather the harvest that comes of the seed of our own sowin' and plantin'."[11]

In *The Chainbearer*, Cooper uses the historical opposition between landowner and squatter not only to present an argument about the necessity of maintaining inviolable owners' rights in the emerging American republic, but also to comment directly on the Anti-Rent Wars then taking place in New York. During the 1840s and 1850s, New York farmers who lived as tenants on large estates owned by the patrician class built an insurgent movement aimed at destroying these estates and redistributing the land among themselves. By 1845, the Anti-Rent movement had tens of thousands of active, sometimes militant supporters.[12] Leaseholders responded with their own political program, forcing a national discussion about whether land should rightfully belong to those who lived on it or those who held juridical title to it. Responding to this political context in *The Chainbearer*, Cooper espouses conservative ideals and assails squatters' rights, portraying the landless tenant as a malicious extortioner and usurer. Tenants may have "taken the field in a literal sense," but they hold no claims comparable to "those who have taken it in the moral," the absentee landlords who legally own it.[13]

Ideologically, the landowner and the squatter are foils in Cooper's novel, but the real enemy of the landless tenant is the sidekick of the aristocratic hero, the gentle, loyal surveyor, Andries Coejemans, called Chainbearer for his skill in measuring land. As Cooper's narrator explains, "The man who measured land, and he who took it to himself without measurement, were exactly antagonistic forces, in morals as well as in physics." Though Timberman's opposition to surveying is general and philosophical—"A curse on all lines, in a free country, say I . . . they're an invention of the devil"—he is particularly resentful of the class-based alliance between the surveyor and the socioeconomic status quo. In the view of the Yankee squatter, the measurer of land is "born the servant of the rich, and will die their servant." As the Chainbearer himself surmises, Timberman wants "no chains and no chainbearers, no surveyors and compasses, no lots and no owners." This sounds like anarchy to the novel's gentleman protagonist, a man of property who does battle with forces of disorder that Cooper saw as a potential threat to the class system. The political alliance between Chainbearer and Littlepage symbolizes the mutually supportive relationship between surveyors and landowners in the late-eighteenth- to mid-nineteenth-century United States.[14]

What makes Cooper's novel unique and interesting is not its plot or assumptions about social class, which are quite conventional, but its depiction of the surveying profession in relation to a number of racial and cultural divisions operant in the novel's period of production. Among these is an explicit contrast between the value systems of the acquisitive New England Yankee and those of the country's "older money," the more genteel culture of the New York Dutch. As a young man, Chainbearer had been cheated of his land by a Yankee speculator; he is now able to contrast his friend and client Littlepage with Yankee landowners: "Yankees are the whole time trying to cut off a little here and to gain a little 'ere, so it is as much as a man's worth to carry a chain fairly between 'em." Toward Yankee surveyors, Cooper's novel expresses special disdain. A spokesman for Cooper's Dutch characters warns a gentleman landowner that "if one of them gets upon the tract, he will manage to carry off half the lant [sic] in his compass box!"[15]

Within the novel, surveying is the exclusive technology of the white male; for Cooper's alter ego, Littlepage, it offers the plainest evidence of the racial supremacy of the Anglo-American. With technologies of land appropriation in mind, Littlepage instructs the Native American Sureflint about the basis of his assumed superiority: "The white man is stronger than the red man, and has taken away his country, because he *knows* most." When the Onondago suggests other possible reasons for the power imbalance, Littlepage is forced to spell out his meaning: "Now, all the knowledge, and all the arts of life that the white man enjoys, come from the rights of property." Later in the novel, Sureflint seems to awaken to this truth, expressing an inchoate sense that, more than the white man's firewater, it is the compass and chain that have brought about the destruction of his culture. Though he despises the rapacious and "lawless" squatter Thousandacres, he cannot disagree with the outlaw's negative view of surveyors. When Thousandacres asks if the red man approves of the surveyor's tricks, Sureflint cannot "deny his own principles" and acknowledges that the Indian nations want no surveyors. He remarks, "It be bad to measure land, [I] will own. Nebber see anyt'ing good in measurin' land."[16]

Chainbearer himself, however, is exempt from Sureflint's scorn. In part because of his simple honesty but also because of his substantial skills as a woodsman, this surveyor occupies a neutral racial category in between the white settler and the Indian. The "habit of running straight lines" in tangled undergrowth has given his eye an accuracy almost equal to the "species of instinct" manifested by the Native American. Moreover, like Henry David Thoreau, another surveyor with a reputation for accuracy and a sympathetic identification with indigenous cultures, Coejemans makes a home in the wilderness, selecting a Walden-like location "surrounded by the magnificence of a bountiful vegetation." In this "deep forest seclusion . . . removed from the comfort, succor and outward communications of civilized life," Chainbearer builds his hut, "a low, solid structure of pine logs, that were picturesque in appearance, and not without their rude comforts." That the surveyor is a woodsman with a professionally destructive but personally nondestructive relation to the land is a key issue in Cooper's text. For the Indian Sureflint, the fact that the Chainbearer "live in wood wid him" makes him "*my* friend . . . one of *us.*"[17]

While Cooper's surveyor clearly shares a number of traits with Thoreau, there are meaningful differences between the two. First, Chainbearer is uneducated. Having no head for mathematics and thus lacking the "intellectual part" of the surveying profession, Andries measures the land with fidelity but is unable to calculate acreage and check his measurements. He therefore relinquishes authority over the results of his work, "employing men with heads better than his own to act as principals, while he still carried the chain." The fact that Chainbearer is "no scholar" makes all the more apparent his subservience to the landowner. The meek and deferential demeanor of the surveyor solidifies the author's depiction of a social order of clear and inviolable hierarchies. In Cooper's

world, the surveyor is heroic to the extent that he furthers American imperialism and serves the propertied classes. Honest, brave and modest
but skilled only in practical work, Andries is fit to reinforce, but not to
challenge, the economic order.[18]

Significantly, Chainbearer is also a slave owner. The reason he does
not live in a *solitary* cabin in the woods, as Thoreau did at Walden, is
that he requires two other cabins: "a place to contain the male slaves"[19]
and a separate hut to accommodate his niece's servant, a black female domestic attendant. The fact that slaves are Andries's only possession other
than his surveying equipment and a keepsake military sword from his
campaigns with Washington is revealing. Realistically, the Chainbearer
is not wealthy enough to own slaves. In order to make him more useful
to the political purposes of the novel, however, Cooper directly associates
the surveyor's upholding of land ownership with his upholding of slave
ownership. By the mid-nineteenth century, a major political question involved the extent to which the U.S. Constitution did the same thing. In
the 1840s, Cooper was not alone in recognizing that the constitutional
enshrinement of absolute owner autonomy effectively intertwined all
forms of property, including human, under the uniquely American legal
umbrella of absolute owners' rights.

Cooper's decision to locate this fundamental nexus in the person of
a land surveyor is by no means an ideological stretch or a far-fetched artistic maneuver. Uniting the two major forms of property in the character of Andries Coejemans aptly underscores a similar linkage made not
only in the Constitution but also in pre–Civil War discourse of sectional
conflict. During the two decades before the war, proslavery Southerners insisted on this association. Out of concern that their property rights
were being questioned by Northerners, they argued that national law explicitly protected both land and slaves, and that the federal government
could not discriminate between them. Cooper, realizing the broad con-
ceptualization of property at the core of the New York Anti-Rent Wars
and Southern proslavery doctrines, chose a slaveholding surveyor—an
open admirer of fellow slaveholding surveyor George Washington—to
embody his version of official American ideology. If, in Cooper's view, the
symbolic defender of juridically defined property in land also served well
as an exemplar of the right to own human chattel, it was because these

principles were joined in the Constitution and not separated until just after the Civil War.[20]

The Chainbearer, the literary product of a political context that included not only the New York Anti-Rent Wars but also an increasingly viable abolitionist movement, is both a landowners'-rights novel and a proslavery novel, a work of the mid-1840s that jointly champions property in soil and in human beings. At the center of Cooper's manifesto is a land surveyor whose work supports both causes. At one point in the novel, when the landowner-protagonist is imprisoned by the squatter, he is rescued by the surveyor, who is aided by a compass as well as his "long familiarity with the woods." When Chainbearer is mortally wounded while fighting for the landowner, his only expressed regret is that he dies "before the patent has been fully surveyed." For his role in the physical and ideological battle to maintain the antidemocratic social and legal strata of his community, the surveyor-hero Chainbearer is given "a warrior's grave."[21]

Thus in the mid-1840s one individualistic squatter and nascent literary figure was surveying the Walden woods for conspicuously antimaterialistic motives, not wanting to get his "fingers burned by actual possession,"[22] while another and very different land measurer was offered for public approval by an important establishment writer. As the personification of land law, Cooper's Chainbearer illustrates the inverse of Thoreau's squatter at Walden, whose surveying cleansed rather than created land boundaries. Though Chainbearer's life in the woods shares some traits with Thoreau's, Coejemans is politically the dark twin of the Walden surveyor, illustrating orthodox surveying practice, along with the role of such practice in perpetuating a transparently conservative political program. Cooper's conformist Chainbearer is the type of surveyor the American socioeconomic order could put to use, a competent and compliant lackey whose function is to preserve a romantic sense of Caucasian racial preeminence at the same time he *benignly* appropriates land, and *benignly* holds slaves. Though Cooper's novel was not widely read or reviewed, it took for granted the importance of land measurement to the development of American society while registering fascinating public perceptions of the surveying profession.

At about the time Cooper published *The Chainbearer*, Ralph Waldo

Emerson was sufficiently interested in the tug-of-war over absolute and limited conceptualizations of property to make them a central theme of his 1844 essay "Politics." This treatise, allegedly a direct influence on the political sentiments Thoreau expressed in "Resistance to Civil Government" and *Walden*, begins in the manner of many arguments over slavery in the 1840s: with the axiom that persons and property are "the two objects for whose protection government exists."[23] Adopting the vocabulary of labor- and land-reform movements as well as some terms of the incipient abolitionist cause, Emerson states that "doubts have arisen whether too much weight had not been allowed in the laws" to property in the maintenance of a structure that has "allowed the rich to encroach the poor, and to keep them poor."[24]

With land distribution apparently in mind, Emerson then notes the highly unequal existing allocation not only of property but of the power that accrues from it: "One man owns his clothes, and another owns a country." Using terms applicable to the discussion of both land and slaves, Emerson broaches the possibility that "the whole constitution of property, on its present tenures, is injurious . . . its influence on persons deteriorating and degrading." In the process of enumerating the legal guarantees that are under debate as he writes, Thoreau's friend refers pointedly to the role of the land surveyor, who physically enacts the distributive process: "This truth and justice," he observes, "men presently endeavor to make application of, to the measuring of land, the apportionment of service, the protection of life and property." Among the selected agents of the state's authority are by implication its surveyors, who facilitate land apportionment.[25]

Emerson's framing of the political crisis over forms of property, an issue of particular moment in the essay's period of production, remains general and superficial, like the essay's single-word title, which fails to convey an ideological agenda. Once we concede the strong association between politics and property in the 1840s, however, the almost-coded discourse comes into better view, and we realize that Emerson's argument, like Cooper's polemic in *The Chainbearer*, is about owners and owning. What Emerson means when he asserts that "property should make the laws for property and the person the law for persons," is that slave law and land law must be separated, but that they currently are not. That the discussion of the one entails the discussion of the other complicates attempts to mitigate the negative effects of either. Because the two have "mixed themselves in every transaction," inordinate power has accrued to the proprietors.[26]

"Politics" offers little guidance about exactly how to sunder such noxious conditions and few specifics about what a system free from such restrictive bonds should look like. Emerson remains content at this stage to wonder aloud whether the state ought not to align itself with the rights of persons to the exclusion of all else. "The tendencies of the times," he observes, seem to predict "a recognition of higher rights" than the inviolable nature of individual property in either of its two major forms. Seemingly anticipating Thoreau's sentiments in "Resistance to Civil Government," Emerson proposes that "good men must not obey the laws too well" and laments that he cannot recall "a single human being who has steadily denied the authority of the laws, on the simple ground of his own moral nature."[27]

In some ways, Thoreau would take it upon himself to heed the call, implicit in Emerson's treatise, for a man who would put conscience firmly before law. Doing so while becoming a serious land-surveying professional, however, was a complicated balancing act that certainly carried dilemmas and at times ethical compromise. "I am concerned to trace the effects of my allegiance," Thoreau declared in "Resistance to Civil Government."[28] His pursuit of commercial surveying would often prompt Thoreau to trace this particular allegiance to effects that were environmentally and politically awkward.

On the face of it, the choice of a surveying trade seems a particularly apt one for Thoreau, who exhibited a lifelong propensity for measuring the natural world, who stated unequivocally his belief in "the forest, and in the meadow"—who avowed that he could not stay in his chamber for a single day without acquiring rust. The lengthy outdoor excursions required of a surveyor accorded well with Thoreau's natural habits and with his strikingly broad scientific interests that eventually included such diverse disciplines as plant ecology, systematic botany, animal behavior, ichthyology, anthropology, geomorphology and limnology.[29] As Thoreau exclaimed in *A Week on the Concord and Merrimack Rivers*, "What wonderful discoveries have been, and may still be, made, with a plumb-line, a level, a surveyor's compass, a thermometer, and a barometer!"[30] From one perspective, Thoreau should have valued surveying because it allowed him to analyze environmental characteristics while earning money, or, as he put it, "answering to the bread and cheese which make my dinner."[31] From another perspective, however, surveying contradicted the preservationist ethos at the core of Thoreau's enduring legacy as our greatest nature writer. Imposing straight lines and mathematical formulae upon natural irregularities, marking off and subdividing the landscape near Walden Pond, laying out houses, barns and roads in Concord, Thoreau undeniably participated to some degree in civilized encroachment and environmental defacement.

Surveying work also gave rise to significant questions about Thoreau's relation to the political issues of his period. Thoreau seems to have recognized that surveying forced the notorious nonjoiner to identify himself with local authorities and participate in the maintenance of a civic order based firmly on wealth accumulation through property. As Leo Stoller observed in his study of Thoreau's economic life, "No other occupation for which Thoreau qualified would have been as adequately symbolic as was surveying of the decision to accept life within an economic order based on profit."[32] Once it is acknowledged that acceptance of the profit motive and sanctification of owners' rights were indexed to the dominant political issue of Thoreau's day—the debate about slavery—such a decision becomes especially consequential. Slavery polarized the nation and eventually put Thoreau firmly on the side of "radicals" who viewed the U.S. Constitution as a transparent sanctification of owning-class interests, a morally flawed proslavery document, "an agreement to serve the devil."[33] Surveying work, on the other hand, forced Thoreau to compromise his anti-institutional persona, not only by selling his time and labor but by doing so in a role that explicitly exerted the rights of both individual and institutional proprietors.

Part of Thoreau's lasting reputation as a great anti-institutionalist derives from his consistent and proactive evasion of any type of formal or official relation to communities, including the community of his birth. In "Resistance to Civil Government," Thoreau claimed to have asked the Concord selectmen to expunge his name from the governmental register, submitting to the town clerk his declaration, "Know all men by these presents, that I Henry Thoreau, do not wish to be regarded as a member of any incorporated society which I have not joined." Among his most profound repudiations of state authority in the essay is his subsequent description of the short reach of the state, its utter inability to impinge on his life or consciousness once he arrived at his sanctuary of woods and meadows. After being released from the Concord jail, Thoreau joins a huckleberry party and soon finds himself in a field on a hilltop, where "the State was nowhere to be seen."[34]

The assertion in the same essay that "I meet this American government, or its representative, the state government, directly, and face to face, once a year—no more—in the person of the tax-gatherer" may have been true in 1848.[35] But the author's successful and celebrated estrangement from authority clearly ended the moment he allied himself with his government in a mutually beneficial financial relation. In 1851, for example, Thoreau the surveyor earned sixty-four dollars from the Town of Concord, paid by the town's selectmen for laying out a road, perambulating the Acton and Bedford boundary lines, and producing a "survey and plan of the line between Concord and Carlisle."[36] A journal entry written before his service to the selectmen noted with ambivalence that the work was "authorized by the central government of the town."[37] By becoming the town's favored surveyor, Thoreau accepted designation as an employee of the "corporation" he had once shunned, compromised his hard-won noncompliance with civic authority, and forfeited his institutional anonymity. As journal entries on the 1851 perambulation show, he realized at once that he had "crossed the line" and "walked not with God but with the devil," compromising what he termed the "charmed circle" he had drawn around his life in exclusion of the trivial and superficial.[38]

"There are different ways of surveying," Thoreau wrote in "Life Without Principle," a statement suggesting that there was room to maneuver, some flexibility about the kind of professional he could be.[39] But there was in fact no viable way for Thoreau to both work as Concord's land surveyor and avoid a form of association with the state. From the beginning of his career, Thoreau's name appears frequently in the fiscal records of Concord, and not always as a mere recipient of "miscellaneous" wages. In legal documents and reports produced in connection with official surveys and the frequent practice of local-boundary demarcation, his signature even appears as a "legally appointed" substitute for the selectmen of Concord.[40] Carrying out a responsible, specialized and legally binding administrative function, Thoreau personally negotiated in behalf of Concord with officials from neighboring townships about the placement and maintenance of civic boundaries in relation to roads, buildings and natural landmarks.[41]

To the self-satisfied cultural majority represented by the selectmen, Thoreau probably seemed an aloof personality but a valuable employee. To the selectmen themselves, the public identities Thoreau cultivated, those of abolitionist and surveyor, probably seemed rare and oxymoronic, and they would have been right in thinking so. Having rejected church membership, the payment of his poll tax, and all other non-consensual associations, Thoreau accepted surveying, not without severe misgivings, as his official tie to his political community.

For the land surveyor in the mid-nineteenth century, Cooper's Chain-bearer was one kind of model, and until Thoreau was forced to earn money, the unpaid, powerfully symbolic, environmentally harmless surveying he did at Walden Pond was another. Later, when he bought equipment, advertised services, ran boundary lines and kept accounts, Thoreau would have to negotiate contradictory demands on his spirit and situate himself among business models, looking for a place where an enlightened individual conscience and sometimes dubious functions could coexist. Once he was no longer financially free to be only a surveyor of the soul, as at Walden, there were questions for Thoreau to answer. Would he accept a role as an implicit standard-bearer for the sociopolitical status quo and all it implied? Would he be a scientist-surveyor, using the compass to investigate the earth and stars? Would he be, like the militant abolitionist John Brown, a surveyor-revolutionary, drawing on the status of the profession with political creativity? Would he be a naturalist-surveyor, tempering his accurate measurements of man-made boundaries with more meaningful natural facts and dimensions? Would he be a disgruntled surveyor, resenting the time sacrificed to arduous fieldwork and the petty claims of clients? At one time or another between 1846 and the end of his life, Thoreau would be all these things. During an excursion in the Maine woods in 1857, Thoreau remarked, "I have a surveyor's eyes," an assertion that in its context meant simply that he was able to detect a slope in the landscape invisible to his companions.[42] Applied in retrospect to his life and literary output, having a surveyor's eyes meant significantly more.

A good way to begin an analysis of Thoreau's diverse surveying-related incarnations is to step outside the literary-critical field and consider observations made by experts on land surveying. Professional civil engineers, assessing the author's legacy and character from a vantage point beyond the ken of literary researchers, have consistently expressed respect for Thoreau's work and continue to claim him as one of their own. Surveying historians, presumably evaluating Thoreau solely on the basis of his engineering merits, sometimes place him in quite distinguished company. In 1985, Donald A. Wilson classified Thoreau as one of only a handful of surveyors deserving to be called "pioneers in their own right, who played a very important role in the development of our country." Wilson claimed that Thoreau was "a man who believed in doing what he wanted" but was ultimately compliant with the legal system, serving as an expert witness in property-related court cases and holding what Wilson considered political office as his town's "surveyor-in-chief."[43] Similarly argued essays about the man referred to as "the quintessential surveyor" have appeared with some regularity in professional engineering journals. Not surprisingly, they paint a picture of Thoreau that is in some ways at variance with the author known to literary scholars.[44]

In his article "Henry Thoreau, Surveyor," in the June 1965 *Journal of Surveying and Mapping*, Harry B. Chase acknowledged the obvious in stating that "the world remembers him as transcendental philosopher, nature lover, and author, not as a land surveyor." Chase sifted Thoreau's journals for evidence that would restore Concord's best mid-nineteenth-century surveyor to the historical record, locating references to his paid fieldwork on at least 160 separate occasions in the journals between 1849 and 1860. To make his experiences recognizable to twentieth-century surveyors, Chase offered revealing glimpses of Thoreau at work: Thoreau's clients complained that he walked too fast for them; he had the great advantage to a surveyor of being immune to poison ivy; he dressed for work in tattered corduroy trousers and joked with his chain man that "it wasn't everybody who could afford to have fringe around his legs." While he was surveying in the "Great Fields" in July of 1853, Thoreau's line of sight was interrupted by a herd of grazing cows and he had to time his compass sightings to peer between them. "What present-day surveyor hasn't had the same experience with cars on a highway or pedestrians on a busy sidewalk?" Chase wondered. Another incident familiar to surveyors took place in December of 1849, when Thoreau "had the experience of losing a pin [a chaining pin used to mark measured ground] and then hunting for it a long time in vain." As Chase notes, Thoreau's surveying assistants were a varied and interesting lot. Sometimes a property owner or one of his hired hands carried the surveying chain, sometimes an illiterate Irish immigrant, but his chain bearers also included his great friend Bronson Alcott and Concord sheriff Sam Staples. Concerning Thoreau's attitude toward his work, Chase speculated that he "tolerated surveying because it allowed him to observe nature" and quoted journal passages in which surveying and environmental sensitivity coexist. While running a line in the woods with a young helper on June 3, 1856, Thoreau found a chickadee nest and "called off the boy in another direction that he might not find it."[45]

Like Wilson, Chase compares Thoreau to famous surveyors, observing that "a number of noted men—Washington, Lincoln, and John Brown among them—at one time or another plied the chain and compass, but only Thoreau was a lifelong professional." Given that Thoreau did not work regularly until he was in his thirties, the reference to him as a lifelong surveyor may be a slight exaggeration. Chase's readiness to call him one, however, is a symptom of the eagerness with which the profession has adopted Thoreau. For the modern engineer, the author of *Walden* has been put to frequent use as a reminder of the profession's proud history, a man who proved that it is indeed possible to love the land while lotting it off for sale and development. Thoreau worked seriously at surveying for about thirteen of his forty-four years, but the consensus is that he was more skilled than either Washington or Abraham Lincoln, who worked at the profession only briefly and intermittently in the 1830s. Anticipating a number of engineers who would write about Thoreau's surveying, Chase conveys palpable respect: "A modern land surveyor would find it interesting, even instructive, to accompany Henry in the field."[46]

In the March 1976 issue of *The Journal of Surveying and Mapping*, Danish surveyor Thorkild Hoy noted that Thoreau had much to teach contemporary surveyors about the keen observation of detail: "One could have wished him to study a modern topographic map." Hoy found Thoreau's ability to detect old boundaries by studying the growth of trees and bushes especially impressive. The Danish surveyor implicitly reminded his colleagues in the profession to sharpen their perceptions accordingly, drawing attention to an assertion Thoreau made in his journal that "even after many years . . . lines were still discernible when closely observed." If Thoreau may be considered a model engineer and cartographer, it is in part because his work successfully combined both rational and intuitive faculties. His professional descendants should emulate the imagination and emotional engagement evident in Thoreau's surveying work: "Let us take care," Hoy counsels, "that too much rationalization never again results in maps lacking in detail."[47]

Acknowledging the accuracy of the Walden Pond survey, Hoy expressed amazement that some mid-nineteenth-century readers of *Walden* thought it a hoax. He seems exasperated at their not being able to understand what is obvious to him: "The chart derived from Thoreau's deep delight in exploring nature and was one of many results of his drive to try to penetrate into its secrets." The Danish surveyor grants willingly that Thoreau's "ability for and inclination to precise and accurate observations undoubtedly made him a reliable professional," but he is very aware that a great part of Thoreau's genius was in his ethical reckoning: "It can also be said for certain that his measurements and observations had a deeper meaning for him." Interestingly, Hoy compares the American poet-surveyor to his Danish countryman Søren Kierkegaard, "a controversial character too," reflecting that "those of us who live more than a century after can in good conscience draw upon the riches from such individuals."[48]

In a 1983 issue of *Professional Surveyor* magazine, Richard H. Howard asked, "Many of us know Henry D. Thoreau as a naturalist, but how well do we know him as a surveyor?" Howard is among the few who have mathematically analyzed the degree of accuracy Thoreau brought to his survey measurements. His article "A New Look at Henry Thoreau the Surveyor" attempted to define the specific qualities that marked Thoreau's work, noting with amazement that Thoreau's surveys sometimes give distances to the hundredth of a foot, and that his compass bearings are often recorded to one-eighth of a degree. Howard checked the data of one Thoreau tract and arrived at a calculated precision of one part in 1,300—an almost impossible accuracy for the 1850s. Thoreau once wondered why his services were demanded more often for surveying than for lecturing, claiming that "a hundred others in this county" could survey as well as he. Howard argues that in this statement Thoreau "obviously underestimated" his considerable technical skills.[49]

A recent and ardent response to Thoreau from a surveying professional is Barry Savage's "The Quintessential Surveyor," which appeared in the April 2003 issue of the surveying journal *Point of Beginning*. Savage, an instructor of surveying at East Tennessee State University, traveled to Concord with a student surveying team in May of 2002. He did so not only to sharpen his students' field skills by retracing some of Thoreau's measurements, but to make pedagogical use of the values discernible in Thoreau's surveying work, teaching his students to understand "the vital roles integrity, truth and thought play in becoming a surveyor."[50]

During an interview for this book, Savage commented on his use of Thoreau's field notes in the surveying classroom, explaining that he begins his unit on Thoreau with an illustration of professional ethics, drawing his students' attention to a particular field-notes entry from early in Thoreau's career.[51] In the notes for the survey of Daniel Shattuck's cottage house lot on June 19, 1850, there is a notation in light pencil indicating that Shattuck "agreed in presence of A.C. Collier, to accept my survey." One might imagine the posing of the question, perhaps by Collier, "Will you accept the results of Henry's work?" followed by Shattuck's binding assent, "Yes, I will trust his work." During a period when a land register was not in existence and there were no licensing requirements for the persons who carried out surveys, a reputation for integrity, which Thoreau clearly possessed, could be the primary factor in enabling a surveyor to fulfill the crucial role of legal arbiter.

In their retracement work in Concord, Savage's crew believed they had discovered two split stones left by Thoreau as monumentation in a survey of Emerson's lot near Walden. They also located Thoreau's bean field north of the cabin site, confirming the statement in *Walden* that its rows were each fifteen rods in length. They verified the accuracy of a few of Thoreau's measurements with modern GPS surveying equipment. The primary purpose of Savage's fieldwork, however, was to "learn more than the mechanics of Thoreau's work." They sought to explore his attitudinal as well as his mathematical greatness. Savage prefaces his analysis by stating a belief that the surveyor's art of measurement is "as much philosophy as science," then gives several reasons for viewing Thoreau as a model of ethically grounded and environmentally sensitive professionalism.[52]

According to the Tennessee surveyor, Thoreau was a born chain man. His proclivity for what Emerson termed "mensuration" was seemingly innate; he was almost never not measuring. Inferring this trait from the location descriptions in *Walden,* Savage offers a substantive insight for literature scholars: "It was in Thoreau's very nature to begin describing any place he wrote about by giving dimensions first." Savage takes seriously the surveying profession's often-overlooked responsibility to carefully document and describe landscape detail. Because a surveyor almost always begins his work from points established by his predecessors, his duties are an important element of property conveyance, enabling the next generation of owners to quantify their holdings. But Thoreau's historical awareness had both concrete and abstract purposes that modern practitioners would do well to emulate. Clearly, his natural inclination to study the environment and learn the histories of its fields, ponds and woodlands helped Thoreau to locate old boundaries. Alluding to the sensitive and discerning consciousness that infused Thoreau's fieldwork, Savage asserts that "history and surveying go hand in hand . . . the profession requires each surveyor to 'follow in the footsteps' of those who have gone before." Essentially, Savage urges his surveyor colleagues toward a deeper awareness of the past while extolling an ethically transcendent paradigm for the profession. Downplaying the surveyor's role in supporting property law and landscape exploitation, he glorifies Thoreau as a personification of its redeeming purposes.[53]

In the process of addressing the "dilemma every surveyor has faced"— a landowner who assumes the surveyor will tailor his work to maximize the owner's profit—Savage claims a fundamental experiential kinship with Thoreau. Thoreau epitomized the professional who took spiritual satisfaction from work performed the "most correct" way rather than the way that would give his client the most land. He serves as a reminder to his descendants in the profession that they must "tell the truth . . . even if it's not what our clients want to hear."[54] In the field, as in his literary efforts, Thoreau's standards were impeccable; his first allegiance was neither to the rapacity of his clients nor to civilizing processes but to his sense of integrity. This approach stresses the surveyor's potential for individuality, aligns surveying with truth seeking, and shifts the categorization of fieldwork from an ethical neutral to an ethical positive.

At the close of his article, Savage weighs the consequences of honest surveying: "To a surveyor always telling the truth has two universal outcomes. One is a good night's sleep; the other is a guarantee that half the people he/she encounters will dislike the surveyor." Deducing practical precepts for modern-day fieldwork from Thoreau's moral commitments, the surveyor concludes that "Emerson was correct when he described Thoreau's dedication to truth as a catalyst for confrontation."[55] Admittedly, Emerson probably did not have Thoreau's surveying in mind when he described his friend as "a speaker and actor of the truth; born such . . . and ever running into dramatic situations from this cause."[56] But Savage has done fieldwork. He knows how often a surveyor raises hackles by serving professional standards rather than a client's land hunger. From the standpoint of a professional who clearly places a high value on the spiritual aspects of his calling, Thoreau emerges as a heroic figure and embodiment of traits essential to the proper performance of the measurer's art—a patron saint for surveyors.

The place of honor Thoreau has attained in land-surveying history is an interesting codicil to his status as canonized literary giant. Thoreau's literary stock has risen steadily in the twentieth century, but interest from literary researchers in his reputation as a land surveyor has been intermittent at best.[57] The story of how the author of *Walden* so lived his life as to elicit the admiration of literature scholars, philosophers, environmentalists, antiauthoritarians *and* future land surveyors is certainly an underappreciated and significant measure of the man. One of the purposes of this study is to adequately describe Thoreau's work in the field and show how the attainment of such skills was not a negligible intellectual accomplishment.

A more pressing concern, and a higher priority in this study, is to shed light on the sociopolitical context in which Thoreau's work was performed. Ultimately, the fascinating issue is not that Thoreau became a competent and sought-after civil engineer, but that he did so while crafting some of the most eloquent cultural criticisms in our language. As students of our national mythology, we should recognize that the respect and sometimes awe with which Thoreau's surveying career has been described is based largely on a clichéd romantic concept: the land surveyor as embodiment of the honest man and good citizen, a builder of the country who loved the wilderness his work helped tame. This George Washington paradigm underestimates Thoreau and would not have satisfied him, nor is it a sufficient description of the meanings his surveying eventually expressed. Thoreau would have been much more pleased to be classified with John Brown, the most subversive of all surveyors, who overturned standard connotations of the profession by using the compass and chain as weapons in a war against state-sanctioned injustice. One of my central aims is therefore to explain how Thoreau's fieldwork was closer to Brown's than to Washington's—how the best surveyor in Concord often managed to combine civil engineering with civil disobedience.

2

Material to Mythology

I am thankful that this pond was made deep and
pure for a symbol.

—Thoreau, *Walden*

I too would fain set down something beside facts
—They should be material to the mythology which
I am writing. Not facts to assist men to make
money.... Facts to tell who I am—and where I have
been—or what I have thought.

—Thoreau, *Journal*, November 9, 1851

BY ANY CRITERION EXCEPT ECONOMIC, Henry Thoreau's surveying
career began at Walden. "Desirous to recover the long lost bottom of
Walden Pond," he "surveyed it carefully, before the ice broke up, early in
'46, with compass and chain and sounding line."[1] The sole reason Thoreau gives for the survey—that he wanted to make sure the pond had
a bottom—is insufficient and intentionally disingenuous. Sounding the
depths of the pond was only a part, perhaps the simplest part, of an am-
bitious task with profound justifications. This task, along with almost

everything about the extensive surveying work Thoreau did in his lifetime, deserves a closer look.

To analyze nineteenth-century land surveying is to study Henry David Thoreau's primary nonliterary pursuit, an activity that took up a large portion of his adult life. Conceding that Thoreau truly did make what he referred to as "wonderful discoveries" while surveying, this book attempts to isolate and explain those discoveries, along with the procedures and methods that produced them. What did one have to do, for example, to survey a pond or river, or lay out a new road, or divide up a woodlot, or establish a town boundary? What did the surveyor observe, feel and experience? After completing a job, what did the surveyor know that nonsurveyors did not? What were the political conditions and social attributes of the profession in the mid-nineteenth century and how did Thoreau respond to them? All these questions are important, primarily as a means of getting at the central issue: how an understanding of Thoreau's engineering work and his long-term self-identification as a surveyor help to know him better as a person and artist. We can't accompany Thoreau on a surveying job, but we can speculate in informed ways about what he did with compass and chain, what the work meant to him, and what it should mean for interpreters of his legacy.

For starters, it seems essential to know how Thoreau actually made the Walden survey, a three-dimensional pond map that is now one of the most important images in American literary history. Surveying the sixty-one-acre pond presented significant technical challenges, but it was also a physically arduous process requiring days, perhaps weeks of toil, some of it quite exhausting.

Making "more than a hundred" sounding holes in ice that was sixteen inches thick was in itself a substantial feat, requiring of Thoreau's relatively small frame considerable cardiovascular stamina and physical power. The Harvard grad, writer and woodsman was also an athlete whose methods of environmental inquiry were appropriately physical. Amazingly, the hard work did not blunt Thoreau's perceptions but stimulated his speculative and interpretive faculties, grounding an epistemology that was as much corporal as cerebral. At Walden and after, labor in the open air was a source and basis of the writer's acute phenomenological discernment.

The pond survey was a rare type of work, an experiential episode in

Thoreau's life whose processes are now somewhat hard to imagine. Walking and working on the vast open ice, nestling the wooden legs of the tripod into the snow and leveling the compass on the frozen pond surface, squinting through the compass sight vanes at hundreds of points on the horizon and every contour of the Walden shoreline must have produced sensations bordering on the surreal. Taking in the surrounding hills and embankments from isolated points in the middle of a vast smooth plane, Thoreau would have been acutely conscious of the stark emptiness of the space. Confronted by an upward-sloping topography and the steep wall of the twenty-foot-high railroad embankment to the immediate west, the surveyor may have felt like he was working on the bottom of an enormous basin. Even with the sound-muffling blanket of snow on the pond, the concussions of Thoreau's axe on the ice would have reverberated on the substantially treeless surrounding hills, rhythmically sending back the thousands of blows necessary to create his sounding holes. The desolate, enveloping whiteness would probably have produced a heightened aural sensitivity, amplifying the echoes of the relentless chopping, along with the creaking of the shifting ice and the click of the surveying chain.

The prolonged careful examination of the Walden environs surely made an indelible imprint on Thoreau's mind and memory, enabling a depth of sensual, visual and bodily knowledge of the pond and its immediate landscape that perhaps no one else could lay claim to, then or now. Thoreau's comments on the sensory phenomena of this unusual space imply an awareness of its visual strangeness: "Sometimes . . . where the ice was covered with shallow puddles, I saw a double shadow of myself, one standing on the head of the other, one on the ice, the other on the trees or hill-side."[2] To the readily imaginable light and sound effects of working in such a space, the movement of the ice surface added an element that intensified the fantastic. "While I was surveying," Thoreau writes,

> the ice . . . undulated under a slight wind like water. . . . At one rod from the shore its greatest fluctuation, when observed by means of a level directed toward a graduated staff on the ice, was three quarters of an inch, though the ice appeared firmly attached to the shore. It was probably greater in the middle. . . . When two legs of my level were on the shore and the third on the ice, and the sights were directed over the latter, a

rise or fall of the ice of an almost infinitesimal amount made a difference of several feet on a tree across the pond.[3]

As Thoreau's use of surveying equipment and procedures begins, so does
a new form of observation, a merging of manual and intellectual labor
previously theorized in transcendental philosophy but now being actually put into practice.[4] The rise and fall of the pond surface, detectable
only with surveying equipment, compels speculation. Deriving a universal hypothesis from the fluctuation of a level, Thoreau asks, "Who knows
but if our instruments were delicate enough we might detect an undula-
tion in the crust of the earth?"[5]

Not having confronted the pond with the methods Thoreau used, we
normally live, as *Walden* explains, by "notions of law and harmony" that
are "confined to those instances which we detect"—presumably without
mechanical aids.[6] To passively experience a world like Walden is one
thing, to *survey* it is another. The former is what we normally do, either by hiking its paths, swimming its deep clear waters, listening to the
sounds of its wildlife, breathing its pine-scented air. The latter, however,
requires the purposeful acquisition of detailed topographical and hydrographical information, the lexical systematizing and careful recording of
environmental facts, and the formalizing of data pinpointing the relation
of observed locations for presentation in visual form.

The 1854 Walden map is now ubiquitous, having been reprinted in
many editions of *Walden* and academic studies of Thoreau. An interesting "fair copy" of the pond-survey map Thoreau made in 1846 has also
appeared in scholarly texts, most notably Stowell's *A Thoreau Gazetteer*
in 1970. But the full story of precisely how the pond was surveyed is accessible only by looking at the more crudely drawn preliminary draft, the
first attempt to render the pond in visual form. This document indicates
that in measuring and mapping the pond, Thoreau used a method of
angle intersection, a procedure that enabled satisfactory accuracy but required a minimum of actual measuring with the surveyor's chain. Instead
of chaining around the pond's long and irregular perimeter, he took advantage of the fact that the pond was frozen and used compass bearings
taken from its open surface to locate selected positions on the shoreline.[7]

As this draft survey also shows, Thoreau began at the southernmost
tip of Walden and measured almost due north for about 1,300 feet,

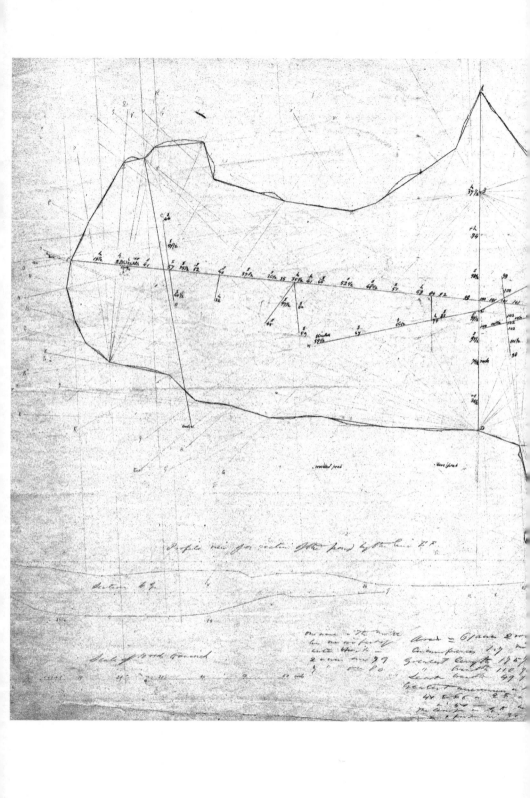

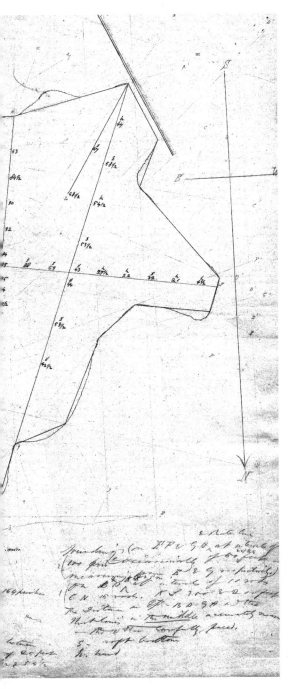

FIGURE 2.1. Preliminary draft of Walden Pond survey, 1846. Ink and pencil, 16 × 21″. Courtesy Concord Free Public Library. The notes below the drawing read as follows:

One acre in the middle has over 100 feet of water upon it.

2 acres over 99, 7 [acres] over 80.

Area = 61 acres, 2 roods 23.164 perches.

Circumference 1.7 miles.

Greatest length 175½ rods.

Greatest breadth 110½ [rods].

Least [breadth] 49½ [rods].

Greatest increases on the bottom between 41 and 66 on EF a descent of 25 feet in 50 [feet]. The least on GK between 53½ and 54½, 1 foot in 30 rods.

Soundings on EF & GH and shorter lines at intervals of 100 feet, occasionally of 50 and 25 feet measuring from E & G respectively. On BD & CM at intervals of 10 rods CN 15 rods, K, L 300 and 200 feet. The Distances on EF-BD-GH and the short lines **in the middle** accurately measured - the others carefully paced.

s - soft bottom

h. hard

bisecting the pond with the line *BCD*. This was the baseline of his survey—the line that would serve as the verification base of all adjoining measurements, the first line he would draw in transforming his data to visual form, and one of the few distances he had to measure with extreme care and precision. As the notes on the pond sketch indicate, the line *BCD* was "accurately measured," while other distances were "carefully paced"—walked off rather than measured with the chain.[8]

Next Thoreau established traverse stations, points on the pond surface from which all or nearly all of its perimeter could be seen. Points B and D—at opposite ends of Thoreau's baseline and providing a full panorama of the pond—became the primary traverse stations or hubs. After setting up the tripod and leveling the compass at station B, Thoreau recorded a series of horizontal angles or bearings to significant points along the edge of the pond where the shoreline changed direction or formed coves.

Interestingly, Thoreau labeled the bearings with letters of the alphabet. His first piece of data was the angle from station B to point A1, where the pond met the south edge of the Fitchburg railroad embankment. This field note would have read "B-A1 S 76¼ W," meaning that the line from station B to point A1 had a bearing of seventy-six and one-quarter degrees west of south. Remaining at station B, Thoreau then turned his compass sight to the next significant shift in the pond's outline at the north extremity of the railroad embankment. To this point, labeled B1, he recorded a bearing of about N 89 W, or eighty-nine degrees west of north. Point C1, a spot where the shore angled into a cove, was about eleven degrees north of B1, or N 78 W.

And so on. Thoreau took at least twenty-eight readings of bearing from station B, filling out his data by locating four objects in the surrounding topography—a tall tree at the pond's eastern edge, a tree in the distance to the northeast, and the wooded peak and bare peak on the north side of the pond. In the process of gathering data from this initial hub, Thoreau turned his compass in a complete circle, surrounding himself with symbols that overlaid and partitioned the 360 degrees of the pond's physical space. His last bearing, labeled Z on the draft, was within a degree of his first. The final degree of the horizon was the final letter of the alphabet. The coupling of numeric with linguistic signification systems was strangely appropriate in this survey, for in gathering mathematical data about Walden, Thoreau was also producing and inscribing the literary text of *Walden*.

When all coordinates were taken from station B, the second hub, D, was occupied. Immediately after setting up at this station, Thoreau took a back sight or reciprocal bearing to the location he had just left. If the bearing was 180 degrees apart from the one taken from B to D, it indicated that there was no local magnetic attraction affecting the compass. Thoreau could then proceed to sight the twenty-four points on the pond that were visible from both B and D. When he took the bearing from D to point A1, which read approximately thirty-eight degrees west of south or in his field notes "D-A1 *S 38 W*," he had all the data he needed to locate this point on his pond map. Lines drawn from stations B and D using his recorded bearings would intersect exactly at point A1. When the bearing lines taken from all his traverse stations were redrawn on paper, their thirty-eight points of intersection would produce a connect-the-dots outline of the pond.

Whether Thoreau had assistance in mapping Walden is unclear. With patience, he could certainly have made this large survey entirely on his own. To use the chain to measure his baseline—along with the pond's greatest length, greatest breadth and least breadth, all of which are re-corded on the survey draft—he would have had to drive an iron pin or perhaps a railroad spike into the ice to hold the chain as he pulled it taut. After tallying a chain length, he hammered in another spike at the chain's terminus, then returned to its back end to remove the first spike and swing the chain around to get the next distance on his line. In order to take his measurements working alone, Thoreau would have been re-quired to perform this procedure at least 108 times.

But he was in no hurry, and with planning and preparation Thoreau could also have managed to take readings of bearing without help. To view through the compass his several dozen points along the perimeter of the pond, he could have fashioned a collection of twenty or so sighting posts—what surveyors sometimes call targets. These were made from sturdy branches improvised in the field, probably three or four feet long, with a piece of red cloth flagging attached for visibility. Thoreau would have made a careful circuit of the pond and its immediate environs, se-lecting locations that were visible from his sighting stations on the pond surface and setting the flags firmly in the frozen ground. Once his targets were in place, Thoreau could locate them through his compass sights from the stations on his baseline.

If Thoreau did have a helper, his distance measuring was much easier and his method of taking bearings somewhat different. A chain man would certainly have increased speed and efficiency while reducing the possibility of error in the processes of creating a 925-foot baseline and measuring almost 2,900 feet in 66-foot increments across the pond. The task of sighting specific points on the pond's perimeter, some of which were more than a thousand feet away, could be accomplished by having an assistant stand at the selected point and identify it by waving and then holding in place a vertical leveling stave, or Jacob staff. Thoreau could directly sight the staff, record the bearing and wave his assistant to the next point. The text of *Walden* offers some evidence that the survey was at least a two-man job. In "The Pond in Winter," Thoreau describes standing at the pond's edge and directing his level toward "a graduated staff on the ice."[9] While it is possible that the staff was somehow fixed to the surface, it is much more likely that an assistant held it. It seems probable that an anonymous chain man, perhaps recruited from among the Irish railroad workers living in shanties in the Walden woods, helped to survey Walden Pond.

In a modern survey of the type Thoreau made at Walden, electronic equipment measures the lengths of all radiating lines, thus establishing each point using both bearing and distance. With or without a chain man, measuring the great number of long lines from Thoreau's traverse stations would have been an almost impossible task. As most nineteenth-century surveyors did in projects of this type, Thoreau compensated for not measuring each radial line by taking a large number of bearings, including some to landscape features outside the immediate area of the traverse. These reference azimuths helped establish the accuracy of angles read with the compass. In addition, the reference azimuths oriented the primary area or object of the survey in relation to significant features of local topography.

As an azimuth mark crucial to the completion of his Walden survey, Thoreau chose an intriguing object: the front door of the cabin he was living in to the north of the pond. With his tripod and compass at point C, the center of the pond, Thoreau sighted his cabin and recorded a bearing probably in the neighborhood of N 16¾ W. He then turned his compass about ninety-seven degrees to point B1, the spot where the railroad runs nearest to the pond, and took a bearing of *S 66 W*. The draft survey shows that he later moved with his compass to point B1, setting up his tripod at the base of the railroad embankment on the pond's western extremity and taking a bearing from here to his cabin that read about *N 24 E*. This final piece of data created a triangle within Thoreau's survey that enabled him to check for closure. If the sum of the internal angles of the three-sided figure was near to 180 degrees, Thoreau knew that the bearings he had taken were consistent enough to be trusted. He also knew exactly where to draw on the Walden map the tiny dot that represented the house he had built the previous summer. He could thus survey the pond with increased confidence, and place *himself* within its environs with increased precision.

The pragmatic purposes of using his cabin as a reference point are interesting, but so are the philosophical inferences that may be drawn from it. By sighting his cabin from the center of the pond and the railroad embankment, Thoreau created a three-sided figure that brought key locations into a form of contact with each other. As all good readers of *Walden* know, the deepest part of the pond provides Thoreau with his "rule of the two diameters," a metaphysical axiom suggesting that the "height or depth" of a person's character is located, as with the pond, at the intersection of length and breadth. That the pond's greatest length, width and depth were concentric was in Thoreau's view a remarkable coincidence, enabled by a surveying chain and sounding line and of substantive importance to his great book.[10]

Creating the pond-cabin-railroad triangle at the core of the Walden survey has similar implications. Obviously it confirms Thoreau's awareness that station C, the nucleus of Walden, bore a relation worth discerning to point B1, where the pond met the railroad. The statement Thoreau made in *Walden* that the railroad "touches" the pond is in a way only true once an association between the two objects has been made. As the draft survey suggests, the pond-to-railroad linkage was established in survey form before it was established in literary form. Through the process of visually tracing the faintly radiating lines on the Walden Pond draft, we learn that, as early as the winter of 1846, Thoreau recorded a numerical bearing between these points and used that bearing to create his sketch.

On the draft survey as well as on the finished map, Thoreau made sure he clearly identified his cabin site. He wrote the word "House" at the point where the bearing lines intersected and gave the single line running from the pond's center through the cabin the same verbal designation, scribbling the word a second time where the line terminated to the far north of the pond. As Thoreau asserts in *Walden*, knowing the realities around the man, the limiting or liberating factors in his environment, can be revealing. If it is true of a man that "perhaps we need only to know how his shores trend and his adjacent country or circumstances, to infer his depth and concealed bottom,"[11] then determining one's exact place in the environment becomes an urgent matter. As always for Thoreau, to know the self was to study nature. Since self-analysis and environmental observation were the same thing, finding the bearings directly from one's front door to significant landscape features was a logical and perhaps crucial endeavor.

We might have assumed that Thoreau would want to locate with exactitude the relative positions of his cabin, the railroad and the pond center—vital locations in the microcosm of Walden. A look at the survey draft, however, compels a recognition of the ways the three locations were tied to each other. The idea that the surveyor determined the position of each location *using* the other two—that each location was a vertex of a planned triangle—is thought provoking. Considering the purely inquisitive rather than practical purposes of the Walden survey, it would not have made sense for Thoreau to ignore the connotations of this geometric association. What purpose did the map serve, and why the inclusion of the pond survey in the literary text, if not to deduce and display such analogies?

After Thoreau had created his triangle, he may have considered what the numbers meant. He may have wondered whether the ninety-seven-degree angle at the pond's center, with adjacent sides extending to his cabin and the railroad, expressed something important. He may have thought about the degrees of each angle, and what these indicated literally about where he stood in his "border life" between nature and civilization. Looking at his survey data, he would certainly have noticed that the angle of about forty-two degrees from the railroad to the pond's center was close but not quite equal to the angle from his cabin to the same spot. With field notes in hand, he may have positioned himself for contemplation, perhaps standing at the door of his cabin, at the threshold of

his self-created existence, and gazed first at station C and then at point
B1. Here he would have noted that the other two points of his triangle
were within his field of vision, and that they were only about forty-one
degrees apart. Did it occur to him that if one stood at the railroad embankment, the same was true? From his knowledge of Euclidean geometry, one intriguing fact would surely have dawned on him: the linear distances from the railroad to the pond's center and from his house to the
pond's center were nearly the same. He had surveyed a scalene triangle of
unequal sides, but it was *almost* an isosceles, with two equal base angles
and two equal legs. These legs, he surely noticed, converged at an apex
that was at once the pond's center, very nearly its deepest point, and the
intersection of its length and breadth.

Spatial relationships and precise locations were significant to Thoreau
at the pond, where he thought it important that he did not need to go out
of doors to take the air, where he became neighbor to the birds by having
caged himself near them—where he proclaimed, "I dwelt nearer to those
parts of the universe and to the eras in history which had most attracted
me."[12] Though the view from his cabin door is described in *Walden* as
more confined than that available from nearby Heywood's Peak, it nevertheless provides "pasture enough for [his] imagination,"[13] justifying the
notion that the cabin served well as a figurative vantage point. Learning
from the draft survey that it was a literal marker as well—a reference
azimuth—indicates the extent of the surveyor's formal awareness of the
location he had occupied within the pond landscape.

Cultural-materialist literary critics have examined formal similari-
ties between mapmaking and the creation of literary texts, looking at the
ways both types of documents may be read as artifacts of cultural practices. Maps and surveys purport to be neutral representations of the real,
but they are in fact both image and narrative, displaying "not only representations of the world but metaphors of the world."[14] Like literary texts,
maps are symbolic conceptions, the product of selective design values
and culturally constructed priorities, and they therefore function politically, within discourse and ideology. The lines on maps and surveys are in
effect stories in which topographical features become characters and directional trajectory the equivalent of plot. Their substantial narratologi-
cal function requires reading and interpretation. Even their blank spaces
or "silences" speak loudly. To the extent that maps and surveys function

allegorically, they may be classified along with literary texts as arguments that are embedded in social practice and re-present the world's meaning from a given authorial perspective.[15]

With these insights in mind, we might subject Thoreau's cartography to a political reading, analyzing the narrative aspect of the lithograph that appeared opposite page 307 in the first edition of *Walden*. What story does the Walden map tell, how would readers have reacted to it, and how may it be read as a cultural artifact? Upon initial discovery of the map in the text, a predictable reaction would probably have involved the understanding that Thoreau simply wanted his readers to *see*—not just read about—the place where he lived. But one of the first things a reader of the Walden survey notices is that it is upside down: north appears at the bottom edge of the document, reversing the traditional compass rose that designates north as the upper portion of the map. On the most famous image Thoreau ever produced, north is south and east is west—the world is reversed on its axis. Whatever the rationale for the upside-down image, it could initially have raised questions about the author's intent, perhaps even his competence or credibility. Present-day Thoreau admirers have probably seen the document so many times that it no longer registers as an object at odds with the canons of mapmaking. But if early readers of the Walden map, as Robert Stowell observes, misunderstood its purpose or "thought it was included for humorous reasons,"[16] it may have had something to do with the fact that its orientation was radically discontinuous with reader expectations. Less familiar with Thoreau's now-established reputation as a great iconoclast, early readers of *Walden* might not have expected the map to tell a story that seems in conflict with the phenomenal world.

Before publishing his map, Thoreau had several chances to easily reverse the orientation of the document, making at least three copies of it—the initial preliminary draft, a fair copy shortly thereafter, and a reduced plan in early 1854, just before he sent the book to press.[17] In revising the map over several years, Thoreau left it upside down, so we can only conclude that he was satisfied with its perspective. He did, however, make a significant change to its directional orientation. In early 1854, he repositioned the drawing and redrew its directional arrow to incorporate the magnetic declination of his compass from true north. The 1854 reduced plan of Walden thus includes the customary pair of directional arrows—one for true north and one that shows the magnetic declination of the compass from north at the time the survey was made. Adding the declination to the plan of Walden in 1854 essentially finished the document, making it look like the many other surveys Thoreau had been making since seriously taking up the profession five years earlier.

On the final version of the Walden map, however, Thoreau removed the declination indicator, leaving only the eye-catching and boldly drawn arrow marked clearly along its shaft with the words "True Meridian." Arguably, this was an aesthetically pleasing change, simplifying the look of the map and investing it with a more assertive tone. The fact that it made no sense in land-surveying terms seems not to have mattered at all to Thoreau. In the mid-nineteenth century, a surveyor might draw only a magnetically determined directional arrow and indicate "bearings magnetical" on the document. More skilled and careful members of the profession included arrows for both magnetic and true meridian, specifying the difference in degrees between the two. A surveyor would not, however, indicate only the true north designation. In itself, such a designation was not related to the conditions under which the survey was made and was of little practical use. Not surprisingly, the plan of Walden is the only Thoreau survey that bears exclusively the true north designation.[18] By withholding the information that had made the document readable and usable as an actual survey, Thoreau explicitly forfeits the pretense of practicality, asserting instead the symbolic priorities of the project. Moreover, removing the declination arrow expresses themes in the map's general narrative. Magnetic declinations are expressions of time, and they are usually recorded as a function of time, informing the "reader" of conditions existing when the directional readings were determined. They are therefore the products of a particular historical moment. Removing the declination and using only a single arrow that oriented the document to an unchanging feature of the environment, Thoreau de-emphasized the temporal in favor of the eternal.

Significantly, the directional arrow at the bottom of the map also oriented the "point" directly at the reader, and thus figuratively at the residents of Concord, Thoreau's intended audience. The title page of the original Walden manuscript unambiguously identified the target of Thoreau's book, declaring that it was addressed "to my Townsmen."[19] The arrow on the Walden map seems a parallel form of direct address, targeting the same audience insistently. Albert McLean once speculated that the rationale for Thoreau's unusual directional arrow was to indicate "the correspondence of his own life at Walden with the true direction of Nature itself."[20] Though this could have been accomplished with a right-side-up Walden map, keeping things upside down also enabled the author to locate the directional arrow near his house, approximating its position with Thoreau's, in the quadrant of the image where the map title would have been had he reversed the drawing. Moving the arrow to the top of the map might also have entailed reducing its size; the arrow on the underside could be larger and bolder.

As a didactic prompt, the arrow may be understood as both interro-

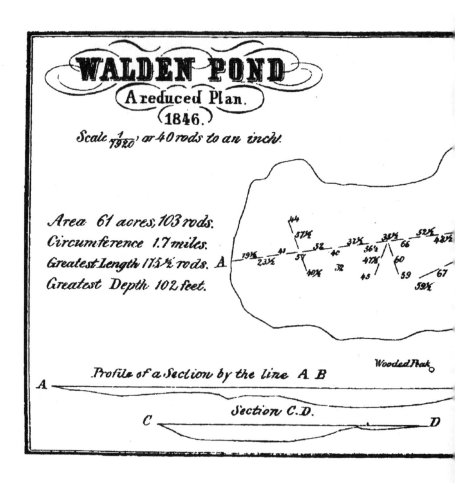

gating and instructing, first through the drastic maneuver of turning the world upside down, then by "redirecting" the way we habitually read. It not only points out a "true" and invariable course but implicitly challenges what Herman Melville referred to as "the doctrine of assumptions"[21] by which a complacent society habitually views the world. In geometric terms, the shift of orientation to true north was slight, turning the document only about nine degrees eastward from its original position. Where the document's internal narrative was concerned, however, the change was radical.

Maps and land surveys were and are documents meant to establish and preserve certain social, economic and political circumstances. Pri-

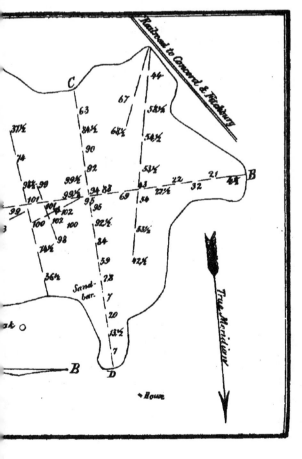

FIGURE 2.2. "Walden Pond. A Reduced Plan." Lithograph: original plate by S. W. Chandler and Bros., Boston. The image appeared opposite page 307 in the first edition of *Walden*. On this version of the survey, Thoreau removed his magnetic north and added the "True Meridian" directional arrow. He simplified his point-numbering system and printed fewer soundings. Though he removed the abbreviations "s" and "h" to indicate a soft or hard pond bottom, he added the location of a submerged "Sand-bar" at the entrance to the northern cove.

mary among these circumstances are boundaries of a national, civic and proprietary nature. Lines on maps are only thinly disguised as natural fact, but we accept their existence in accordance with legal and ideological conventions. Thoreau's Walden survey does not honor these conventions. At the time the document was created, the land area around the pond was entirely owned. Cyrus Hubbard and other surveyors had already divided the Walden woods into fairly regular rectangular lots averaging about thirteen acres and described on deeds held by the likes of Richardson, Heywood, Moore, Hosmer, and of course Emerson, whose boundaries Thoreau knew well. On the Walden map, however, no property lines appear and no form of ownership is acknowledged. Not only are known lot corners absent, the possessive denotation for landscape features also disappears. Heywood's Peak, about forty rods to the southeast of Thoreau's cabin, becomes simply "Bare Peak" on the Walden map. The cabin that Thoreau had built with his own hands and perhaps had a right to call his own is not referred to as "My House" but simply "House." Objects exist on the map, but they are located in a realm beyond possession where minimally descriptive denotations suffice. If John Richardson, who owned a thirteen-acre lot adjoining Emerson's property, had bought a copy of *Walden* and studied the map, he might have noticed that Thoreau had assumed a right to physically traverse his boundaries and then blatantly ignore them in his cartography.

Thoreau's map also ignores a significant civic boundary. The Lincoln-Concord town line—established in 1754—cuts across the southeastern edge of Walden Pond. Since 1829, monumentation in the form of split stones marked with the initials of Concord and Lincoln had been set up near the edge of the pond, establishing the town limits in a manner "agreeably [*sic*] to the laws of the Commonwealth."[22] The conclusive signification of political jurisdiction is among the most basic purposes of land surveying, but Thoreau self-consciously flouts this justification. Perhaps as much as the absence of property lines, the omission of the town border is a meaningful silence in Thoreau's cartography.[23] The Walden map is not a socially empty commodity, for the home of at least one acknowledged resident is included, but it is empty in a proprietary and institutional sense, a space where there are suddenly no property lines and no discernible personal or civic claims.

An interesting corroborating expression of these priorities is that neither lot corners nor the town boundary were used—even as points of reference—while Thoreau was actually in the field recording his data. It would have been useful and convenient for the surveyor to turn his compass toward a readily available stake and stones at a lot corner near the water's edge or to use the well-established town line as a point of reference. So far as can be determined from the draft survey, however, this never happened. In the hands of a professional surveyor, the compass follows lines and uses previous boundaries as points of beginning and back sights. Under Thoreau's control at Walden, the compass steers clear of boundaries, follows instead the contours of the pond, and references objects that are either natural or clearly symbolic—trees, hills, the cabin, the railroad.

Rather than locate boundaries on his survey, Thoreau locates himself, symbolized by his tiny cabin. Thoreau's inclusion of the ten-by-fifteen-foot man-made object indicated his conviction that his self-created domestic life was substantial enough to locate amid topography. Man-made structures are commonly included on surveys, but almost always for the purpose of spotting them in relation to the limits of the land parcel. Locating or spotting his house not within lines, but within woods, hills and waters, was another unorthodox move. Like landscape artists who invested their work with heightened realism by including in the foreground of their paintings evidence of themselves at work, Thoreau built into his survey visual testimony to his presence, adding an individual referent to the mythological landscape he was measuring. Putting himself in the foreground was a way of signifying his hand in the production of both the literary and cartographic texts while suggesting the ways both were shaped not by existing boundary conceptualizations but by a notably boundless perspective.

At what point does a willful disavowal of legal claims and lines of political demarcation become subversive? In plane surveys, the landscape is understood as essentially meaningless—only artificially created markers matter. Fundamentally, the surveyor's compass and chain exist in order to ascertain limits, substantiate owners' rights, or proclaim political authority over an area. The Walden survey fulfils none of these functions. Rather, it seems to go out of its way to offer nothing of conventionally economic or political value to anyone. Accurate surveys lubricate the wheels of commerce, solidify possession and help bring order to civic life. From the Walden survey, no one, not even the surveyor himself (who received no pay for his laborious efforts) derives pelf or profit. According to the reigning economic paradigm, unsurveyed land is unowned land; surveyed land is owned or about to be. Since the land around Walden was already deeded away (even the surface of the pond was being harvested for profit by ice merchants), Thoreau made a drawing that in a sense took it back, reclaiming it from its possessors and undoing the work of previous surveyors. To say simply that Thoreau's priorities differ from professional norms seems inadequate. In turning his map upside down and eliminating property lines, he gave his readers a cartography that was the inverse of utilitarianism, rejecting key tenets of both map-making and land surveying as accepted cultural forms.

What happened to Thoreau's work when it was included on H. F. Walling's 1852 map of Concord is a revealing indication of its eccentric motivations. In order to make the survey conventionally useful, the Lincoln-Concord town line had to be added; several of Thoreau's geographic features, including the location of his cabin, had to be removed; and of course, the map had to be turned right side up. No one had ever denied that Thoreau's survey was accurate; its design principles and aesthetic priorities, however, had to be substantially reorganized for public consumption. The story told by the Walden map is thus a forcefully iconoclastic narrative, saying to the citizens of Concord, landowners, and perhaps even the selectmen who cut across his favorite pond with what Thoreau called a "petty" and "insignificant" town limit,[24] "Here is the phenomenal world as I know it, not as you know it." With the Walden map, Thoreau gave visual evidence of an aesthetic not only dissimilar but opposed to social norms—as diametrically opposed as south is to north.

The numerical data or field notes for the Walden survey no longer exist, but they may be reconstructed with fair precision using documents Thoreau did leave behind.[25] From the preliminary sketches of the pond, distances and bearings taken in the field can be ascertained, and the accuracy of the reobtained data checked by redrawing the map itself. The Walden field notes constitute a point of intersection between the literary and surveying inclinations of a great American writer. These data, gathered through Thoreau's considerable physical exertions, have remained latent in the survey document, untranslated and unread. They are valuable as a product of his intellectual life, a remnant of his personal material culture, and a fragment of *Walden*, dictated intact across more than a century and a half.

It is possible, perhaps likely, that the production of the literary text of *Walden* actually began with the surveying notes—that before Thoreau wrote a line of his book, he measured lines across the pond.[26] If the field notes are the earliest recoverable fragment of the book, an urtext of Thoreau's masterpiece, it should be emphasized that this text originated in an unusual way. The field notes, after all, were authored as much by the compass needle as by Thoreau. They, and therefore the first component part of *Walden*, were a materialization of the earth's magnetic field, emerging from a hybrid assortment of morphemes transcribed while in contact with the shifting surface of the pond itself. There is perhaps no other book with a germination so richly metaphysical. Prompted by a desire to know and shape reality for visual rather than verbal representation, Thoreau began not with words of his own making but with symbols for which he was merely a conduit, not with the drafting of sentences but with the drafting of a landscape.

The reconstructed field notes for the Walden survey, along with a diagram showing the baseline, lines of bearing, and reference points Thoreau used to survey the pond, appear at the end of this chapter. Figure 2.3 shows clearly the meshlike network of facts with which the surveyor blanketed his environment. Using compass readings from at least six stations, Thoreau took many more bearings than were necessary, probing fastidiously into the pond's corners and projecting his concentrated vision over its surface like beams of light. Engineering software and the reconstructed field-notes data were used to create this image, but anyone with a good protractor and a straightedge could apply the same field notes to establish Thoreau's baseline, determine his angles, locate his points of intersection, and in essence redraw the Walden map.

Thoreau wanted his readers to know that drawing a pond for its own sake, with no reason other than love for it, could be a worthwhile endeavor. Having sketched Walden in the same manner, and with the same motivations, I can argue that he was right. For me, the drafting process

did not simply underscore the versatility of Thoreau's intellect; it en-
forced awareness of the physical skills that were cultivated, and the rational faculties that were applied, in the careful creation of one vital page
of *Walden*. Redrawing the pond could not reproduce the sensations of
wintry afternoons spent chaining and chopping on a vast sheet of ice, but
it offered a compelling kind of access to the writer who performed such
work, and to the origins of his great book.

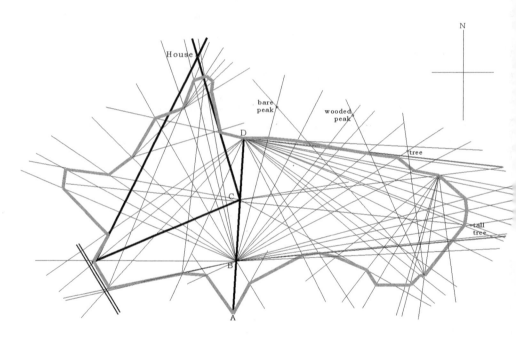

FIGURE 2.3. Schematic of the Walden survey, showing Thoreau's method of angle
intersection. Lines of bearing originate from stations B, D and midpoint C on the
survey baseline, with secondary stations along the pond edge. The Fitchburg Railroad is shown with parallel lines at lower left. The core triangle appears in bold,
with vertices at Thoreau's house, the railroad, and midpoint C.

TABLE 2.1. Reconstructed Field Notes for the Walden Survey

Walden Pond, surveyed 1846			
AB	N 3 E	5.94 chains	
BD (baseline)	N 3 E	14.06 chains	
BC	N 3 E	7.085 chains (midpoint of BD)	
B-a1	S 76 ¼ W	B-y	S 62 ½ W
B-b1	N 89 ½ W	B-z	S 75 ¼ W
B-c1	N 78 W	B-G1	N 12 W
B- d1	N 64 ½ W		
B-e1	N 59 W	D-a1	S 38 ½ W
B-f1	N 52 ½ W	D-b1	S 47 W
B-g1	N 42 W	D-c1	S 52 W
B-j1	N 26 ½ W	D-f1	S 73 W
B-i	N 17 W	D-g1	S 78 ½ W
B-G	N 8 ½ W	D-j1	N 76 W
B-D	N 3 E	D-w	S 24 E
B-Bare Peak	N 11 ½ E	D-v1	S 30 E
B-Wooded Peak	N 34 ½ E	D-u	S 45 ½ E
B-f	N 39 E	D-s	S 48 ½ E
B-g	N 46 ½ E	D-q	S 52 E
B-k1	N 52 ½ E	D-p	S 61 E
B-e	N 24 E	D-o	S 66 E
B-tree	N 54 ¼ E	D-tall tree	S 66 ½ E
B- J	N 56 E	D-n	S 70 E
B-k	N 60 E	D-m	S 73 E
B-1	N 72 ¾ E	D-1	S 76 ½ E
B-m	N 76 E	D-k	S 78 E
B-n	N 80 E	D-j	S 82 E
B-o	N 83 ¼ E	D-h	S 82 ½ E
B-tall tree	N 84 E	D-f	S 83 E
B-w	N 86 ¾ E	D-e	S 86 ½ E
B-x	S 28 E	D-z	S 21 ½ W

STATION C AT POND CENTER

C-House	N 15 W
C-Railroad(b1)	S 64 ½ W
C-G	N 66 ½ E
C-e1	N 79 ½ W
C-v	S 58 E
C-k1	N 81 ¾ E

continued

Station k1 on NE edge of pond

k1-p	S 7 E
k1-q	S 7 W
k1-r	S 13 W
k1-s	S 15 W
k1-t	S 26 ½ W
k1-u	S 33 ¾ W
k1-v	S 49 W

Station R on SE edge of pond

R to Bare Peak	N 38 W
R to Wooded Peak	N 21 W
R to tree	N 8 W

Station A at apex of baseline

A-West edge	N 32 W
A-East edge	N 26 E

Station b1 (Railroad)

b1 to House	N 23 ½ E

North Cove

a1-G	N 20 E
G-j	N 30 W
G-k	N 38 W
G-1	N 44 E

Note: Since Walden and nearby White Pond were surveyed using the same method, the notes Thoreau made for the White Pond survey, located on pages 39–41 of his "Field-Notes," offer an indication of how this data would have been organized. To create a 16 × 21 inch map of the pond with these notes, use a protractor and ruled T square. Make station C the center point of the map and exact midpoint of the baseline BCD. Make the baseline 5.63 inches long and draw it at a bearing of three degrees east of north. Trace and label the lines of bearing from stations B and D. The outline of the pond, and the location of other stations where bearings were taken, will become apparent as the lines intersect.

3

Walden, Cape Cod,
and the
Duty of the Coast Survey

R.W.E. told [of] Mr. Hill, his classmate, of Bangor,
who was much interested in my "Walden," but rel-
ished it merely as a capital satire and joke, and even
thought that the survey and map of the pond were
not real, but a caricature of the Coast Surveys.

—Thoreau, *Journal*, January 5, 1855

THE ORIGINAL OBJECTIVES OF THE U.S. Coast Survey, authorized
by Congress in 1807, were military and economic. Accurate maps and detailed geographic knowledge of the eastern seaboard were necessary to
systematize coastal defense and safeguard the nation's growing commercial maritime traffic. The first superintendent of the Coast Survey was
Swiss-born mathematician Ferdinand Hassler, who directed the project
from its inception in 1816 until his death in 1843.[1] Hassler was one of
the most skillful measurers in history and the ingenious method he con-
ceived for implementing the vast survey was his greatest achievement. He
devised a plan to measure the Atlantic seaboard by laying out a network

of enormous consecutive triangles, the sides of which ranged from ten to sixty miles in length. The precise baselines of the triangles—sometimes up to nineteen miles long and accurate to within inches—were to be measured manually with a carefully constructed base apparatus, an assemblage of four two-meter-long bars of brass and iron, meticulously calibrated and finished with a chemical coating to reduce expansion or contraction from temperature fluctuations. Using astronomical determination of prominent points, a triangulation to connect the points, and a hydrographic survey based upon the triangulation, Hassler began measuring in northern New England and worked southward, mapping every feature of shoreline topography and charting the depths of all usable harbors and coastal waters within commercial shipping routes.

Hassler was a much better scientist and surveyor than he was a lobbyist; his tenure as superintendent was marked by frequent conflict with the government, which had commissioned the project and held the power of the purse. Work on the survey was broken off for long periods by legislative indecision over its budget and disputes about whether the military could do the work more efficiently.[2] Believing that scientists and not politicians should judge his efforts, Hassler was never willing to fully cooperate with military engineers or to express goals for the survey that would appeal to Congress or the general public. Over the more than three decades he spent on the project, he could not proceed quickly enough for elected officials who wanted immediate results from appropriations. At his death in 1843, Hassler's work had reached only as far as the southern border of New Jersey.

Hassler's successor as survey superintendent was Alexander Dallas Bache, who reinvigorated the project, in part by better articulating its impressive scientific achievements and in part by explicitly linking surveying fieldwork to popular cultural concerns.[3] Realizing that the lofty scientific goals of the work were "somewhat in advance of public opinion,"[4] Bache negotiated an accommodation between the interests of the survey and society by emphasizing the mutually supportive relation between the nation's commercial growth and its scientific prestige. In one instance of inspired public relations, he recruited testimonials from a group of elite scientists, then brought the scientists to Wall Street to explain to leading merchants and insurance agents how the survey project would improve investment security.[5] Conceiving of science as a cultural endeavor, Bache framed the survey as a national responsibility, a validation of Manifest Destiny, and an expression of American aspiration toward new discoveries in astronomy, geodesy and the natural sciences. Strongly motivated by patriotism, Bache described the project not only as a working merger of technology and commerce but as an opportunity to demonstrate to Europeans that American-trained scholars could command a world-class scientific institution. In this respect it helped that Bache was native-born—he was the great-grandson of Benjamin Franklin and could therefore "stamp upon the work the character of Americanism."[6]

Admiring descriptions of the Coast Survey appeared frequently in scientific journals and popular literature during the period immediately prior to Henry Thoreau's 1846 survey of Walden Pond. In 1844, the prestigious *American Journal of Science and Arts* had celebrated the Coast Survey as a great enterprise and extolled the intellectual qualifications and "great practical wisdom" of its charismatic superintendant.[7] Just as Thoreau was taking up residence at Walden in July of 1845, the same periodical acknowledged the heightened significance and visibility of the work: "The interest which the readers of this Journal must have always felt in the condition and progress of the United States coast survey, has been very much . . . increased by the appointment of Dr. Bache to the office of superintendent." Since the survey was now "exclusively under American control," its progress supported "a just pride in the scientific reputation of this country."[8] An April 1845 article in the *Biblical Repertory and Princeton Review* claimed that the work of the Coast Survey "affects the whole civilized world" and that its importance was "evident to everyone who reflects on the nature of the art of navigation and its connexion with . . . the prosperity of our nation." In terms that would become a frequent refrain in later debates over funding for the project, the journal described the Coast Survey as "a duty," an obligation "which every nation owes to every other, and to humanity in general."[9]

One of Bache's improvements to the survey was to publish its results as soon as possible rather then waiting, as Hassler had done, until a work phase was complete.[10] Another was to democratize the coastal survey. To expand the support base and social legitimacy of the national mapping project, Bache made it possible to employ common citizens, often with equipment no more sophisticated than a weighted cod line, to provide preliminary soundings for Coast Survey use. While gathering their data, survey employees often worked by themselves, in areas far from the authority of Bache and other Coast Survey managers. Beginning in the 1840s, Bache instructed his corps of volunteer "tidal observers" to study "the movement and deposit of sandbars and banks" along with "the environment in which lighthouses may be located."[11] Exhorting citizen-surveyors to maintain a high level of accuracy, he also reminded them that they "cannot be too careful to note the facts *precisely as they occur*."[12] Bache's use of local residents as Coast Survey "correspondents" increased public involvement in the science of the survey and offered nonprofessional naturalists a means of vicarious participation in the great national endeavor. Benjamin Peirce, an acquaintance of Thoreau's and the Coast Survey's leading mathematician, saw this type of participation in the project as "the solemn duty of every scientist, who has a drop of patriotism in his veins."[13]

A large number of Coast Survey projects were going on, and a large number of Coast Survey maps published, while Thoreau was living at Walden Pond. In 1844–45, Bache published long-awaited maps of New York Bay and New York Harbor. In 1846, new and accurate maps were published of New Bedford Harbor and New Haven Harbor. Surveys of Fisher's Island Sound, Holmes Hole and Oyster Bay were under way. The mid-1840s also marked great progress in the geodetic work of the project. Thoreau surely knew that the Coast Survey had established the exact longitude of the nearby Harvard Observatory in 1845, aiding the astronomical observations that were essential to the accuracy of its triangulations.[14] A major hydrographic achievement of 1846 was the survey of Nantucket Shoals, which located and charted long-hidden dangers to commercial traffic, greatly increasing maritime safety in the crowded shipping lane to the south of Nantucket Island. These advancements made it easy to proclaim, as the *Literary World* did in September of 1847, that the work of the Coast Survey "promoted the best interests of the country, by contributing to lessen the loss of life and property on the water, and we have no doubt that other discoveries as valuable as this remain to reward its labors."

Just as Thoreau's two-year stay at Walden was coming to a close, *Literary World* editor C. F. Hoffman had produced a widely circulated Coast Survey appreciation that emphasized the nationalistic implications of Bache's work. After praising the "minuteness of detail and miniature accuracy" of the survey, Hoffman proceeded to note the impressive magnitude of the project then stretching from Massachusetts to the Gulf of Mexico. Like the Lewis and Clark expedition or the reports of scientific surveys of Fremont, Pike, Kane, Perry and Lieutenant Herndon,[15] the Coast Survey bespoke a responsibility that was "part of the moral tenure upon which every civilized nation holds its territory." As a journey of discovery, the Coast Survey was intertwined with our national myth, supporting the general ideology of Manifest Destiny and continental conquest by expressing "the duty of improvement and cultivation, and so of exploring the national possessions."[16]

In the decade immediately preceding the publication of *Walden* in 1854, the U.S. Coast Survey was the most important and highly publicized scientific institution in antebellum America,[17] dwarfing in scale and cost any previous government-sponsored foray into science and attracting some of the country's best minds in fields ranging from astronomy to botany to marine biology.[18] The annual reports of the Coast Survey published not only new harbor maps but findings about marine plant and animal life, coastal climatology, ocean tides and currents, and terrestrial magnetism. As both an important abstract intellectual pursuit and a specifically American cultural activity, the Coast Survey became a focal point for the nation's ideas about economics and the environment, an arena in which higher mathematics and elevated scientific strivings interacted with patriotic impulses and profit-driven interests on a large scale.

The public discourse and models of scientific procedure generated by the Coast Survey in the 1840s and 1850s provide an interesting background for Henry Thoreau's geographic explorations in *Cape Cod* and *Walden*. During the period when these works were produced, the Coast Survey gave a platform to contending philosophies about a workable alliance between American science and American commerce and theorized the place of the surveyor's work in relation to both. A close look at surveying-related passages in these works, alongside published documents and print media from the period, situates the author's initial desire to measure the landscape—as well as the vocabulary of his self-identification as a surveyor—within a context informed by Coast Survey ideologies.

The visits to the Massachusetts coast upon which Thoreau's posthumously published *Cape Cod* was based took place in October of 1849,

June of 1850 and July of 1855, while Bache's project was at its peak of activity and national influence. Chapter 8 of *Cape Cod*, entitled "Highland Light," adumbrates a topographic survey during which Thoreau acts and thinks as a Coast Survey correspondent. The chapter's focus on a lighthouse echoes the practices of the Coast Survey, which regularly used the lofty and permanent heights of lighthouses as "high tripods" or instrument stands. In accordance with Coast Survey priorities, Thoreau's opening sentences geographically locate the Highland Light, stating that it is "forty-three miles from Cape Ann Light and forty-one from Boston Light." Possibly paraphrasing one of Bache's annual survey reports, Thoreau refers to the location as "one of our primary sea-coast lights" and immediately afterward relays topographic information: "It stands about twenty rods from the edge of the bank, which is here formed of clay."[19] Since the Highland Light was actually used as one of the Coast Survey's many triangulation points, it was listed in its 1851 charts in relation to two nearer positions—4.39 miles to Cambria and 7.08 miles to Griffin's Island. The two reference locations given by Thoreau emulate such charts but position his triangulation point using more familiar stations.

Bache's coastal charts also give the exact latitude and longitude of the light, along with precise bearings figured to the second or one-sixtieth of a degree, from the Highland Light to the Cambria and Griffin's Island lights. Unequipped to conduct such long-range operations or to match Bache's precision, Thoreau is nevertheless determined to obtain and record landscape data, beginning with the vertical height of the lighthouse:

> I borrowed the plane and square, level and dividers, of a carpenter who was shingling a barn nearby, and using one of those shingles made of a mast, contrived a rude sort of quadrant, with pins for sights and pivots, and got the angle of elevation of the bank opposite the light house, and with a couple of cod-lines the length of its slope, and so measured its height on the shingle.[20]

Here Thoreau's "rude sort of quadrant" was a wooden quarter-circle panel with degree graduations drawn on its ninety-degree arc. At opposite ends of the panel's top edge were two pins or small nails that served as sights. Suspended by a string from the center of the arc—attached by means of a pin according to Thoreau's description—there would have been a surveyor's plummet or plumb bob, but Thoreau may have substituted a string with a small stone attached.

Determining the height of the lighthouse was a simple operation. Using the cod lines, Thoreau first measured the distance from the structure's base to the point where he would take his quadrant sighting. This gave him the length of one side of the triangle he was creating with the base of the lighthouse, the top of the lighthouse, and his point of observation. In order to measure the angle of elevation to the top of the lighthouse tower, he viewed this point through the sights on the top edge of the quadrant, holding the instrument so that its plane was vertical. The weighted string was allowed to hang vertically and indicate a degree reading on the arc's graduations. After he had determined this angle, he had enough trigonometric information to calculate the height of the beacon.

Thoreau was also very interested in the extent of the erosion on the cliff between the light at Truro and the shore. This gave him another reason for using the quadrant to determine the bank's angle of elevation. He discovered that the bank of "mixed sand and clay" between the lighthouse and the shore was thirteen feet high, that it "lay at an angle of forty degrees with the horizon" and that it seemed to be, like the much-higher bank a mile to the south, "fast wearing away." By questioning the lighthouse keeper Thoreau learned varied theories about the rate of erosion, including the possibility that the Cape coastline was "wasting . . . on both sides" and that "erelong, the light-house must be moved." The surveyor and the lighthouse keeper then "calculated, *from his data*, how soon the Cape would be quite worn a way at this point." [21]

This 1849 "survey" of the coast at Truro was only the beginning of Thoreau's long-term study of the location. Returning to the same spot in June of 1850 to find that the bank had lost about forty feet in one place, Thoreau theorized that the rate of erosion was not as rapid as many believed: "I judged that generally it was not wearing away here at the rate of more than six feet annually." The actual rate of erosion was probably then just over three feet per year,[22] but Thoreau's basic hypothesis—his intimation that "any conclusions drawn from the observations of a few years or one generation only are likely to prove false, and the Cape may balk expectation by its durability"[23] —has been somewhat validated by subsequent history. It took 140 years, until the early 1990s, for the erosion of the Truro coast to move another 230 feet and reach within 100 feet of the lighthouse. The Highland Lighthouse was not moved back from the bank until 1996.[24]

Thoreau could feel confidence in his judgments about coastal geography in part because of what he had learned from his own explorations but certainly as well from his attention to the techniques of the Coast Survey. The Highland Light chapter directly alludes to a recent treatise on ocean tides by Charles Henry Davis, the well-known commander of one of the survey's hydrographic parties. "According to Lieutenant Davis," Thoreau wrote, "the forms, extent and distribution of sand-bars and banks are principally determined, not by winds and waves, but by tides."[25] On his 1855 visit to the Cape, Thoreau probably had Davis's theories in mind as he conducted yet another rudimentary hydrographical survey—this time looking into the effects of a single storm with a high tide. Perhaps with help from William Ellery Channing, Thoreau took soundings that revealed that the sand on the beach opposite the lighthouse had been inundated with six feet of water within an area "three rods in width as far as we could see north and south."[26] During the same visit, he discovered "a bar wholly made within three months; first exposed about the first of May; as I paced, now seventy-five rods long and six or eight rods wide at high water."[27] With these operations, Thoreau personally tested Davis's conclusions about the influence of tides on land formations.

Another example of overlap between *Cape Cod* and the ongoing maritime survey is the chapter "The Beach." In a single paragraph that typifies Thoreau's priorities at the Cape, a sandbank is described as "the height of a hundred feet" and a dozen rods in width; moreover, a "desert of shining sand" is from thirty to eighty rods in width. The "Table Lands" of Eastham are described as full fifty rods in width, rising "full one hundred and fifty feet above the ocean . . . for two and half miles, or as far as the eye could reach . . . as regular as a military engineer could desire."[28] Unhindered by the absence of compass and chain on his coastal excursions, Thoreau is nevertheless able to pace out distances and conduct topographical studies with pretensions to mathematical precision, the processes and results of which form a significant part of his literary manuscript.

Chapter 5 of *Cape Cod*, which recounts Thoreau and Channing's overnight stay at the cottage of Wellfleet oysterman John Newcomb, is particularly rich in surveying terminology, beginning with Thoreau's casual noting of the boundary between Wellfleet and Truro, "a stone post in the sand." This is followed immediately by the more subjective and interested comment that "even this sand comes under the jurisdiction of one town or another."[29] The process of locating a land boundary, followed by an innuendo about the futility and impermanence of the landscape's official domestication, is a visible pattern in the book. The oysterman's remark about the incompetent surveyors of his own property—that "they who surveyed his farm were accustomed, where the ground was uneven, to loop up each chain as high as their elbows; that was the allowance they made, and he wished to know if I could tell him why they did not come out according to his deed, or twice alike"[30]—suggests the arbitrariness of boundaries while also providing Thoreau with the chance to disparage bad surveying procedures. Rather than explaining the inaccuracies that would result from such crude slope-chaining techniques, however, Thoreau maintains an ironic stance by commenting that Newcomb "seemed to have more respect for surveyors of the old school, which I did not wonder at."[31] The particular surveyor of the old school referred to in this conversation is King George the Third, who is described by Thoreau's host as having "laid out a road four rods wide and straight the whole length of the Cape." The fact that the king's road is gone—"where it was now he could not tell"[32]—provides another bit of humorous local color, but it has a deeper meaning as well, identifying the surveyor as a metonym of state authority and hinting at the transient nature of the lines established by that authority.

Thinking about the conversation in relation to the time line of Thoreau's career evokes other, perhaps essential inferences and suppositions about how Thoreau saw himself and his work. In response to Newcomb's questions about his position and background, Thoreau gives a curious answer: "I told him that I was a surveyor." The statement is interesting because at the time this conversation took place, Thoreau was not a surveyor, at least in the professional sense. Other than the as-yet-unpublished Walden map and some work for Emerson, Thoreau had produced perhaps only one known survey before 1849.[33] He had not yet purchased his field notebook, advertised his services or begun to regularly hire himself out—all of which took place just after he returned to Concord from Provincetown in mid-October 1849. The first entry in Thoreau's surveying field notebook—the November 1849 plan of Isaac Watts's woodlot made with Cyrus Hubbard's compass and chain—came in the month following this trip to the Cape.

To the Wellfleet oysterman, however, Thoreau presents himself as a surveyor, and in keeping with this assumed persona, he accounts for himself to the oystermen in part by sharing surveying stories. Along with the anecdotes described above, Thoreau tells of a Long Islander who, "when he came to a brook which he wanted to get over . . . held up one leg, and then, if his foot appeared to cover any part of the opposite bank, he knew he could jump it." Skeptical of the man's homespun science, Thoreau had introduced real trigonometry to the issue by asking him "how he knew when he had got his leg at the right elevation." Since the Long Islander regarded his legs as a kind of "ordinary quadrant," with the leg on the ground perpendicular to the plane of the horizon and the other held up at a right angle, Thoreau suggested he use a string to connect his two ankles to make the chord of an arc. Perhaps, Thoreau mused, the measure of the string would enable him to measure his "jumping ability" on horizontal surfaces.[34]

The tale of the Long Islander's "geometry in the legs" is a seemingly digressive anecdote in *Cape Cod*. It is nevertheless a story that Thoreau claims to have been interested to hear of, probably because he was then beginning to seriously refine many other field applications of Euclidean geometry.[35] The mathematics in question bore an obvious relation to that of his makeshift quadrant at Truro, and perhaps it also mattered that nineteenth-century surveyors regularly applied the science of precise chord measurement in the field. When a surveyor needed to measure an angle but suspected that his compass bearings were unreliable (as often happened), he could find angles by measuring one chain length along the two sides that composed the angle, then taking the distance between the two sides. This last measure was the chord of the angle formed by the two lines. Using a table of chord lengths or subtendents to the radius of one chain, the surveyor could then determine, often with more accuracy than with a compass, the degree of the angle and the bearing of the lines. That Thoreau is reminded of the eccentric Long Islander by the oysterman's equally unconventional "story of the surveyors" is an indication that, in addition to having a surveyor's eyes, Thoreau was beginning to display a surveyor's priorities and mind-set.

Thoreau and Channing's stopover at the cottage of the Wellfleet oysterman had been preceded by a recent visit from employees of the Coast Survey. The oysterman takes pleasure in teaching his guests the names of ponds in the vicinity, in part because he has done so before, when "the coast surveyors had come to him for their names and he had told them of one they had not detected."[36] Thoreau was surely already aware of how his Cape Cod excursion followed in the footsteps of the Coast Survey, but after this conversation, he may have wondered if the oysterman saw him and Channing as just another surveying party. He may also have considered whether his spontaneous measurements with makeshift equipment were closer to the work of the ineffectual surveyors who carelessly looped up the chain to compensate for a slope or to the magnificent accuracy of Bache's project. Though a good deal of the chapter's humor derives from the implicit comparison between Thoreau's competence and less sensible methods of measurement, Thoreau himself was still a rank amateur. The fashioning of his own quadrant from a shingle and pins at Truro, the borrowing of a compass and chain for the Walden survey, even the surveying of Jesse Hosmer's hundred-acre farm with a tape rather than a Gunter's chain because he did not yet own one—all present a good idea of the dubious conditions under which Thoreau's self-identification as surveyor began.

The conclusion that Thoreau saw himself as a kind of surveyor, in particular a type of informal Coast Survey correspondent, before he began working professionally is inevitable. Where his sense of himself and his identity were concerned, he had been a type of surveyor since his early twenties, when he and his brother took their students into the fields to teach mathematics and geometry through measuring—or since 1846, when he had mapped Walden. He had been a surveyor—but not truly a professional one—in 1847, when he included surveying among his numerous avocations on his Harvard alumni questionnaire, and in October 1849, when he gathered coastal environmental data on the Cape with homemade equipment. To some extent, he had been a surveyor in his worldview for his entire adult life, and running lines for his neighbors, or emulating Bache, were indications of a habit of mind that had been there from the beginning.

One gets the sense, however, that the surveying expedition to Cape Cod was on the whole less than fruitful in terms that mattered to Thoreau. One of his immediate problems after arriving on the Cape is the distortion of perceptions and distances. In the chapter entitled "The Plains of Nauset," he notices a solitary walker on the beach who "loomed like a giant" due to the absence of proper perspective against the background of the sea. "The landscape is a constant mirage," Thoreau observes, and objects are distorted, "there being no object by which to measure them."[37] Though it is hard to argue that learning distances and recording spatial relationships are not an essential component of *Cape Cod*, it appears that Thoreau's ideas about measurement were challenged on his trips to the Massachusetts coast, prompting him to experiments more refined than those of a mere "tidal observer." At the start of his adventure, he acts as if knowing land measurements is the surest way to apprehend the landscape itself; what ultimately troubles him is the inadequacy of his own perceptions to fully do so. But if the coastal landscape, as Richard Schneider observes, "represented the shifting, unsurveyable wilderness of illusions that humans can never fully penetrate in this life," Thoreau does not seem to have despaired in the face of this realization. After encountering the Cape, Thoreau would, as Schneider notes, redouble attempts to "measure desperately the objects in the Concord woods."[38] He would also, however, begin to measure them professionally, with his own professional equipment. Simultaneously, he would pursue increasingly sophisticated inquiries about geography and environmental science.

Soon after Thoreau returned from his first visit to Cape Cod in October 1849, reviews of *A Week on the Concord and Merrimack Rivers* began to appear in popular journals alongside the type of articles about the progress of the Coast Survey that had proliferated since the early 1840s. Thoreau's personal library included a copy of the widely read *American Almanac and Repository of Useful Knowledge* for the year 1849, in which the earlier-mentioned Lieutenant Davis—who joined the Coast Survey in 1842 and became famous for his discovery of Nantucket's New South Shoal in 1846—gave perhaps the quintessential Coast Survey manifesto. Davis's long essay provided a detailed firsthand description of the progress and practical operations of the project. It also offered an eloquent philosophical discussion of the value of surveying work "in every country where science and its application to the arts of life are justly appreciated."[39]

The opening sentence of Davis's article reads like a formal preamble carrying grandiose historical pretensions: "It was to be expected that a

people devoted to the pursuits of commerce, and depending, in some degree, on the sea as a means of communication between distant parts of
the national territory, should demand, at an early period of their history,
a competent survey of their coasts and inland waters." After asserting that
the project would aid the process of the country's acceptance of its role
as a global citizen, helping to integrate the country into a broader web
of commercial and diplomatic relations, Davis argues that it has been "of
service to the farmer as well as the navigator." Responding to budget-mo-
tivated attacks on the Coast Survey by congressmen and journalists, he
acknowledges that the long-term project is sometimes misunderstood by
the public, then enumerates its considerable economic uses as "a subject
identified with the commercial welfare of the country."[40]

But Davis's real subject, the one that calls forth his most impassioned prose, is the scientific basis of the survey. Clearly taking cues from
Bache's portrayals of the work, Davis notes that "in abstract science it has
also its mission, equally useful and distinguished." The "great triangles of
the survey," Davis explains, employed knowledge of the "elongations of
Polaris in its eastern and western digressions" along with determination
of azimuths through multiple telegraphically synchronized readings of
the circumpolar stars. While Davis's descriptions of the hydrographic
aspects of the survey would certainly have resonated for Thoreau, the
foregrounding of these abstract scientific purposes, including investigations into local gravitation and the phenomena of terrestrial magnetism,
were probably just as compelling to the novice Concord surveyor. Davis's
message was that, while the practical consequences of the work were
connected to political and commercial interests, the national survey also
possessed a purely scientific element—untainted by economics—that
superseded all others: "The investigations involved by the Coast Survey
are of the most abstruse science, requiring computations of the highest
order of mathematics and physics."[41]

Prompted by financial necessity to accept relatively routine fieldwork
but certainly also cognizant of the sophisticated rationale, cultural significance and epic labors of the Coast Survey, Henry Thoreau began regular
employment. Throughout the early 1850s, while toiling in the fields of
Concord and while perfecting the manuscript of *Walden*, he continued
to demonstrate curiosity about the science of surveying as a national
enterprise and evinced a long-term interest in published Coast Survey

products. Performing small surveys for local clients, he remained apprised of Bache's work through his subscription to the annual *Report of the Superintendent of the Coast Survey*, which he received without fail for every year from 1850 to 1858. Thoreau also owned the *Sketches* published by the Coast Survey in 1851, which presented land, water and climate data along with remarkably detailed coastal maps. Thoreau's journal of July 1850 expressed an appreciation for Lieutenant Davis's *A Memoir upon the Geological Action of Tidal and Other Currents in the Ocean*, a work that grew directly out of his explorations for the Coast Survey.[42]

The Concord surveyor also seems to have missed few opportunities to learn from Bache's assistants. As early as 1847, Thoreau had discussed astronomical discoveries with Benjamin Peirce, one of the survey's principal scientists, who later succeeded Bache as superintendent.[43] While in Boston in 1851, Thoreau conversed with John Downes, an engineer connected with the Coast Survey, asking Downes about the "tables for astronomical, geodesic, and other uses" he was compiling as one of Bache's civilian officers.[44] With Harvard astronomer William Cranch Bond, one of the Coast Survey's chief scientists, Thoreau cultivated a scholarly association.[45] When the two met in 1851, Bond's investigations of the phenomena of terrestrial magnetism on behalf of the survey had been internationally recognized and celebrated as evidence of American achievement.[46] Thoreau had several meetings with the famed astronomer, apparently for the purpose of gaining individualized instruction on magnetic phenomena from the leading American authority on the subject.[47] These tutorials nearly bore literary fruit; Thoreau was sufficiently intrigued by the subject to produce a fascinating but unfinished manuscript that described and commented on the historical development of investigations into earthly magnetism over several centuries.[48]

While Thoreau never pretended to Bond's level of scientific expertise, he looked for ways to apply Coast Survey discoveries in the many property surveys he had begun to perform as a professional civil engineer.[49] He also, it seems, inquired about actual rather than merely vicarious participation as a survey correspondent. An entry in Thoreau's journal of July 1851 describes a visit with Bond at the Harvard Observatory, during which the conversation turned to the cataloguing of the stars and other astronomical data then being compiled. Apparently referring to the work of the correspondents then making tidal and astronomical observations,

Thoreau asked Bond "if an observer with the small telescope could find employment." Bond replied, "Oh yes—there was employment enough for observation with the naked eye—observing the changes in the brilliancy of stars, etc., etc., if they could only get some good observers."[50]

Since he was obviously a sensitive observer with a clear interest in Bond's investigations, we might wonder why the Concord surveyor left the Harvard astronomer's apparent job offer on the table. The logical answer is that in asking about the types of observation accepted by the Coast Survey, the purpose had not actually been to seek part-time employment. Rather, Thoreau's aim was to determine where his own less sophisticated work stood in relation to the most advanced geodetic research. Bond's response satisfied Thoreau because it confirmed the linkage, always important to him, between comparatively simple field operations and the great science of the day: "One is glad to hear that the naked eye still retains some importance in the estimation of astronomers."[51] If interdependence among forms of observation was a viable concept, Thoreau was in a way already working for Bache, as Bache was working for him.

Acknowledging correspondences between complex national science and unpretentious local inspection with the naked eye supports several inferences affecting our appreciation of Cape Cod. The frequency and pervasiveness of Thoreau's topographical observations on the Cape suggest that Bache's methods were well integrated into Thoreau's thought processes and that his identity as a surveyor derived in part from the perceptual attitude of a tidal observer. The Coast Survey may well have had an important cross-disciplinary influence, both prompting Thoreau to conduct measuring experiments and offering him precedents for affording them meaning. The national survey emphasized cultural interrelations, boldly articulating a rationale for geographic exploration that was at once commercial, scientific, philosophical and patriotic. In Cape Cod, Thoreau's reconnaissance of the New England coast—characterized by a strong interest in its maritime commercial history, close attention to botanical science, and an evident pride in the area as "a place of wonder"—is recognizable as a microcosm of Bache's culturally complex work.[52]

In Walden, Thoreau's visceral response to Coast Survey methods and models is even more apparent. The physical discovery of the pond, along with the tropes Thoreau used to describe that discovery, accord well with the Coast Survey's heralded goals and processes. Bache's hydrographic work had clear significance for American commerce and culture at large, but it somehow mattered also at Walden, where pond surveying was explicitly modeled on harbor surveying, and where Thoreau's enumerated tasks included "charts to be studied, the position of reefs and new lights and buoys to be ascertained, and ever and ever, the logarithmic tables to be corrected."[53] Thoreau's interest in determining as clear a picture as possible of the slopes and contours of the pond bottom is analogous to the attempts of the Coast Survey to not only establish the depths of coastal waters but to locate the treacherous shallows and irregularities that could and often did spell disaster for maritime commerce. Accuracy and scientific precision were crucial to Bache's awe-inspiring project but were equally indispensible in the nautical world of the pond, and for the same reasons: "For by the error of some calculator," Thoreau wrote in Walden, "the vessel often splits upon a rock that should have reached a friendly pier."[54]

As an amateur engineer, naturalist, and scientist with broad competencies and environmental interests, Thoreau possessed the skills to decipher Coast Survey results, understand their significance, and field-test some of the survey's tangible and theoretical insights. To a considerable extent, Thoreau's account of his pond survey in *Walden* reads like the annual reports of the Coast Survey. Perhaps aware of this correlation, Thoreau seems to work out comparisons between his small-scale hydrographic work and the deepwater surveying being carried on by Bache: "As I sounded through the ice I could determine the shape of the bottom with greater accuracy than is possible in surveying harbors which do not freeze over." Eager to derive practical principles from his observations, the Walden surveyor is surprised at the general regularity of the pond bottom. The hypothesis that follows—"I could calculate the variation [in the pond's depth] for each one hundred feet in any direction beforehand within three or four inches. . . . The effect of water under these circumstances is to level all inequalities"—could easily be appended to one of Bache's tide tables or reports on the effect of ocean currents on bottom configuration. Thoreau also reports the somewhat bold deduction that "the regularity of the bottom and its conformity to the shores and the range of neighboring hills were so perfect that a distant promontory betrayed itself in the soundings quite across the pond, and its direction could be determined by observing the opposite shore." Finally, the

Walden surveyor arrives at a synthesizing insight that might have interested the coast surveyors as a rudimentary principle. Linking elements of geographic and hydrographic science, Thoreau proposes that "cape becomes bar, and plain shoal, and valley and gorge deep water and channel." As if proclaiming an association between the waters of Walden and the frontiers of surveying science then being explored by Bache, Thoreau asks, "Who knows but this hint would conduct to the deepest part of the ocean as well as of a pond or a puddle?"[55]

A visual comparison of the Walden map (figure 2.2) with a typical Coast Survey publication (figure 3.1) strengthens Thoreau's analogy, showing fundamentally similar cartographic procedure and lexicon. Bache's "Preliminary Chart of Ship and Sand Shoal Inlets" on the Virginia Coast, published in 1854, includes a prominent true north and depth soundings at frequent intervals "so as to represent the figure of the [ocean] bottom." It designates the character of the bottom—"Sand, Mud, Shells, Gravel or Specks"—with abbreviations similar to the "s—soft bottom" and "h. hard" bottom descriptions Thoreau used on his initial drafts of Walden. A close look at Bache's work helps explain why Thoreau took the trouble to locate and pencil in on his finished survey the submerged "Sand-bar" at the entrance to his pond's northern cove; the finding and publication of such shoals and shallows was a chief purpose of the Coast Survey. Bache's products, like the pond survey, consisted of both topographic and hydrographic information but prioritized the latter.

For both Bache and Thoreau, precise geographic observations had philosophical potential. Bache's annual report for 1853 observed that "the charts furnished by the surveys are its most important practical results," but "in the course of the minute investigations required for this purpose, facts of a striking kind are ascertained."[56] By accurately determining that the greatest depth of Walden Pond was "exactly one hundred and two feet," Thoreau gave the lie to legends and superstitions about its bottomlessness, but the real meaning of this critical datum was universal: "What I have observed of the pond is no less true in ethics."[57] As Bache saw it, the Coastal Survey provided facts that spoke a universal language and observed "strict fidelity to nature," practices that meshed seamlessly with beliefs about the correspondence between physics and ethics expressed in the pond survey. In Davis's description of the survey as exhibiting a "philosophical regard to minute details" and a reliance on "the higher

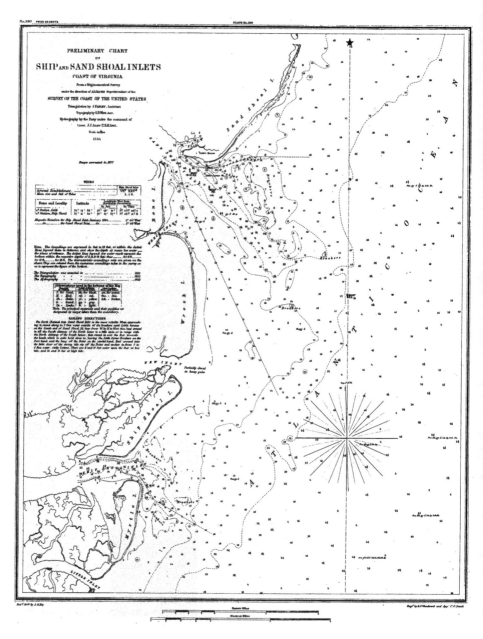

FIGURE 3.1. "Preliminary Chart of Ship and Sand Shoal Inlets, Coast of Virginia," published by the U.S. Coast Survey in 1854. A typical Coast Survey product, providing sailing directions and information about water depths and sea-bottom composition.

mathematics,"[58] Thoreau would have recognized a relation to his own painstaking and principled explorations, which also served purposes at once scientific and sublime, though only figuratively commercial.

Readers of *Walden* have often expressed curiosity about the author's persistent efforts to describe his experience at Walden using economic metaphors. "Why would a writer," Judith Saunders once wondered, "choose to convey the joys of a natural and spiritual life with the language of business and commerce?"[59] Inclusive responses to the question should take note of the prestige and significance of the Coast Survey in antebellum popular culture, along with its role in concurrent discussions of national economic policy. A key passage appears in the opening chapter of *Walden*, "Economy," in which Thoreau indicates that at Walden he will oversee an imaginary business of worldwide trade and export, with the pond as his harbor. Assuming the role of "at once pilot and captain, and owner and underwriter" of the excursion, Thoreau will "buy and sell and keep up a steady dispatch of commodities" while also aiding the free progress of trade by "speaking all passing vessels bound coastwise." Thoreau's work at Walden will require "taking advantage of the results of all exploring expeditions, using new passages and all improvements in navigation."[60] This multifaceted persona—guiding ships to safety, commanding vessels at sea, distributing and marketing goods, insuring as underwriter, taking profits as owner—synopsizes the varied Coast Survey interests and justifications and seems derived from the vocabulary of its supporters in the popular press.[61] Thoreau's impersonation of a Coast Survey correspondent was thus a reconfiguration of a preexisting cultural metaphor. As reshaped in *Walden*, this persona visibly contrasted with the mundane commercial motives of the national survey but closely approximated the scientific goals of Bache's administration. The self-described nautical explorer of the pond is an *inner* correspondent to the Coast Survey, "opening new channels, not of trade, but of thought."[62]

Also potentially intriguing to the philosophically engaged surveyor was Lieutenant Davis's theorization that as Coast Survey science progressed and causes of miscalculation were eradicated, a rare form of perfection was within grasp: "The source of error and its correction being recognized, there is no other limit to accuracy than the possible."[63] In Thoreau's worldview as well, it was assumed that the patient application of measuring technology would hone skills to the point where they would yield not only data but attributes more elusive and abstract. His apparent desire to pursue elements of surveying that were more sophisticated than called for in his small-scale work around Concord derive in part from the romantic formulations of extraordinary accuracy publicized by Bache's survey.

In the text of *Walden*, revised over several years in the early 1850s, Thoreau intermittently seems comfortable with presenting himself as a theoretical brother of the coast surveyors. Like the data Thoreau reported in *Walden*, the national survey did exhibit a philosophical regard for minute details, and privileged the important fact for more than just its benefits to "local and general commerce of the country and the world," but as evidence of the aspiration toward harmony with the entire natural world. As Davis noted, the charts of the Coast Survey, much like Thoreau's map of Walden, would "enable the future hydrographer and the future engineer . . . to cooperate intelligently with natural laws, instead of blindly opposing their effects." Coast Survey charts exhibited "a view of the topographical formation of the bottom of the sea" that was visually analogous to Thoreau's cross-section view of the pond: both produced results "highly interesting to the naturalist."[64] And in both surveying expeditions there was, as the opening chapter of *Walden* openly contends, "universal science to be kept pace with."[65]

Reading *Walden* through the lens of the Coast Survey adds significance to Thoreau's pond experiment, offering ways of understanding its relation to the cultural context of the United States at midcentury. In "Economy," Thoreau explicitly compares the Walden coast with the continental coast, explaining that the yet-to-explored pond shoreline constitutes both "a good place for business" and "a good port."[66] It therefore seems appropriate that Thoreau infuses his lengthy description of his "business" at the pond, including its surveying work, with precepts reconstituted from the Coast Survey. Bache's project was based in part on a lifesaving rationale; it was often framed as a means to prevent or diminish the waste of life and property that was annually occurring in American waters. Thoreau's attainment of simplicity, his avoidance of material threats to life, is salvational as well: "In the midst of this chopping sea of civilized life, such are the clouds and storms and quicksands and thousand-and-one items to be allowed for, that a man has to live, if he would not founder and go to the bottom and not make his port at all, by dead reckoning, and he must be a great calculator indeed who succeeds."[67] With his extended metaphor of maritime surveying at Walden, Thoreau seems to pay homage to Bache, positioning himself as an imitator of the superintendant whose efforts were understood as a sophisticated merger of scientific, commercial and spiritual ends. Referring to his own endeavor but also characterizing the exertions of the coast surveyors, Thoreau proclaims, "It is a labor to task the faculties of a man,—such problems of profit and loss, of interest, of tare and tret, and gauging of all kinds in it, as demand a universal knowledge."[68]

In the epigraph that begins this chapter, Emerson's friend Mr. Hill correctly intuited that Thoreau's surveying and the Coast Survey had something to do with each other. That Hill's misreading of *Walden* was based in part on a misreading of the Walden survey—and specifically a misunderstanding of its relation to the national work in progress—is significant. Perhaps not believing that Thoreau had actually done the work described, not knowing how seriously the author took his measuring, Hill saw the Walden survey as either a frivolous or ersatz textual element that colored Thoreau's book with irony.

If Thoreau was disappointed to learn that the product of his fieldwork could be understood as not "real" but a "caricature," it might have been because his book had plainly indicated the map's purpose and context. In "The Pond in Winter," Thoreau expounds his geometry-based "rule of the two diameters" but also elucidates a significant philosophical conceit that might be called the "rule of coastal geography." At the midpoint of his description of the pond survey, Thoreau effectively states that the outer geography of the pond stands for the inner geography of the individual. The pond's every cove represents a "particular inclination" of the self, a "harbor for a season, in which we are detained and partially land-locked." Under the terms of this conceit, the general mass of humankind is represented by the ocean, from which the individual gradually withdraws as his poetic thoughts take shape. Individuality thus begins as a barely submerged "bar" at the entrance to an inlet; the bar "is gradually increased by storms, tides, or currents" so that finally, "when there is a subsidence of waters," the self emerges. "At the advent of each individual into this life, may we not suppose that such a bar has risen to the surface somewhere?" Thoreau wonders, anthropomorphically equating the personal with the environmental.[69] Interestingly, the trend of both processes is away from convention and toward severance from the majority. What had begun as an "inclination in the shore in which a thought was harbored" becomes an "individual lake, cut off from the ocean"—a setting "wherein the thought secures its own conditions." At this point, the personality "changes, perhaps, from salt to fresh, becomes a . . . dead sea, or a marsh"—or, like Walden, a "sweet sea" whose measurable profundities harmonize with a "corresponding depth of thought." Though it would seem that successful self-differentiation is already accomplished, the process of studying the landscape is still vital and necessary. We need to examine the "inclinations" of our physical and spiritual worlds, Thoreau says, because they are "not whimsical" or randomly created; rather, their "form, size and direction are determined by the promontories of the shore, the ancient axes of elevation." In effect, geographically derived laws shape both self and soil; if we fail to discern them it is because we are "poor navigators of our thoughts."[70]

Thoreau is suggesting that most of us do not have the courage to plot our own direction or separately locate ourselves within our own philosophical space. "For the most part," he avers, we "stand off and on upon a harborless coast, are conversant only with the bights of the bays of poesy, or steer for the public ports of entry."[71] We are content to become small, nonradical curves or indentations in the shoreline. We haven't yet succeeded in the individuating process of encompassing a closed 360 degrees, as Thoreau has at Walden. Content with the shoreline as is, or with the commonly used ports or harbors, many of us fail to create—and to survey—our separate worlds and separate selves. Others, as Thoreau speculates, succeed observationally but fail perceptually, neglecting the critical *associations* between discovering natural facts and discovering the self. These observers, Thoreau explains, "go into the dry docks of science, where they merely refit for this world, and no natural currents concur to individualize them."[72] While the passage clearly borrows terminology from a scientific enterprise that was then a national priority, it couches the observational method practiced at Walden as a distinct, "natural" activity that goes beyond science.

To the extent that the Walden survey seems consciously modeled on the Coast Surveys, its relation to the real thing it stands for is not satiric or caricatured, as Emerson's friend surmised, but direct and emblematic.

In more than one sense, it constitutes not irony but synecdoche. Framed in simple terms, the image of the pond was a dually significant "part for whole" representation. Thoreau equates the pond with a lake that was once a part of an oceanlike body but is now cut off and compositionally changed—from salt to fresh water. At the same time, the survey document is figured as the product of an exploration of the surveyor's individual spirit. Curiously, the Walden map is also the depiction of a "whole for part" relation: ports and harbors on Coast Survey maps are subordinate bodies, contiguous with larger, unsurveyed waters. Since Walden was contiguous to nothing but itself, Thoreau's map was a finished entity in a way the typical cartographic product of Bache's labor was not. Compared to the maps produced by Bache, the Walden map represented a whole that replaced the linearity of the Atlantic coastline with a finished circle.

Viewed in context, the beautiful outline of Walden Pond may also be understood as a third form of synecdoche—"the material for the thing made from it." As even the spontaneous perceptions of Mr. Hill suggest, the small-scale pond plan showed explicitly the raw material out of which the great measuring science of the day was fashioned. And Hill was correct in comprehending that the map was a replication—though an idiosyncratic one—of an ongoing cultural activity with inherent social meaning.

Thoreau was probably aware that some of his readers might equate his work with Bache's, but he also took pains to illustrate the ways the two endeavors did not equate, showing how his own map was less a cultural responsibility than a duty of self-culture. The Walden map imitates scientific procedure while testifying to the efficacy of, and its maker's preference for, a type of unscientific observation made with the unaided eye. This preference is insinuated in the first chapter of *Walden*, when the author counsels against the "common course" of sending a boy in need of education to "some professor," where he will learn only "to survey the world through a telescope or a microscope, and never with his natural eye."[73] At Walden and on the Cape, Thoreau demonstrated the value of nautical exploration performed with nothing more sophisticated than makeshift quadrants, a weighted cod line, or compass and chain.

Moreover, Thoreau's surveying at Walden does not participate in national Manifest Destiny as much as it epitomizes a retreat from that doctrine's expansive principles. The Coast Survey made it possible to proclaim, as the *Literary World* did in 1848, that the nation possessed "three great maritime fronts—on the Atlantic, the Gulf of Mexico, and the Pacific."[74] Like the formal Survey of Public Lands that was also in progress throughout the nineteenth century, Bache's project was a means of realizing the nation's possessions and consolidating territory. Government surveyors—whether employees of the Coast Survey or the Public Land Survey—embodied the practical means by which an imperialist nation realized its vast material claims. Asked by a congressman when the Coast Survey would be completed, Bache responded, "When will you cease annexing territory?"[75]

One of the ways Thoreau undercuts the identification of his Walden survey with government surveying is by repeatedly depicting himself as a squatter who does not legally own the land he inhabits. Instead, his land use at Walden is based on a professed "squatter's rights" ideology that is diametrically opposed to concepts of state-sponsored ownership. As Cooper's *The Chainbearer* made abundantly clear, squatters and surveyors were adversaries—sometimes mortal ones—because the squatter subverted what the surveyor's work reinforced. Competition, at times violent, between surveyors and squatters marked the entire history of the Public Land Survey.[76] As the Coast Survey progressed into newly acquired territories, its purposes grew to include distinguishing between unmapped and therefore unrealized areas and those that were surveyed and thus formally possessed. In the immense interior of the continent and along the vast American seaboard, measuring was what turned wilderness into property and formally placed it under jurisdiction—either individual or governmental.

To the extent that *Walden* is a book about a squatter-surveyor, the text illustrates contradictory behaviors. "Where I Lived and What I Lived For" is Thoreau's counterinstitutional legal description of his immediate environs at Walden—"Such was that part of creation where I had squatted"[77]—but the book later moves toward a manifesto of *spiritual* squatter's rights, relating specific details of Thoreau's "settling in the world" and finding his figurative "point d'appui" on land he did not own and had declared an aversion to owning. "The Bean Field" chapter illustrates in microcosm the stages of civilizing the American landscape, with the Walden woods as Thoreau's land claim, and the processes of measuring, clearing, building and planting clearly analogous to the processes of continental settlement. While Thoreau's relation to the land resembles unfettered ownership, he is more accurately an interloper whose rights are contingent on "improving" his claim, and whose outlook defies the Yankee stereotype. The art of husbandry, Thoreau asserts, has lost its sacred character and has instead been "pursued with irreverent haste and heedlessness by us."

As much as the New England farmer's implacable manner of land usage irritates Thoreau, the fundamental nexus on which rapacious husbandry is based comes in for sterner criticism: "By avarice and selfishness, and a groveling habit, from which none of us is free, of regarding the soil as property, or the means of acquiring property chiefly, the landscape is deformed, husbandry is degraded with us, and the farmer leads the meanest of lives. He knows nature but as a robber."[78] If property is theft, as Thoreau seems to be saying, the American concept of statutory land ownership is profoundly unnatural. Employing the legal lexicon of proprietorship, Thoreau boldly imagines the possibility of an American land relation in which a true husbandman relinquishes "all claim to the produce of his fields," a move that would require disavowal of both the "first" and "last fruits" (ownership and profit) of land tracts.[79]

A similarly dissenting strategy informs Thoreau's use of economic terms to characterize the geographic exploration of the pond. As allusions to his existence at Walden as a national fiscal enterprise accumulate, they become noticeably incongruous with the author's fanatically nonacquisitive persona, functioning in the text not to glorify the country's financial pursuits but to establish an increasingly explicit contrast between the benign business at Walden and the soul-strangling commercial world outside its confines. The maps and plats made by the Coast Survey and the Survey of Public Lands were material expressions of the reach of the state, but the Walden survey suggested the limitations of such authority. It accomplished this by renouncing legal ownership while simultaneously proclaiming, as Thoreau does after laying out his homestead in the forest, "My right there is none to dispute." Though the Walden map is not a parodic counterpoint to the Coast Survey, it presents in key ways a serious alternative cultural initiative. Metaphorically recasting the commercial justifications of the national measuring endeavor in a decidedly anticommercial setting, Thoreau stresses the need to protect the more precious maritime cargo of individual self-actualization.

"I have always endeavored to acquire strict business habits," Thoreau explained as he began his account of the two years he spent at the pond.[80] In his surveying business, he followed the complex methods and procedures described and inculcated in the technical manuals, textbooks and popular surveying science of his day. In the numerous surveying-related procedures and passages that appear in his literary works, however, Thoreau wrote his own surveying textbook. In doing so, he enriched his literary-philosophical efforts with meanings that did not always contradict or cancel out the norms and standards of his profession but almost never failed to lend them new significance, sometimes in strikingly creative ways. These unconventional rereadings and anti-institutional rewritings of engineering principles comprise ample cultural material and carry considerable political significance. In *Cape Cod* and *Walden*, they offer a sophisticated alternative application of important nineteenth-century procedures as transformed through the alembic of Thoreau's perceptions.

4

The Skillful Engineer

I find when I have been building a fence or surveying
a farm, or even collecting simples, that these were
the true paths to perception and enjoyment. . . . If,
as a poet or naturalist, you wish to explore a given
neighborhood, go and get your living in it.

—Thoreau, *Journal*, October 28, 1857

ASIDE FROM EARLY STINTS as a schoolteacher and an employee of his
father's pencil factory, working as a land surveyor was as close as Henry
David Thoreau ever came to a steady means of income and "legitimate"
profession. His Harvard curriculum included "mensuration of surfaces
and solids as well as surveying,"[1] so we can assume that he picked up the
basics of land measurement as a student. But the record of his experience in the field began with his teaching of surveying principles at the
private school he ran with his brother, John, from 1839 to 1841. In 1840
Thoreau "obtained" a combination leveling instrument and circumfer-
entor, probably by borrowing it from Cyrus Hubbard, and "ascertained
the height of the cliff hill—and surveyed other objects."[2] With the compass and a graduated staff, Henry and a partner—in all likelihood his
brother—spent the better part of a November day measuring the verti-

cal slope from the surface of the Concord River to a "Top of Rock" on the Cliff Hill peak. To arrive at their figure of 231.09 feet as the height of the hill, they executed a well-planned differential-leveling procedure by taking vertical readings at nineteen separate locations as they ascended from the river.[3]

While these activities were apparently done in practical preparation for teaching mathematics in the field, there is evidence that Thoreau made several surveys purely for the pleasure of experimentation. In addition to the surveys of Walden in 1846 and White Pond in 1851, Thoreau apparently made a recreational plan of the Old Marlborough Road sometime in the 1840s.[4] During his paid surveying jobs in and around Concord, Thoreau often conducted "unnecessary" science, recording data that were of value only to himself as writer-naturalist. He often carried portable surveying instruments—a pocket compass, a cloth tape and a notched birch branch for measuring depths—on his almost daily woodland excursions. In *Walden*, he explained why: "For many years I was a self-appointed inspector of snow storms and rain storms, and did my duty faithfully; surveyor, if not of highways, then of forest paths and all across-lot routes."[5] On his more distant explorations to places like Cape Cod and the woods of Maine, Thoreau enriched his natural history with countless surveying- and engineering-related observations that reveal a lifelong intention to use surveying skills as aids for understanding the natural world.

After the first paid Thoreau survey that we know of—the plan of a woodlot owned by Edmund Hosmer in December 1845—there is no record of another until the spring of 1847,[6] when Thoreau used his pocket compass to pace out a rough plan of a newly acquired lot of Ralph Waldo Emerson's near Walden Pond—a job for which he received one dollar.[7] A few weeks later Emerson wrote to his brother-in-law, Dr. Charles Jackson, recommending that Thoreau be included as a chain man on Jackson's government expedition to survey the mineral lands of Michigan. Because the jobs were political appointments, Thoreau wasn't hired, but he had been eager to go and would undoubtedly have been well suited to the work.[8] In the fall of that year, Thoreau answered a questionnaire about his professional activity since graduating from Harvard by announcing that he wasn't sure he yet had a profession or a trade but including "Surveyor" among his numerous occupations.[9]

Emerson's perception, expressed in the eulogy he gave at Thoreau's funeral, that his friend had "drifted" toward land surveying is perhaps misleading. More accurately, he was driven to the business by financial need. In 1848 Thoreau entered into a financially risky contract to pay for the publication of a thousand copies of *A Week on the Concord and Merrimack Rivers* out of the work's sales receipts. When the book sold less than three hundred copies, the author was left with a debt of several hundred dollars.[10] As a result he needed income more substantial than his intermittent honoraria for lectures and published essays and the small amounts he could earn for occasional manual labor.[11] The logical answer to his financial dilemma was an active pursuit of professional surveying. Planning for necessity in the fall of 1848, Thoreau made a list of books and articles he had read or intended to read to prepare himself for the work.[12]

Initially it may have been difficult for Thoreau to find clients around Concord because there was already a trusted surveyor in town, Cyrus Hubbard, twenty-five years Thoreau's senior and seemingly an amiable gentleman, who "studied and practiced surveying almost as long as he lived and was considered very correct in that business."[13] In 1849, his first year of work, Thoreau used Hubbard's compass to make only a few surveys.[14] Nearly all of these were brought about through Emerson's patronage, but there was also a job for Henry's father, John Thoreau, who had proposed to the Concord Town Board that a road be laid out in front of his family's "Texas home," so named for its location on the outskirts of Concord in the grassy plains west of the Fitchburg Railroad tracks.[15]

To prove, perhaps partly to himself, that he was serious about his new business, Thoreau purchased his own equipment in the spring of 1850, including a top-of-the-line compass manufactured by the C. G. King Company of Broad Street, Boston, one of the best instrument makers of the day.[16] The fifteen-inch compass, which would have cost Thoreau about forty dollars, is made of lacquered brass with a silvered five-inch dial or compass card divided into four ninety-degree quadrants. North is indicated by the traditional fleur-de-lis, with east and west reversed in deference to the American surveyor's method of recording directional bearings. The rim of Thoreau's compass is graduated to thirty minutes, or to the half degree. Beneath the blued-steel directional needle on the southern arm of the compass there are two perpendicular vials that were used to level the compass before taking a bearing. The two screw-on sight vanes each had six beveled circular apertures and were unusually tall for a compass of this period. This delicate piece of equipment was kept in a mahogany compass box and tripod-mounted for use with a ball-and-socket adapter that could be tightened to hold the compass in position.

The compass, on display in the Concord Free Public Library, bears interesting indications of how it was used. Around a viewing hole on the north sight vane are visible remnants of a sticky tarlike substance. This is where Thoreau attached a horsehair across the aperture and parallel to the ground to make leveling operations more accurate. In the corresponding viewing hole on the south sight vane, the tar and the horsehair itself are miraculously still in place. Interestingly, the instrument has no vernier. A vernier is a small brass scale that slides along the edge of the compass card and provides surveyors an additional level of exactness by making it possible to take readings of more precise gradations than those on the compass scale. That Thoreau's compass lacked this device is not particularly unusual, but it raises the question of how he sometimes recorded angle readings to an eighth of a degree, which cannot be read with the naked eye. Some surveyors use a pocket magnifying glass to increase the precision of compass readings, but another likely explanation is that Thoreau took several readings of the same bearing and averaged them to get the fractions, an accepted estimation practice. Thoreau's first job with this quality instrument was a plan of Jesse Hosmer's more-than-hundred-acre farm in the spring of 1850, but his field notes reveal that he was still in the improvising stage where some of his field operations were concerned. His notebook indicates that he surveyed this property "with my compass. Though with a tape."[17] Measuring such a large area with a tape that was probably homemade was surprisingly unsystematic of Thoreau, but perhaps his new surveyor's chain was still on order and Hubbard's equipment wasn't available.

Thoreau's surveying field notebook, purchased in 1849 and labeled "Field-Notes of Surveys Made by Henry D. Thoreau Since November 1849," provides interesting details about his more impressive engineering-related accomplishments.[18] This small bound-manuscript volume, kept for the last thirteen years of Thoreau's life and bequeathed to his sister Sophia at Thoreau's death in 1862, includes measurements and calculations, descriptions of work done for various employers, expenses, fees

FIGURES 4.1a and 4.1b. Thoreau's surveying compass and detail of the compass card. Courtesy Concord Free Public Library.

charged, and other materials generated by Thoreau in the preparation of surveys.[19] As essentially the technical record of a working civil engineer, the notebook offers testimony to his professional competence, along with straightforward indications of its author's methods and work habits as they developed from 1849 to 1860.

Evidence of Thoreau's technical proficiency is contained in the following notes for an 1850 survey of a lot owned by Ralph Waldo Emerson in the area just south of Walden Pond:

R.W. Emerson

Woodlot and Meadow by Walden Pond——(that part contained within the Lincoln bounds)—the woodlot being a part of what was known in 1845 as Samuel Heywood's "pasture," and deeded by him as such to his "son Jonathan Turner."

Surveyed March 1850 with unusual accuracy.

Course of Town line, as given on town map, from stone by Walden Pond to stone by Fair Haven S 58 W 326 rods. Variation of the compass used, in running the town-line 5°54'W. Variation of my compass from that used in running the town-line 1°12'W; therefore var. of my compass from the true meridian 7°6'W.

Distances in four-rod chains and decimals of a chain or links—commencing at the northern-most angle, where the town-line crosses the boundary line between Emerson & Bartlett.

cor. for. sag. (The allowance was probably too much.)

Looking at these notes, we might speculate that Thoreau took a special interest in this survey—either because it had legal ramifications for Emerson, or was close to the sight of his earlier sojourn in the Walden woods, or was one of the first he made with his own compass, or a combination of these factors. Thoreau's inclusion of the information that his distances are given in "four-rod chains and decimals of a chain or links" indicates his use of the standard measuring tool of the day, a Gunter's chain, or surveyor's chain, made of iron or steel wire and consisting of one hundred "links," each of 7.92 inches. One "chain" was equal to sixty-six feet, or four rods of 16.5 feet each.[20] Given that such units of measurement had long been standardized in the profession, Thoreau's inclusion of this information, while conforming to canonical surveying procedure, is redundant and unusually careful. In his field notes, Thoreau could show an almost compulsive attention to detail, but the fact that no other of the many entries in the notebook has recourse to this particular explanatory material suggests a legalistic formality stemming from the use of these notes in the protracted Emerson–Charles Bartlett boundary dispute that would not culminate until 1857.[21]

Throughout the surveying notebook, Thoreau made notations about the quality of his measurements, using phrases like "measured with tolerable accuracy," "very rudely surveyed," "tolerably accurate" or even "badly surveyed employees in a hurry" to describe his work. His claim of unusual accuracy in his notes for the Emerson survey seems justified. The phrase "cor. for. sag" near the bottom of the entry refers to Thoreau's use of a mathematical correction for the slight natural sag in the measuring chain when pulled taut between points of measurement.[22] This is the only instance of Thoreau's making such a note in the field. In a later hand, Thoreau penciled in a final observation, "The allowance was probably too much," indicating a degree of meticulousness that might be considered atypical for a surveyor of Thoreau's experience.[23]

Also telling is Thoreau's use of true meridian or true north instead of the slightly less accurate magnetic north that was sometimes used in everyday surveying of the period. Having obtained a recent town map to use as a point of reference to begin his work, Thoreau saw that the survey of the Lincoln boundary had determined a variation of the compass from the true meridian and had indicated the degrees of declination. Thoreau then simply checked the declination of his own compass from this earlier line, added the new diurnal variation ($1°12'W$), and noted the resulting magnetic declination ($7°6'W$) along with the bearings he recorded for Emerson's property lines. Thoreau would later embrace the metaphorical meanings of true meridian, but here in one of his first uses of it in the field, he is able to give Emerson its practical benefits without performing the lengthy operations of locating true meridian on his own. In sum, this notebook entry shows Thoreau as a careful and resourceful civil engineer.

While the bulk of the "Field-Notes" confirms an appreciation now pervasive in Thoreau studies of the author's striking intellectual versatility, the notes also comprise some relatively mundane items. Among these are notes about the prices for surveying paper (on the notebook's inside back cover), and two small handwritten conversion charts for quick reference—one translating rods to feet and links to inches, another showing lengths of departure from a straight line produced by one degree of linear deviation at several intervals. There is also a table of the fees Thoreau collected for surveying jobs, with lines drawn through the names of clients to indicate payment, along with several notes of legal significance made in the field, including the aforementioned testimonial of Daniel Shattuck, who agreed in the presence of his adversary to accept Thoreau's results.

As the "Field-Notes," draft surveys and other surveying-related manuscripts show, Thoreau undertook a remarkable variety of complicated tasks. In the spring of 1850, a major project was the parceling out of sixty lots in the town of Haverhill, on the Merrimac River. In 1851, Thoreau was hired by the Concord selectmen for the job of perambulating and re-establishing the town borders. Satisfied with Thoreau's work, the Town of Concord hired him again in 1853 to lay out a new road from Concord to neighboring Bedford. When the surveys of both Walden Pond and White Pond were used on the 1852 map of Concord by H. F. Walling, Walling appropriately gave credit for these landscape features to "H. D. Thoreau, Civ. Eng." In 1856 Thoreau worked for several weeks in trying conditions to survey the town of Eagleswood in Perth Amboy, New Jersey, laying out an orchard and a vineyard there as well. In 1859, Thoreau was hired by owners of meadowlands along the Concord River to help map the river in the preparation of a legal case against the Billerica dam. He worked assiduously through the summer of 1859, producing detailed charts and drawings that indicated water-level data and flow measurements at dams and bridges, river currents and depths, riverbank contours and soil composition. Applying his encyclopedic knowledge of local flora, he also identified, sketched and located numerous species of meadow plants that were of importance in the legal dispute.[24] A year later, Bronson Alcott referred to Thoreau as Concord's "resident Surveyor-General of the town's farms, farmers, animals, and everything else it contains."[25]

Other than the beautiful compass and tripod, only a few remnants of Thoreau's surveying equipment have survived. Among the more interesting surveying items in the Concord library's Thoreau Collection is a set of chaining pins, sometimes called arrows, which were used in measuring courses with a Gunter's chain. The pins were placed in the ground at the end of each chain by the fore chain man, usually the surveyor's hired helper. The surveyor followed and retrieved them one by one after the next distance had been measured. Usually there were ten pins in a set so when the surveyor collected the final one, which was marked differently from the others, he knew he had measured ten chains. Thoreau's set of chaining pins includes only eight 14½-inch rods. One may have been lost on December 30, 1856; on that date, the surveyor wrote in his journal, "Had the experience of losing a pin and then hunting for it a long time in vain." The remaining pins are carved from oak branches, sharpened at one end and gouged to make a small loophole at the other so they could be strung together and carried on Thoreau's belt. One pin has two circles carved at the top to mark it as the last of the set. Looking at these objects, one pictures Thoreau kneeling down to palm them into the ground, or imagines them hanging at the surveyor's side and clicking against each other as he sauntered through the fields. The tips of the pins still bear discolorations from the Concord soil.

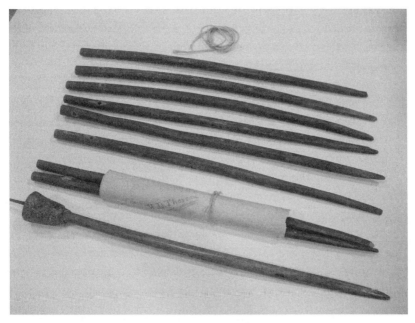

FIGURE 4.2. Chaining pins and sighting pin made by Thoreau. Courtesy Concord Free Public Library.

In the same set of homemade surveying tools there is a 14½-inch sighting pin. Thoreau made this interesting item by casting molten lead into a bell shape at the end of an oak branch, then fixing into the lead a square nail protruding 1¾ inches from the top of the pin. Used as an aid to accuracy, the pin would have been set in the ground at a property corner or point along a line. Thoreau could then use his compass to sight directly on the protruding nail to determine an accurate bearing over short distances. Thoreau once remarked that "the birch is the surveyor's tree" because of its white bark. "It makes the best stakes to look at through the sights of a compass except when there is snow on the ground."[26] This improvised sighting pin would have been useful when snow made birch impractical.

Among other Thoreau possessions owned by the Concord library, there is a thirty-foot measuring tape of thin white cloth, marked in feet, half feet and inches. It looks to have been made by Thoreau, but it is not a device for land surveying and does not show wear from field use. It is almost certainly not the tape he mentioned using in the 1850 survey made before he owned a chain, or the one with which he measured a moose killed by Joe Polis in an event from 1857 described in *The Maine Woods*. Probably this light pocket-sized tape was one of several Thoreau used or intended to use for measuring natural phenomena on his daily walks. The Concord Free Public Library also owns a 3½-inch semicircular brass protractor, a larger 360-degree protractor, 7½ inches in diameter and made of tin, and several six-inch right triangles, all used by Thoreau for drafting surveys. The nearby Concord Museum has a larger set of Thoreau's drafting tools. Their Thoreau Collection includes a wooden T square, a brass protractor, two straightedges and a wood ruler.

The museum also owns a 49.5-foot iron-and-brass engineer's chain that was believed to be Thoreau's surveying chain until my examination of the item suggested otherwise.[27] During a March 2008 visit to Concord, I took a close look at the museum's chain and was surprised to discover that it was a very poor measuring instrument. I later explained to museum curator David Wood the several reasons I had for thinking it very unlikely that this chain was ever used by Henry Thoreau for land surveying. First, the museum's chain is not a surveyor's tool but a device for laying out railroads and canals. Only three rods long, it is impractical for recording distances in the four-rod units that had been legally required of the surveying profession since 1797. Its intervals, or links, are of twelve and six inches—measures that bear no relation to the links of 7.92 inches that give a standard surveyor's chain its ease and precision in calculating acreage.[28] Second, the chain is inherently incapable of producing the precise numbers Thoreau valued and was known for. Some of its rod and half-rod lengths, for example, are haphazardly marked with pieces of white cloth wrapped around the approximate midpoint of a link—a practice that does not make for good surveying data. Third, using this nonstandard chain for fieldwork would have been an almost absurdly complicated task, requiring Thoreau to record distances in three-rod units, then convert his data to four-rod units, then convert each measurement's leftover feet and inches (the only units obtainable with the museum's instrument) into the links of a true surveying chain. These procedures would have produced considerable inaccuracy and greatly increased the likelihood of errors of calculation. There are no computations in the "Field-Notes" that indicate such processes, and it would have been very surprising to have found any; such professional sloppiness was not in Thoreau's character.[29] Finally, many of Thoreau's finished surveys clearly record his use of a standard four-rod surveying instrument. On a plan drawn for Daniel Weston in December of 1852, for example, Thoreau notes that his distances are "in four-rod chains and links or decimals of a chain. 100 links to a chain, 25 links to a rod."[30] It seems certain that Henry Thoreau owned and used a proper surveying chain, one perhaps now lost to history.[31]

Among the more extraordinary relics of Thoreau's surveying is the often-reproduced but seldom-analyzed LAND SURVEYING broadside that he used to advertise his services in the early 1850s. To build his client base and essentially become Concord's busiest civil engineer, Thoreau composed a surprisingly slick marketing message that announced his availability for surveying "of all kinds" and boldly asserted that he used "the best methods known." The text of the ad suggests the surveyor's desire to differentiate himself from his competitors with technologically advanced methods and precision. It also indicates much about the market niche Thoreau sought to fill. In the ad, the surveyor promises to supply data "in order that the boundaries of Farms may be accurately described in Deeds." Thoreau is referring to the metes-and-bounds type of surveying required around Concord. In work of this kind, the surveyor used

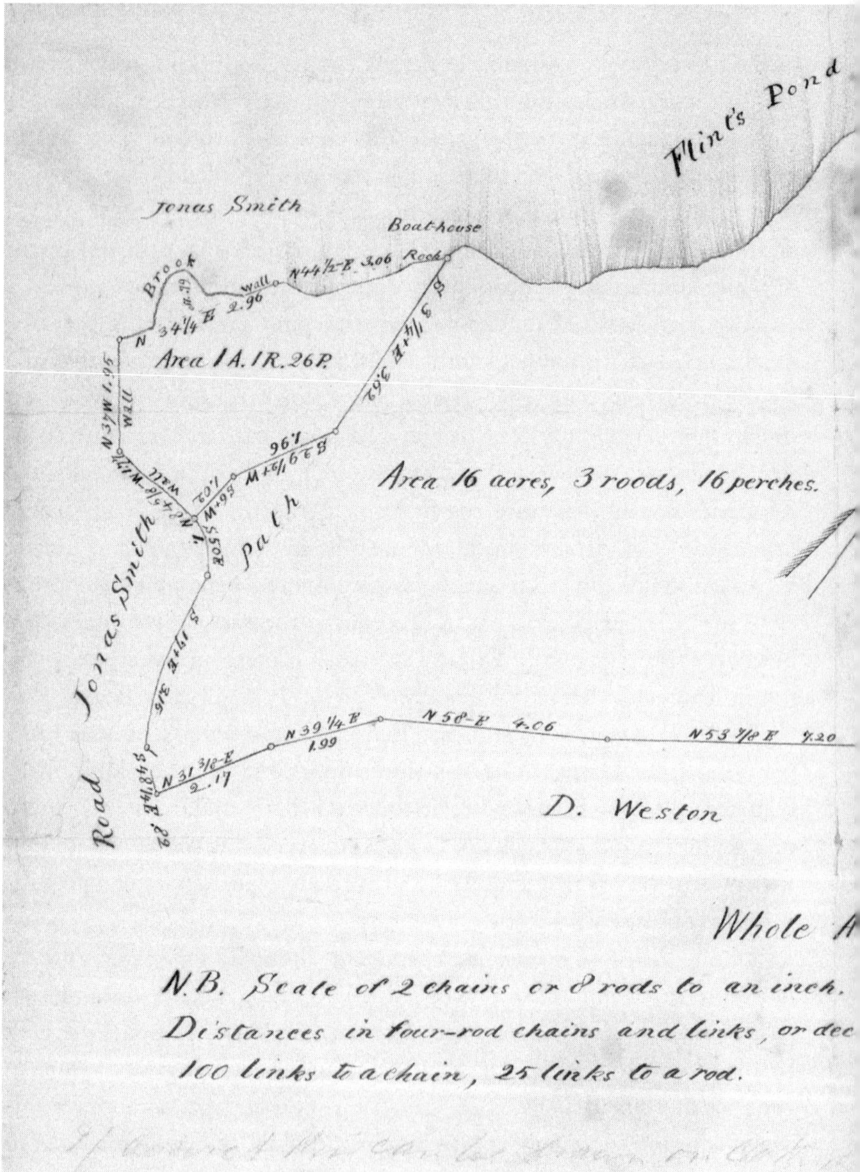

Flint's Pond

Jonas Smith

Boat-house

Brook

Rock

N 44½ E 3.06

N 34¼ E 2.96

Wall

Area 1 A. 1 R. 26 P.

N 37 W 1.95

Wall

S 9¼ E 3.62

N 49½ W 1.10

Wall

S 39½ W 2.07

Area 16 acres, 3 roods, 16 perches.

1.96

S 66 W 1.98

Road   Jonas Smith

Path

S 19¼ E 3.16

N 39¼ E 1.99

N 50 E 4.06

N 53 7/8 E 7.20

S 24 84 S

N 31 3/8 E 2.17

D. Weston

Whole A

N.B. Scale of 2 chains or 8 rods to an inch.
Distances in four-rod chains and links, or dec
100 links to a chain, 25 links to a rod.

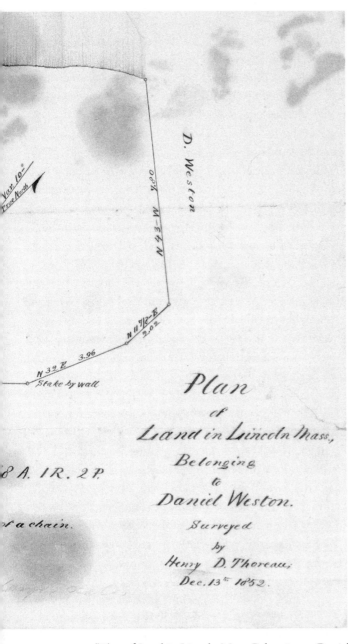

Var. 10°
True North

D. Weston

N 44 W 7.00

N 11 1/2 E
2.02

N 32 E   3.96
Stake by wall

8 A. 1 R. 2 P.

of a chain.

Plan

of

Land in Lincoln Mass.,

Belonging

to

Daniel Weston.

Surveyed

by

Henry D. Thoreau;

Dec. 13ᵗʰ 1852.

FIGURE 4.3. "Plan of Land in Lincoln Mass. Belonging to Daniel Weston" (1852). Thoreau's note at bottom—"Distances in four-rod chains and links, or decimals of a chain. 100 links to a chain, 25 links to a rod."—indicates his use of a standard Gunter's chain. Courtesy Concord Museum.

natural or man-made objects rather than a standard geometrical grid to define the location and limits of surveyed property. A metes-and-bounds plat often refers to landscape features, as for example in an 1851 survey for James Wood, which describes a parcel as "beginning at the northeasterly corner of the middle of a ditch on the pond (Bateman's) thence N 70 ⅝ W 16.20 chains."

Though metes-and-bounds surveying was suited to the irregular lots around Concord, the more orderly and gridlike geometry of superimposed squares and rectangles did figure in some of Thoreau's surveying projects. The advertisement's next marketing sound bite reads, "*Woods* lotted off distinctly according to a regular plan." For property owners wishing to neatly subdivide their woodlands and sell timber-cutting rights to the parcels, Henry Thoreau was the man to contact. This marketing appeal appears to have been particularly well timed and effective, accounting for a large number of jobs over the course of his career. The reference in the broadside to "*Roads* laid out, &c., &c." is perhaps in a similar category, referring as it does to Thoreau's role in building his community's transportation infrastructure. Thoreau performed various types of road-surveying and civil-engineering duties for his most lucrative single client, the Town of Concord, which paid him the substantial sum of sixty-four dollars for various types of surveys in 1851 and rehired him regularly for the next decade.

The LAND SURVEYING broadside also promises to furnish "Distinct and accurate Plans of Farms . . . with the buildings thereon, of any size . . . to accompany the Farm Book." The farm book was a journal or almanac kept by landowners that included financial data, records of crops and harvests, and information about the physical property. For southern farmers such as Thomas Jefferson, whose farm book is now famous as a record of his economic relation to slave Sally Hemmings, it was also the place where bills of sale for chattel were kept—where losses and gains in human property were recorded. Thoreau's mention of the farm book in his ad copy was a purposeful act, suggesting a permanent use and appropriate location for the property-related product he was marketing. A clear and accurate recent survey, he reminded clients, safeguarded one's holdings by forestalling boundary disputes and encroachments. Security in property was thus part of the added value of a Thoreau survey. That Thoreau offered to attach a scale of feet to his surveys was another nod to

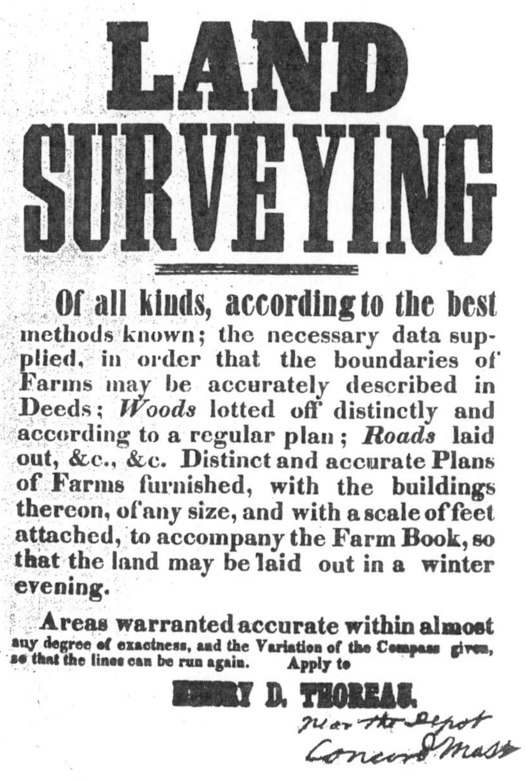

LAND SURVEYING

Of all kinds, according to the best methods known; the necessary data supplied, in order that the boundaries of Farms may be accurately described in Deeds; *Woods* lotted off distinctly and according to a regular plan; *Roads* laid out, &c., &c. Distinct and accurate Plans of Farms furnished, with the buildings thereon, of any size, and with a scale of feet attached, to accompany the Farm Book, so that the land may be laid out in a winter evening.

Areas warranted accurate within almost any degree of exactness, and the Variation of the Compass given, so that the lines can be run again.   Apply to

HENRY D. THOREAU,
Near the Depot
Concord Mass

FIGURE 4.4. Broadside advertising Thoreau's services as a professional surveyor (ca. 1850). Berg Collection, New York Public Library.

his clients' practical needs. Distances on surveys were officially recorded in chain-rod-link units, but owners might also want data recorded in feet, a more readily understood measure that farmers could easily pace out on their own. Thoreau wanted clients to know that he would provide this information upon request.

The most expressive phrase in Thoreau's marketing message comes near the end of the document: "so that the land may be laid out in a winter evening." Here the diction suddenly achieves a lyrical tinge, creating an appealing pastoral image that would not be out of place in the text of *Walden*. In establishing his homestead at the pond, Thoreau had remarked that "an afternoon sufficed to lay out the land into orchard, woodlot, and pasture."[32] His broadside suggests the ways his surveying products facilitate the same process—the founding of one's economic enterprise through the "improving" of a homestead. The language of the broadside might enable a potential client to envision the deeply satisfying process of walking his bounds, of using a well-executed survey to lay out his fields, barn or house lot in the crisp winter twilight. The stock American image might resonate on an emotional level for the surveyor's clients, as it clearly did for Thoreau in laying out a homestead and establishing his rights to Walden. By means of both practical and emotive appeal, by offering security and the full realization of the American form of autonomous land ownership, the author of the LAND SURVEYING broadside is selling the American Dream.

The broadside text closes with a guarantee of the surveyor's work. In stating that his measurements will be "warranted accurate within almost any degree of exactness," Thoreau employs standard advertising hyperbole. Formulated to create an impression of the sophisticated processes of his work, this phrase reiterates his sloganlike opening appropriation of "the best methods known." Thoreau also promises to clients that the "Variation of the Compass [will be] given, so that the lines can be run again."[33] Such information would have been more helpful to future resurveys of the land parcel than of immediate use to clients, but it suggests that the text was likely written after Thoreau's determination of true north by sighting the North Star in February of 1851—an important event in his professional development that enabled him to include his own variation on his surveys.

The Concord surveyor's fieldwork was indeed of good quality, so his claims to precision are not mere hucksterism. Only in comparison to our knowledge of his literary output—or perhaps to a somewhat naive view of Thoreau as a completely antimercantile being—does this example of carefully worded commercial rhetoric ring discordantly against prevailing notions of his life's priorities. That Thoreau knew what his customers wanted and how to appeal to them is clear. Viewing the Walden surveyor as economic man is not only accurate, it increases his relevance to the present day. Overall, the advertising broadside is an uncharacteristic piece of Thoreau's writing, but it should not be ignored as a literary text. It reminds us of the author's special technical abilities and shows how his writing skills could be, and were, tailored to business conditions in shrewd and effective ways.

With the help of the broadside, Thoreau quickly gained a reputation for good work, and his list of clients grew steadily. He completed fifteen known surveying jobs in 1850 and eighteen the next year, working for both the Town of Concord and private property owners, thereby initiating an enterprise that could be counted on for regular income to help offset the large debt from *A Week*.[34] In early 1851, Bronson Alcott's journal noted that Thoreau had lately "taken to surveying as well as authorship, and makes the compass pay for his book on 'The Concord and Merrimac [*sic*] Rivers,' which the public is slow to take off his hands."[35] As late as February 27, 1853, Thoreau claimed to be still chipping away at the debt to his "so-called" publisher, explaining in a letter to Harrison Blake that he had been "almost constantly in the fields surveying of late . . . to pay for that book which I printed."[36]

From 1850 to 1854 Thoreau averaged about fourteen paid jobs per annum, working more often in the winter or early spring months, when there was less vegetation to hack through in running his lines. In 1855, illness forced Thoreau to give up surveying almost entirely for a year, but his career probably gained new impetus when he became acquainted with abolitionist and fellow surveyor John Brown in 1857. Brown, visiting Concord on a tour to raise funds for the antislavery cause, told Thoreau the story of his battles with proslavery ruffians in the Kansas Territory, including, it is very likely, details of how he had impersonated a surveyor in order to spy on proslavery forces. That year Thoreau made his highest-ever annual total of twenty-six surveys, twenty-four of which were completed in the nine months after he met Brown, making this the busiest single stretch of his surveying career. Thoreau stayed active as a surveyor up to the period of his final illness, completing fourteen jobs in 1860 and making the final entry in his "Field-Notes" on January 2, 1861. In all, Henry Thoreau made more than 165 surveys that resolved ownership disputes, aided in the laying out of Concord's roads, regularized notoriously erratic property lines in Middlesex County, and lotted off large stretches of woodland for sale and cutting. By the early 1860s, the pursuit begun as an avocation in November 1840 had become a significant component of Thoreau's perceived legacy and lasting public identity.

Twelve years after Thoreau's death, Henry's sister Sophia donated to the Concord Free Public Library three trunks or boxes containing her brother's unpublished manuscripts, including both substantial literary works and a box containing "a complete survey of almost every farm in town." The account of this event as recorded in the *Reports of the Selectmen* for 1874–75 did not expound on the remarkable literary value of the gift. But it perpetuated the identification of Thoreau as a genuine professional, noting that the lot surveys would be "of great value in the future in regard to the boundary lines of different estates, especially so when we consider the established accuracy of Mr. Thoreau's surveys and measurements."[37]

While these documents no longer have any use in boundary disputes, they are a treasure trove for anyone interested in either Thoreau specifically or antebellum material culture generally. Close to two hundred manuscript surveys are available online at the Concord Free Public Library website. Most are pencil or ink draft versions of plans that were later finished into fair copies for clients. A few, such as the handsome 1857 plan of Bronson Alcott's Orchard House estate, are finished products in ink. The collection includes drafts of Hawthorne's Wayside property, several surveys for Emerson, and a "very accurate" sketch of a seven-acre lot "near Walden Pond" for Sam Staples, the town constable who famously jailed Thoreau for nonpayment of the poll tax in 1846.

The very first survey listed on the website, a complicated September 1851 plan of the Acton-Concord town line, happens to be a particularly good example of Thoreau's careful work and sometimes artistically expressive drafting style. Split stones, pitch pines, blazed oaks, blazed maples and pine stumps mark property corners. Uncut woodlots are indicated by rippling lines drawn in ink. Tellingly, an already clear-cut woodlot becomes an utterly blank space on the survey document. Brows of hills are sketched in undulating parallel lines. Fort Pond Brook is rendered in dashes wending through the property of Henry Hayes. More-prominent dashes trace a "may flower path" that runs through the "Acton Lot" and into Gilbert Webber's property. Wetland areas around the Fort Pond Brook are indicated with vegetation symbols running perpendicular to the water.

While making this survey, Thoreau was unusually fastidious about his compass bearings. In three locations, he observed and noted on the document that there was a local attraction—a magnetic deviation often caused by ferrous anomalies in the soil or surroundings—affecting his compass needle. This was good surveying because once the attraction was discovered it could be adjusted for in recorded data. Along the road to South Acton, Thoreau found a significant attraction, a deviation of thirteen and a quarter degrees in bearings taken over a six-rod section of the line. Even this large anomaly would have been easy for a surveyor to miss or ignore in the field, but it seems the engineering faculties of the future author of *Walden* were razor sharp on this job; penciled notes on the draft state that he found and corrected errors in four lines surveyed on Joseph Derby's lot by John Heywood in 1811.

Sometimes Thoreau's surveying documents give intriguing indications of what he was thinking about as he worked. In the lower left corner of his plan of the Humphrey Hunt lot in the "Easterbrooks Country" to the north of Concord, Thoreau scribbled the note "Upernavik, the most northerly inhabited spot upon the globe."[38] In Thoreau's day, Upernavik was a tiny colony on the west coast of Greenland, an isolated outpost sometimes described as the earth's northernmost permanent settlement. Upernavik was the spot where in 1845 Arctic explorer Sir John Franklin had last gathered provisions on his ill-fated search for the Northwest Passage and the Open Polar Sea. Earlier that year, as Concord historian Steve Ells has noted, Thoreau had been absorbed by reports of the search for Franklin's lost exploring party. Perhaps, Ells speculated, surveying the loneliest edge of the Easterbrooks Country on a frigid winter day may simply have reminded Thoreau of Franklin's faraway icy quest. Whatever form the connection between measuring fields and discovering new worlds took for Thoreau, it seems clear that he "made a metaphorical connection between the North's secular explorers and his own spiritual quest" while surveying the frozen wilderness of the desolate Hunt lot in 1852.[39]

On the Concord library website, a number of Thoreau's maps are also available for viewing. Most are not originally drawn but traced from existing charts in various sources of historical interest to Thoreau. Almost all are of coastal regions: "East Canada" and the St. Lawrence Seaway, Cape Cod, Nantucket Island, and tracings of two sixteenth-century exploratory maps—of the Virginia coast and the North American coast from Canada to Florida. The maps offer further testimony to the long-term fascination with exploration and coastal geography Thoreau had probably imbibed from the Coast Survey. A few surveys on the website have not been identified but might be with further study. Number 160, for example, is listed as unidentified but is almost certainly a draft fragment of the 1851 White Pond survey, showing identical angle-intersection procedures and identical numbering systems for hubs and bearing lines. These observations are only a sample of what may be gleaned from the valuable Thoreau Survey Collection with more attention by researchers.

Land surveying had much to do with the way the world saw Thoreau, but it also profoundly influenced the way Thoreau saw the world. "A Winter Walk," one of Thoreau's first essays, published in the October 1843 number of the *Dial*, reveals an early inclination to study natural phenomena through the lens of engineering principles. Noticing a fallen beech leaf on the shore of a woodland lake, Thoreau at once proposes a mathematical means of determining its place in the natural order:

> A skillful engineer, methinks, might project its course since it fell from the parent stem. Here are all the elements for such a calculation. Its present position, the direction of the wind, the level of the pond, and how much more is given. In its scarred edges and its veins is its log rolled up.[40]

This passage, though it predates the author's measuring experiments at Walden by three years and the onset of his commercial surveying career by a full six years, adumbrates a process that would become habitual to Thoreau: the observation of a natural phenomenon, followed by a recasting of the phenomenon into engineering terminology. Examples of this process are plentiful in Thoreau's literary work, including all essays in *The Maine Woods* and his account of his first trip to Cape Cod in 1849, during which he identifies himself as a surveyor though his surveying business had not yet formally begun.

Throughout the 1850s, even while lecturing against the evils of getting a living, Thoreau acknowledged that he ran a surveying business, but he implied that his method of doing so was somehow compatible with a dissident, antimaterialistic way of life. Because he had chosen work that on one level accorded with his deepest beliefs, he had no need to fully disengage from it during his coastal explorations, his trips to Maine, or his four-hour walks in the Concord woods, where he was always ready to apply skills and practices inculcated by surveying.

That Thoreau's physical perceptions were appreciably sharpened by hundreds of hours of careful observation and "minute-making" in the fields and woods of surveying clients seems axiomatic. Surveying operations and observations permeate Thoreau's published literary works, so it is not surprising that the reverse was true—that some observations of a philosophical nature may be found in his surveying field notes. As this chapter suggests, Thoreau did not always compartmentalize his professional and personal habits of perception while working for pay in the fields and woods. For a man who always believed that facts about the natural world "are truths in physics, because they are true in ethics,"[41] a strict dichotomy between measuring and morality would not have made sense anyway. Apparently referring to the coloring of his environmental observations by the work of keeping surveyor's notes, Thoreau once wondered, "Might not my Journal be called 'Field Notes.'"[42]

The unpaid Walden Pond survey described in chapter 2 is strong material evidence that land surveying was philosophically important to Thoreau, and this document is justifiably a centerpiece of various efforts to reconcile seemingly divergent sides of the writer's personality. But Thoreau's reliance on surveying skills, equipment and data to enrich his nature writing, cultural criticism and political commentary in *Walden* was by no means an isolated occurrence. The large number of references to surveying in Thoreau's published works, the frequency with which he takes on varied surveying-related identities and attitudes in these works, and the extent to which land-measuring vocabulary informs his political and environmental writing—all suggest that surveying was an essential rather than minor or peripheral component of the author's life and character.

5

Serving Admetus

I have lately been surveying the Walden woods so
extensively and minutely that I now see it mapped
in my mind's eye—as indeed, on paper—as so many
men's wood-lots, and am aware when I walk there
that I am at a given moment passing from such a
one's wood-lot to such another's. I fear this particular dry knowledge may affect my imagination and
fancy, that it will not be easy to see so much wildness and native vigor there as formerly.

—Thoreau, *Journal*, January 1, 1858

THE WORDS "I FEAR" OCCUR RARELY in Thoreau's journals and are
decidedly at variance with the prevailing image of the boldly iconoclastic, courageously independent "man of Concord." Here they express his
regret at an apparent loss of independence, an erosion of perceptual faculties that would equate his own discernment with that of the crowd,
that materially focused cultural majority who saw in the beauty of the
Walden landscape merely so many profitable and divisible "men's woodlots." Thoreau understood and repeatedly expressed the dangers to both

individual and community of this mode of thought; his final essays especially assert vehement resistance to the platitudes governing utilitarian exploitation and demystification of nature.

In the passage above, however, Thoreau is honestly afraid, troubled by the possibility that he also could become party to the commodification of the landscape. He proceeds to lament that "no thicket will seem so unexplored now that I know that stake and stones may be found in it." Referring with palpable anxiety to the surveyor's laths he had himself sharpened and pounded in, he confesses complicity in ecological modifications that originate in his own work. As Thoreau knew well, the process that began with "stake and stones" culminated in environmental destruction. The date of this journal entry within the last phase of the author's life, its recognition of a profound paradox in Thoreau's conduct and a threat to his "imagination," its focus on the sacred ground at Walden Pond—all suggest that his spiritual battle to keep his perceptions pure, if won at all, was at least a protracted, intense and problematic struggle.

On a few occasions in his personal writings, Thoreau gave intimations of his distress at even being publicly known as a surveyor. In a pensive letter written from Staten Island to his mother, Cynthia, in 1843, he expressed frustration at having a manuscript rejected and at being viewed by those outside Concord as no more than a businessman: "I go moping about the fields and woods here as I did in Concord, and, it seems, am thought to be a surveyor. . . . One neighbor observed to me, in a mysterious and half inquisitive way, that he supposed I must be pretty well acquainted with the state of things; that I kept pretty close; he didn't see any surveying instruments, but perhaps I had them in my pocket."[1] An 1856 letter written to Harrison Blake from a surveying job in Eagleswood, New Jersey, suggests Thoreau's frustration with the shaping demands made upon him by his chosen profession: "You must excuse me if I write mainly a business letter now, for I am sold for the time,—-am merely Thoreau the surveyor here."[2] Also notable in this letter is Thoreau's allusion in the same breath to a recent reading of his "What Shall It Profit" lecture—-the manuscript that later became his most passionate antibusiness declaration under the title "Life Without Principle."

Thoreau's journals reflect deep ambivalence about his work, referring to surveying at various times as "insignificant drudgery," "a vulgar necessity," "grinding at the mill of the philistines" and "barren work."[3] The journals also record a sense of loss he felt at the extent of New England's environmental transformation.[4] In a particularly moving passage of November 9, 1850, Thoreau is struck by the beauty of "a young grove of pitch pines" but immediately considers their probable demise. The trees, the author laments, are "regarded even by the woodman as 'trash'" and are thus "destined for the locomotive's maw." The great sadness of the passage, however, stems from Thoreau's discernment of the part *he* will play in the destruction of the grove that, he predicts, "erelong perchance I may survey and lot off for wood auction and see the choppers at their work."[5]

Thoreau's "Field-Notes" do not allude directly to the exertions required to open paths for chaining, create sight lines, and mark property corners in densely wooded areas or thick undergrowth. But the clear-cutting of vegetation, the marking of line intersections with permanent monuments, and the blazing or marking of witness trees to identify locations were all standard procedures, required of surveyors on an almost daily basis then as now. It would have been an unusual job that did not require Thoreau to chisel several rectangular divots into the bark of a white pine, oak or hickory, or to gather and arrange fieldstones to erect a knee-high pyramidal monument near a lot corner, or to cut away trees and shrubs in the forest undergrowth in order to get a clear sight line with his compass. Modern surveyors use chainsaws to run line; Thoreau undoubtedly created his own share of unobstructed views using less-menacing equipment.

Reference points described in the surveying notebook directly testify to the scope and frequency of these landscape alterations, performed in service to the need of making land boundaries unambiguous and economically useful. During a single survey of Emerson's lot at Walden, for example, Thoreau recorded using "a stake & stones a short dist from the water" to locate the beginning of a line. Corner and line markers from the same set of notes include a "scarred young oak," "hickory stake and stones," an oak stump, five blazed oaks, two blazed white pines, a blazed walnut, a "heap of stones," one "blazed young oak," a stump and stone near each other, several mounds of stones and several split stones. A field note of 1851 explains that Thoreau moved and used a "stone on the bank of the [Assabet] river" to run a line. An entry in Thoreau's journal records that, while surveying the Richardson lot at Walden Pond in 1857, he "turned up a rock near the pond to make bound with."[6] While the picture of Thoreau hacking away at the vegetation, gouging and scarring trees, and rearranging topography near Walden Pond and in the fields around Concord may not square with our image of the preservationist nature writer, these actions were part and parcel to the long-term compromise with professional and material necessity that Thoreau's surveying career entailed.

Interestingly, Thoreau's prose journals allude only rarely to blazing and cutting, but they do describe his making an opening with "axe and knife" through shrub oaks and birches in order to "get the exact course of a wall" while surveying the Tommy Wheeler farm in April of 1856.[7] Though he tells of "cutting off the limbs of a young white pine in the way of my compass," only three days before he had remarked on "a little blue slate butterfly" that "fluttered over the chain."[8] Thoreau once wrote, "I should not be ashamed to have a shrub oak for my coat of arms,"[9] and so his remarks concerning this specific plant are revealing. On May 17, 1856, the journal celebrates their beauty: "The shrub oak and some other oak leafets [sic], just expanding, now begin to be pretty." But Thoreau is capable of treating the same plant as an obstruction. Surveying the woodlot of John Hosmer about two weeks later, he describes "clearing a line through shrub oak."[10] Thoreau was once moved to speculate about the resemblance between the scars made on trees by the blazing of an axe while surveying and those caused by "natural disease,"[11] but neither the field notes nor the journals offer extended theorizations of these acts of self-inscription upon the landscape. It would be logical to presume, however, that the fear of contaminating his perceptions that Thoreau felt because he had left "stake and stones" in forest thickets would result as well from his having personally cut paths through such thickets. In the chapter of *Walden* entitled "The Ponds," the surveyor truthfully acknowledged that "the wood-cutters, and the railroad, and I myself have profaned Walden."[12]

How then, did the author of the pronouncement "In Wildness is the preservation of the world"[13] negotiate inconsistencies between his protoenvironmentalist, anti-institutional ideals and his professional practices? Evidence of a search for spiritual-emotional compensation, along with signs of an environmentally aware consciousness at war with itself, appear throughout Thoreau's journals. Troubled by the dichotomy between two selves, "the morning surveyor and afternoon seeker,"[14] Thoreau weighed the effects of his surveying on body and soul. In a particularly self-conflicted passage from February 1853, after several days of surveying work described as "comparatively insignificant drudgery with stupid companions," Thoreau is struck by a "remarkable echo" he hears after calling to his chain man on the Hunt farm. He interprets the sound as evidence of nature's generosity in providing him with someone to talk with other than his employee. "It was encouraging and soothing to hear it," Thoreau relates, because it sympathized with "the better part of me . . . somebody, I pined to hear, with whom I could form a community." These echoing repetitions, described as "suggesting thoughts unutterable" to the surveyor, reflect feelings obviously responsive to the natural world but held in check while surveying. Accordingly, Thoreau's impulse is to give up his work in response to the better part of his nature: "I did wish rather to linger there & call all day to the air & hear my words repeated." On this day, however, the side of Thoreau in less-than-ideal relation with the landscape wins out: "A vulgar necessity dragged me along round the bounds of the farm—to hear only the stale answers of my chain man shouted back to me."[15]

An intensely disenchanting encounter with the debasing side of surveying work came in the fall of 1851, when Thoreau was hired for several days by the Town of Concord to verify the town boundaries with the neighboring communities of Sudbury, Lincoln, Bedford and Carlisle. The custom of perambulating the borders was an annual ritual for the selectmen of many New England towns, but because there had recently been disputes about the boundary lines and threats of lawsuits from neighboring communities, Concord had for the first time called on an experienced surveyor to arbitrate the process.[16] The survey of the Acton-Concord town line analyzed in chapter 4 was one of the products of this job. Thoreau had actually looked forward to this project because he believed it would afford him the type of ancillary benefits he had sought when deciding to pursue his business. In a journal entry written three days before the perambulation, he expected that the project would put him precisely where he wanted to be, bringing "the surveyor into contact with whatever wild inhabitant or wilderness its territory embraces."[17]

A second anticipated benefit of the perambulation was that it would require Thoreau to violate more boundaries than he adhered to: "As I am partial to across-lot routes, this appears to be a very proper duty for me to perform, for certainly no route can well be chosen which shall be more across-lot, since the roads in no case run round the town but ray out from its centre, and my course will lie across each one."[18] Always uneasy with the spiritual implications of an owner's right to bar access, Thoreau sometimes assumed the privilege of leaving beaten paths and trespassing, as he did while visiting Canada in 1850, hiking "across lots in spite of numerous signs threatening the severest penalties."[19] Doing so physically counteracted what Thoreau understood as the historical progression toward enclosure of open lands, a trend in which the surveyor's work played a vital role. Largely because of his surveying work, Thoreau envisioned in his journals the coming of a bleak era of complete land appropriation in which "practically a few will have grounds of their own, but most will have none to walk over but what the few allow them."[20] In "Walking," he would develop the choosing of cross-lot routes into an overarching metaphor for his ideal of "sauntering," the inspired activity that, even if it happened while on a paid surveying job, could somehow purify the work, offsetting boundary demarcation with boundary denial. Showing his responsiveness to this ideal, Thoreau notes with pleasure in the days before the 1851 perambulation that there is no "public house" near the line he will establish. Accordingly, he conceives of his surveying as a pastoral sojourn, a cross-lot walk that is more leisure than labor: "It is almost as if I had undertaken to walk round the town at the greatest distance from its centre and at the same time from the surrounding villages."[21]

In the same sanguine preperambulation journal entry, Thoreau seems to have been planning to incorporate the full implications of the term *perambulation* into a mature philosophical program. Apparently searching for a neologism that would express what he most desired to do in the fields and woods, he researched the history and etymology of *perambulation*, learning that

> this appears to be a very ancient custom, and I find that this word 'perambulation' has exactly the same meaning that it has at present in Johnson and Walker's dictionary. A hundred years ago they went round the towns of this State every three years. And the old selectmen tell me that, before the present split stones were set up in 1829, the bounds were marked by a heap of stones, and it was customary for each selectman to add a stone to the heap.[22]

The Johnson's and Walker's English dictionary Thoreau used actually included several meanings for *perambulation*, defining the act as "a traveling survey" or "a survey of the bounds of the parish annually performed." To perambulate was "to walk through," but it also meant "to visit the boundaries of a parish."[23] Among these meanings was the basis of Thoreau's willingness to view the procedure—and thus his supportive role in it—as an affirmative social ritual and an exercise that furthered legitimate communal ends. Though he eventually settled on *sauntering* as the invented term that best expressed his relation to nature while walking and working, it seems *perambulation* was the early candidate for a key word that would justify the surveyor's role in society. In effect, the anticipatory journal entry suggests that Thoreau was pleased with the prospect of government-paid work that would provide him with an enlightening "reconnaissance of [Concord's] frontiers" and confirm how well his chosen occupation accorded with his life's project. At this early stage in his career, he looks forward, hopefully and perhaps naively, to achieving a seamless reconciliation of his moral code with the claims of economic necessity and state authority.

Thoreau was to be quickly and severely disillusioned. What he actually discovered on the perambulation was the power of authority to warp morality. Immediately following his four days of work for the town, it becomes clear that the selectmen themselves, as the personification of his culture's dominant values, have made a damaging imprint on Thoreau's psyche. His September 20 journal entry speaks of the need to recover his "tone and sanity and to perceive things truly and simply again" after "dealing with the most commonplace and worldly-minded men, and emphatically *trivial* things." Judging the communities in his immediate vicinity as fairly represented by these men, Thoreau intuits lives that are "cheap and superficial," concerned inordinately with the crude economic functions of getting and holding. "What can be uglier than a country occupied by grovelling, coarse, and low-lived men?" he asks mean-spiritedly, expressing a disgust for the selectmen that seems as much personal as professional.[24]

An equally distressing insight comes when the surveyor turns the focus of his examination on himself. "Though I have been associating with the *select* men of this and the surrounding towns, I feel inexpressibly begrimed," Thoreau writes. "My Pegasus has lost his wings; he has turned a reptile and gone on his belly." Giving himself over to the selectmen's intentions has at least temporarily robbed him of both his freedom and a part of his humanity: "Since I perambulated the bounds of the town, I find that I have in some degree confined myself,—my vision and my walks," he complains. "I feel as if I had committed suicide in a sense." [25]

In his later address "Slavery in Massachusetts," Thoreau would famously assert, "My thoughts are murder to the state." Here the state is murder to Thoreau's thoughts. Initially expecting some form of vital discovery from the perambulation excursion, he has instead undergone a numbing of imaginative faculties analogous to spiritual if not bodily death, produced by not only attention to but subservience to men and things he found repugnant, a condition similar to the intellectual and moral suicide he warned of in "Life Without Principle." The result of "mixing in the trivial affairs of men," Thoreau learns, is "a fatal coarseness." The final implication of the passage, the didactic message Thoreau derives for himself, is that "the poet must keep himself unstained and aloof. Let him perambulate the bounds of Imagination's provinces, the realms of fancy, and not the insignificant boundaries of towns." [26]

The strong aftereffects of the perambulation prompt inevitable questions about what actually happened on this job to produce Thoreau's disgust and perceived self-abasement. While his journal does not give details, a witness to the September 16 fixing of the Sudbury boundary recalled that the selectmen became embroiled in a heated disagreement over the exact course of the town line. Despite the presence of a trusted surveyor, "there were grave disputes, and law suits seemed probable. . . . The real trouble was owing to the variation of the compass, the old lines having been run some 200 years before." [27] At this moment Thoreau's calculations of the variation between magnetic and true north, made in February and rechecked in March of 1851, proved useful. He pointed out to the selectmen that on the town map Concord's boundary lines had been projected using a variation of nearly eleven degrees, and that the current variation, which naturally changes over time, was now just under ten degrees. [28] A difference of one degree was insignificant in the survey of a house lot, but such a discrepancy applied to the more than five miles of the Concord-Acton boundary would produce an error of over 470 feet. Having compiled in his surveying field notebook a reference chart that indicated the error produced by one degree of variation for lines of various lengths, Thoreau was well prepared to address this problem. As Concord selectman Horace Hosmer later recalled, "Thoreau understood his business thoroughly and settled the boundary question so that peace was declared."[29]

Thoreau's postperambulation nausea was therefore the result not of a surveying problem but of a philosophical problem. What he had envisioned as an affirmative ritual had devolved into the worst kind of empty preening by the selectmen, who had made the town boundary into a site of either materialistically or egotistically motivated political contention. In preparing for the job, Thoreau had learned that a perambulation had two historical meanings. Though in its broadest sense it could be simply a "walking through, a walk, a journey on foot," this was obviously not the activity for which he had been hired. If Thoreau had been able to consult the *Oxford English Dictionary* rather than the Johnson's and Walker's dictionary, he would have found *perambulation* defined in a narrower, more political sense: "the action or ceremony of walking officially round a territory for the purpose of asserting and recording its boundaries, so as to preserve the rights of possession."[30] Was it a walk in the woods or an organized display of hegemony? Obviously, the latter expressed what the selectmen were all about, the former what their hired employee had in mind.

The Concord surveyor seems to have taken several lessons from this experience. The first simple moral had to do with the aforementioned divergence in priorities. Expecting, if not a liberating retreat to the margins of society, at least a dignified communal ritual—perhaps one that emphasized the uniting rather than dividing effects of boundaries and displayed a benevolent form of civil authority—he had instead observed men "tenacious of their rights and dignities and difficult to deal with."[31] He may also have derived the more complicated insight that sauntering for official purposes was a self-defeating practice, a philosophical contradiction of terms. It naturally followed that a walk in the woods while surveying, to the extent that it reinforced rather than traversed boundaries, presented a thorny paradox. In essence, paid perambulation and official walk were oxymoronic concepts.

Painfully aware that in serving the selectmen, he had abetted the political and economic order he despised, Thoreau was conscious of having faltered. Contemplating the material needs that had made him a hireling of the state, he compared his plight to the fable of Apollo serving King Admetus. Sentenced by the gods to a year of servitude as punishment for killing the Cyclops, Apollo became the slave of Admetus in exchange for food and clothing. Recoiling from his own slavery to "mean and narrow-minded men" in exchange for a livelihood, Thoreau wrote in his journal that he was "forcibly struck with the truth of the fable . . . its universal applicability."[32] The difference, perhaps, was in the mental and moral character of the surveyor's bondage, his aversion not toward work itself or the demands it made on his body, but toward its tainted karma—the unhealthy cultural values it made manifest.

Similar sentiments were expressed in journal entries throughout the early phase of Thoreau's career. On November 25, 1850, he becomes alarmed at the recognition that he had "walked a mile into the forest bodily without getting there in spirit." Referring to surveying as his "morning's occupation," he tries but fails to forget obligations to society, among which the demands of clients figure prominently:

> Sometimes it happens that I cannot easily shake off the village; the thought of some work, some surveying, will run in my head, and I am not where my body is, I am out of my senses. In my walks I would return to my senses like a bird or a beast. What business have I in the woods, if I am thinking of something out of the woods?[33]

Probably the most lyrical expression of generalized disillusionment with getting a living—and particularized displeasure with government-sponsored labor—came in late 1851, as Thoreau was physically recovering from an unusually busy period of fieldwork:

> I have been surveying for twenty or thirty days, living coarsely, even as respects my diet,-for I find that that will always alter to suit my employment,-indeed, leading a quite trivial life; and to-night, for the first time, had made a fire in my chamber and endeavored to return to myself. I wished to ally myself to the powers that rule the universe. I wished to dive into some deep stream of thoughtful and devoted life, which meandered through retired and fertile meadows far from towns. I wished to do again, or for once, things quite congenial to my highest inmost and most sacred nature, to lurk in crystalline thought like the trout under verdurous banks, where stray mankind should only see my bubble come

to the surface. I wished to live, ah! as far away as a man can think. I
wished for leisure and quiet to let my life flow in its proper channels,
with its proper currents; when I might not waste the days, might establish daily prayer and thanksgiving in my family; might do my own work
and not the work of Concord and Carlisle,-which would yield me better
than money.[34]

These thoughts, obviously sincere in their melancholy, acquaint us with
the profundity of Thoreau's intermittent aversion to land surveying, perhaps even prompting questions about why he did not find another means
of income, or how he kept up his professional energies for another ten
years and hundred or so more jobs. How could Thoreau's life ever "flow
in its proper channels" if he were regularly compelled to "waste the days"
for Concord or Carlisle?

As he composed the above journal entry, it seems the surveyor himself
confronted this question. The honestly expressed depth of his anguish
must have prompted an immediate mental adjustment, for it did not take
long for him to return to the issue with different conclusions. One of
Thoreau's strongest expressions of job satisfaction came exactly one day
after his lament about the harmful effects of surveying. On December 13,
in the fields of Carlisle, something happened:

> While surveying to-day, saw much mountain laurel for this neighbor-
> hood in Mason's pasture, just over the line in Carlisle. Its bright yellow-
> ish-green shoots are agreeable to my eye. We had one hour of almost
> Indian summer weather in the middle of the day. I felt the influence of
> the sun. It melted my stoniness a little. The pines looked like old friends
> again.[35]

The opportunity to physically encounter nature and the outdoor world
is frequently cited as a factor in Thoreau's choice of a surveying livelihood. Twenty-four hours removed from despair, he is here affirmatively
resensitized, quite clearly made happy by what he sees and feels while
surveying in the open air. As the journal entry continues, however, Thoreau dives deeper, surpassing the acknowledgment of surveying as merely
a job that allows him coincidental contact with natural phenomena:

> Cutting a path through a swamp where was much brittle dogwood,
> etc., etc., I wanted to know the name of every shrub. This varied em-

ployment, to which my necessities compel me, serves instead of foreign
travel and the lapse of time. If it makes me forget some things which I
ought to remember, it no doubt enables me to forget many things which
it is well to forget. By stepping aside from my chosen path so often, I see
myself better and am enabled to criticise myself. Of this nature is the
only true lapse of time.

. . . To be able to see ourselves, not merely as others see us, but as we
are, that service a variety of absorbing employments does us. I would
not be rude to the fine intimations of the gods for fear of incurring the
reproach of superstition.[36]

Based on this passage, theorizations of what surveying could mean to
Thoreau may be taken to a new level. In all Thoreau's journals there is no
better indication that his work in the fields could and did have profound
effects—on his temperament, his view of the world, his view of himself,
his ability to perform the tasks to which his life was dedicated. Surveying the Concord-Carlisle boundary line, Thoreau is forced to cut a path
through a specific growth of vegetation but moved toward curiosity and
interest in all vegetation—he "wanted to know the name of every shrub."
The necessity of small-scale environmental harm is at least partially compensated for by the desire for more inclusive knowledge of the environment in its entirety. In a way, the process is not very different from the
realization that many trees have gone into the making of Thoreau's published books, but the effect of reading them has undoubtedly saved an
appreciable number of trees. Whatever Thoreau learned about the land
through the process of surveying, when translated into observations that
became part of his environmental writings, helped offset the destruction
he confessed to having caused or abetted.

Moreover, as the passage affirms, surveying liberates Thoreau. As an
activity that enables the forgetting of what he periodically "should forget,"
it has restorative purposes where his analytical powers are concerned.
This is not so simple as to say that it allows him to stop thinking ab-
stractly and instead engage physical problems of mathematics and geometry. When Thoreau avers that surveying is akin to foreign travel, he is
also referring to the transference of meaning-making processes from one
language or signification system to another, in this case the verbal symbolic order of his literary life to the numerical taxonomy of engineering.

That such "foreign travel" was beneficial—that the mathematic approximations of reality could function in synergy with linguistically based insights—is borne out in *Walden* as in perhaps no other American book. Thoreau is famous for metaphysical journeying, for having "traveled a good deal in Concord"; what is less widely acknowledged is that the code switching required by his surveying livelihood was frequently his means of doing so.

Once Thoreau returns from surveying work to the "chosen path" of his life, the remunerations of spiritual travel and the passage of time with compass and chain are even more apparent. After surveying, "I see myself better and am enabled to criticise myself," he declares. The work to which "necessities compel," though indeed a diversion from the "highest inmost and most sacred nature" of the artist, makes possible a return to the self that Thoreau recognizes as crucial. Where the writer's critical consciousness is concerned, surveying is among the "fine intimations of the gods," speaking to him in ways he could not have foreseen and would not have chosen, but that are essential to his growth. What Thoreau means when he observes, "Of this nature is the only true lapse of time," is that the spirit develops only by "stepping aside" from its established course, perhaps even occasionally in order to cut a path through a swamp or set a town boundary. Wise acquiescence to the exigencies of surveying, acceptance of "this varied employment" along with concomitants that included both sacrifices and blessings, made Henry Thoreau a better writer.

Evidence that surveying could be productively channeled and made useful in a literary way occurs in the period just prior to the publication of *Walden*. While he was occupied with making final corrections to the manuscript in the spring of 1854, Thoreau was also busy in the fields, making extensive plans of several properties on the Bedford Road and completing smaller jobs for Abel Hosmer and Samuel Hoar. Speaking about the revision process of his masterpiece, Thoreau states, "When I do not see it, for instance . . . I make a little chapter of contents which enables me to recall it page by page to my mind, and judge it more impartially when my manuscript is out of the way." The literary text has been out of sight for a while, but not out of mind. Taking up the *Walden* proofs and his journal after several days surveying, Thoreau seems surprised to discover that his perceptions are sharpened rather than dulled: "I find that I can criticise my composition best when I stand at a little

distance from it." In the process of fulfilling obligations demanding substantial physical and mental labor, Thoreau has actually been editing and
rewriting, with favorable results: "The distraction of surveying enables
me rapidly to take new points of view," he observes. "A day or two of surveying is equal to a journey."[37] After the publication of *Walden*, Thoreau
once more declared his ability not only to balance the mental demands of
field labor and literary labor, but to derive pleasure and edification from
their mutual influence: "Again, so many times I am reminded of the advantage to the poet, and philosopher, and naturalist . . . of pursuing from
time to time some other business than his chosen one—seeing with the
side of the eye."[38]

Other journal entries substantiate the idea that surveying was a spiritual influence Thoreau had learned to regulate. Three years after the
perambulation that prompted his venomous comparison of surveying
to the punishment of serving Admetus, Thoreau revised his assessment.
Working in Carlisle on a beautiful spring afternoon in 1854, the surveyor
momentarily feels sorry for himself; he is still the god Apollo serving a
mortal king. But when he hears the shrill notes of a tree frog on an early-
spring day, his rancor dissipates:

> Whatever year it may be, I am surveying, perhaps, in the woods; I have
> taken off my outside coat, perhaps for the first time, and hung it on a
> tree; the zephyr is positively agreeable on my cheek; I am thinking what
> an elysian day it is, and how I seem always to be keeping the flocks of
> Admetus such days—that is my luck; when I hear a single, short, well-
> known stertorous croak from some pool half filled with dry leaves. You
> may see anything now—the buff-edged butterfly and many hawks—
> along the meadow; and hark! while I was writing down that field note,
> the shrill peep of the hylodes was borne to me from afar through the
> woods.[39]

For all its descriptive interest, what the passage most strikingly records
is Thoreau's emotional self-mastery—a triumph over self-destructive
resentment of his dubious "luck," enabled by a sudden awareness of its
compensations. That the awakening occurs while he is inscribing a field
note is a pertinent detail, symbolizing emancipation from burdens purely
commercial.

At the peak of Concord's deforestation in the mid-1850s, during a correspondingly busy time in his surveying career, Thoreau wrote, "I hate the present modes of living and getting a living." The professional trades, he declared, were "all odious to me."[40] Contemplating man's incursions on the landscape several months later, he broached the fundamental question: "Is the earth improving or deteriorating in this respect? Does it require to be improved by the hands of man?"[41] For the Concord surveyor, the crux of the dilemma was obviously the lot-corner monumentation he had constructed in remote corners of the Walden woods—the stake and stones he left behind while measuring landscape features "so extensively and minutely" that he had physically or metaphysically destroyed them.

Within Thoreau's feelings about his work, there is quite a paradox. For every expression in Thoreau's writings of either discontent at "profaning Walden" or disdain for the process of getting a living, especially under the auspices of civil authority, there is an equally eloquent passage attesting to the positive values or at least temporarily uplifting influences of land surveying. Thoreau could claim that viewing the landscape through the sight vanes of his compass was like putting a veil over his faculties that "shut out nature"; he could also classify surveying as one of the "honest arts of life," one of "the true paths to perception and enjoyment" of his beloved natural world.[42]

In working out the enigma that dwells in Thoreau's identity as businessman, civil employee and instrument of environmental change, it may help to recall that in concluding his description of the psychologically disastrous perambulation of 1851, Thoreau suddenly pulled back from self-censure. Righting himself spiritually, he rendered a calming image of boundlessness and imaginative flight: "I scare up the great bittern in meadow by the Heywood Brook near the ivy. He rises buoyantly as he flies against the wind, and sweeps south over the willow with outstretched neck, surveying." This, it seems, is the type of *surveying* to which Thoreau wished to dedicate himself. Heeding his own call to "perambulate the bounds of Imagination's provinces . . . and not the insignificant boundaries of towns,"[43] Thoreau rejects despair, implicitly renewing a commitment to achieve or embody a personal-professional synthesis that would offset the worldly and environmentally destructive in his work.

6

The Science of the Field Notes

It is impossible for the same person to see things
from the poet's point of view and that of the man of
science. The poet's second love may be science—not
his first—when use has worn off the bloom.

—Thoreau, *Journal*, February 18, 1852

EARLY IN MARCH OF 1853, Thoreau received a printed circular letter
from Spencer F. Baird, secretary of the Association for the Advancement
of American Science, inviting him to join the association and asking him
to fill out a questionnaire about his interests and activities. Founded in
1848 by a cadre of engineers and scientists including Alexander Dallas
Bache and Louis Agassiz, the AAAS was an outgrowth of the Coast
Survey's scientific efforts and one of the means Bache used to put the
work at the service of the nation's eminent naturalists. In accordance with
its stated mission of bringing together and combining the labors of the
emerging scientific community of the United States, the association was
recruiting laypersons to provide them with natural-history specimens
from different regions of the country.[1] Thoreau was identified as a poten-

tial member probably because he was known to Agassiz, having collected numerous plants and animals for the famous zoologist-geologist in 1847.

As a self-identified "observer of nature generally," Thoreau was a good candidate to accept the organization's summons and acknowledge the interests he shared with the foremost natural scientists of the day. Instead of immediately returning the questionnaire, however, Thoreau reflected on it in his journal, where he pondered its meaning as an indication of how his intellectual priorities diverged from mainstream scientific thinking. On March 5, Thoreau wrote that the most important question Baird had asked was "what branch of science I was especially interested in." The seemingly straightforward inquiry prompted a strong reaction:

> Now, though I could state to a select few that department of human inquiry which engages me, and should be rejoiced at an opportunity to do so, I felt that it would be to make myself the laughing-stock of the scientific community to describe or attempt to describe to them that branch of science which specially interests me, inasmuch as they do not believe in a science which deals with the higher law.[2]

What might have been a gratifying opportunity for Thoreau to express his enthusiasms was instead a measure of his somewhat painful alienation and lack of philosophical kinship with the several hundred members, primarily scientists and engineers, of the association. Telling the truth about his observational principles, he seems to have believed, would provoke mirth and derision. For an audience in the "scientific community," truncated and enfeebled responses were necessary: "I was obliged to speak to their condition and describe to them that poor part of me which alone they can understand. . . . How absurd that, though I probably stand as near to nature as any of them, and am by constitution as good an observer as most, yet a true account of my relation to nature should excite their ridicule only."[3]

It took quite a while for Thoreau to decide exactly what to do with the association's membership offer. But in mid-December, almost ten months after receiving Baird's questionnaire, he filled out the printed form, wrote a brief letter expressing his "hearty thanks" along with "an interest in the Association itself"—and politely declined the membership. Compared with the acerbic thoughts he had recorded in his journal, the excuse Thoreau gave for not signing on was uncharacteristically bland. He couldn't join, he explained, because he "should not be able to attend the meetings, unless held in the immediate vicinity."[4]

Given his earlier-expressed disdain, it might seem strange that Thoreau even returned the questionnaire. In March Thoreau had claimed an inability to express himself to the association, yet in December he obviously wanted to communicate with it on some level. His journal had declared that conveying his essential convictions was an impossibility: "I should have told them at once that I was a transcendentalist. That would have been the shortest way of telling them that they would not understand my explanations."[5] Writing to the association later, he avoided the term *transcendentalist*, withheld his criticisms, and gave the organization what it expected—an account of his science that was at least superficially consistent with its priorities.[6]

Thoreau's response to the AAAS questionnaire was in fact formulated to be read on more than one level. In the space next to *Branches of science in which especial interest is felt*, he wrote, "The Manners & Customs of the Indians of the Algonquin Group previous to contact with civilized man." This response, composed at a time when the greatest real-estate transfer in history was in full operation as one Native tribe after another was being displaced by white settlers, necessarily participated in cultural debates about the "Indian question" that vexed both anthropologists and politicians in the mid-nineteenth century. Much of the prevailing theory—espoused in studies by Agassiz, Henry Rowe Schoolcraft and especially Samuel G. Morton—had promoted pseudoscientific conclusions about the supposedly inferior racial characteristics of Native Americans.[7]

Thoreau, however, was "one of the first Americans to view the Indian with anything other than disdain."[8] While recent research into Thoreau's racial attitudes has produced debate over the extent of his empathy for Native Americans, the argument that he developed feelings of respect for Native cultures while gradually rejecting the racist assumptions of his scientific contemporaries seems viable.[9] During the last decade or so of his life, Thoreau consistently kept up with the racially charged discourse on Native Americans while copying down hundreds of pages of extracts from texts both new and old in his voluminous Indian notebooks. By the mid-1850s, as Jessie Bray notes, Thoreau had become "frustrated with the hegemony inherent in his source materials" on the Native American question.[10] Beginning as early as September 1853, when he met with Penobscot Indian Joe Aitteon in the Maine woods, Thoreau progressively cultivated an understanding of Native Americans that rose above the racial discourse of mainstream anthropologists.

Thoreau's use of the words "previous to contact with civilized man" to characterize his interest in Native culture for the AAAS is therefore significant. In his encounter with Aitteon, Thoreau had been surprised at the cultural hybridity of the Penobscot, symbolized by his guide's penchant for whistling "O Susanna."[11] Seeking contact with an authentic Native, he had found one who had adapted by necessity to historical change. When Thoreau heard Aitteon use the Penobscot language, however, he became fascinated by the possibility of recoverable culture and realized that "the Indian was not the invention of [presumably white] historians and poets."[12] Thoreau's declaration of an interest in precontact Native culture three months after meeting Aitteon may be read as an effort to evade the ideological lens through which his own culture constructed "Indians."[13]

The frustration Thoreau felt at not being able to directly express himself to the association on the all-important topic of his scientific interests is all the more understandable in light of the professional identification he gave. Appearing on the same sheet of paper with Thoreau's avowal of special curiosity about precontact indigenous culture is a statement of his occupation as "Land-surveying," a profession that has historically been a *means* of initial contact between whites and indigenous peoples. While Thoreau never surveyed land for the purpose of wresting it from Native Americans, he certainly understood that the existence of surveyors was a function of cultural precepts antithetical to the Native American worldview. Robert Sattelmeyer once empathized with the "methodological difficulty" faced by nineteenth-century scientists in trying to assess Native cultures while relying for their information on texts created by whites whose very presence altered the cultures they described.[14] Thoreau's expressed commitment to pursue knowledge about Algonquin tribes previous to interaction with whites suggests his awareness—somewhat in advance of the thinking of the day—that the cultural presence embodied so often by the surveyor inevitably marred what it touched.

Thoreau closed his response to the association by naming works of natural science he admired and encouraging his audience in the scientific community to draw appropriate conclusions. In the space below

Remarks, he added the note, "I am an observer of nature generally, and the character of my observations, so far as they are scientific, may be inferred from the fact I am especially attracted by such books of science as White's Selborne and Humboldt's 'Aspects of Nature.'"

If the association had actually taken the cue to make inferences from the books Thoreau was especially attracted by, they might have acquired a pretty good idea of his priorities. Gilbert White's *The Natural History and Antiquities of Selborne,* first published in 1788, is a compilation of natural-science discoveries obtained through minute observation of the flora and fauna around White's native town of Selborne in the English county of Hampshire. White was Britain's first ecologist; he believed adamantly in the acquisition of scientific knowledge through careful observation of living animals rather than the laboratory examination of dead specimens. Considering that Baird's letter to Thoreau had also included directions for killing and preserving specimens of local birds and fishes, the reference to the author of *Selborne* seems calculated to suggest one of the reasons Thoreau could not join the association. Though he had collected and killed birds and other animal specimens for Agassiz in 1847, Thoreau had since reconsidered this means of study. By 1854, Thoreau's journal referred to such collecting as a form of "murder" that was "inconsistent with the poetic perception." As the "Higher Laws" chapter of *Walden* asserts, "There is a finer way of studying ornithology than this."[15]

By aligning his interests with those of Gilbert White, Thoreau also conveyed substantial information about his lifestyle choices. Known to his neighbors as a philosophical bachelor, White had "spent the greater part of his life in literary occupations, and especially in the study of Nature." He passed up opportunities to join the scientific academy and "earn a college living" because he could never persuade himself to leave his beloved native town, which he considered a peculiarly advantageous locale for an observer of the natural world.[16] In effect, Thoreau's indication to Baird that he could not attend association meetings unless they were in the immediate vicinity of Concord echoed White's conviction that a small town could provide scope enough for significant discovery.[17]

Both White and Thoreau used land surveying as a methodology in the writing of natural history. Many of the observations in *Selborne* are based on meticulously gathered landscape data, including most notably a careful survey "made with good exactness" of Wolmer Pond, a sixty-six-acre

body of water only slightly larger than Walden Pond. The opening chapter of *Selborne* records the length, width and circumference of the pond
while situating it geographically, remarking on its wildlife, and noting
"the clearness of its water."[18] In this context it is worth mentioning that
Thoreau expressed his affinity for the British naturalist, scientist, ecologist and fellow pond surveyor—along with his rejection of membership
in his country's scientific association—at a key moment. In December
1853, he was in the last stages of work on the *Walden* manuscript.

Alexander von Humboldt's *Aspects of Nature* was also cited by Thoreau as an indication of the character of his scientific interests. *Aspects of
Nature*, the English translation of which appeared in 1849, is described in
its preface as "an artistic and literary treatment of subjects in natural history" in which Humboldt elucidates "the unfailing influence of external
nature on the feelings, the moral disposition, and the destinies of man."[19]
In framing the work's purpose, Humboldt emphasized his effort "to in-
spire and cherish a love for the study of Nature, by bringing together in a
small space the results of careful observation on the most varied subjects,
[and] by showing the importance of exact numerical data."[20] As might
be surmised from this preamble, much of Humboldt's actual geosci-
ence in *Aspects of Nature* is based on meticulous measurements. These
include trigonometric surveys of landscape features, determinations of
linear distances between geographic anomalies, and hypsometric or sea-
level-based measurements of the height of mountain ranges and natural
promontories.

Such methods were quite commonplace in the science of the period,
but Humboldt sought pointedly to draw attention to the ways his work
dissented from the scientific academy. According to its author, the work
constituted a "combination of a literary and scientific object" that presented a "semi-poetic clothing of severe scientific truths."[21] In terms Thoreau embraced but the association might have viewed skeptically, Humboldt underscored the idea that *Aspects of Nature* comprised a merger
of the poetic and scientific that was intended as an implicit reproach to
the scientific establishment. Touting values a transcendentalist could espouse, Humboldt expressed vehement opposition to "the dogmatic half-
knowledge and arrogant skepticism which have long too much prevailed
in what are called the higher circles of society."[22] Considering the anties-
tablishment stance of Humboldt's preface, we might wonder if Thoreau's

decision to invoke the work and its author while declining association membership was a premeditated criticism.

Overall, the strategies behind Thoreau's public and private responses to the Association for the Advancement of American Science seem clear. Because he believed he could not give the academy a true account of his "relation to nature," he had resorted to a journal entry about the questionnaire to effectively translate these pursuits into their actual terms: "The fact is," he wrote in his journal, "I am a mystic, a transcendentalist, and a natural philosopher to boot."[23] As Thoreau's thinking went, an amalgamation of writing, science and surveying so undertaken as to accord with higher principles was something he simply could not safely explain.

Since his philosophy was in fact not exceedingly radical or abstruse, Thoreau's reluctance to share it with the AAAS constitutes striking evidence of how little confidence he had in the judgment of the scientific establishment by late 1853. As Laura Dassow Walls concluded from her analysis of the AAAS questionnaire, "One of Thoreau's ways of seeing a thing was to measure it"; the purpose of Thoreau's constant measuring was "to reveal patterns that enabled insights into all sorts of unsuspected connections."[24] Persuaded by Humboldt's proposal of accuracy in measurement as a serious research precept, Thoreau enacted this principle through persistent quantification of natural phenomena in the field. Rather than expounding the theory to an impervious audience, he presented himself in a way that complied with conventional expectations but gave intimations of heterodoxy to those willing or able to read discerningly.

If Thoreau had been inclined toward a full-fledged effort to present and describe the breadth of his interests, he could have sent the AAAS a copy of his surveying notebook, "Field-Notes of Surveys Made by Henry D. Thoreau Since November 1849." The observations he recorded while pursuing his literary-scientific-surveying vocation might have helped verify the claim made in his journal that his named activities were merely proximal terms for endeavors that were at once practical and those of a "mystic." Measurements and data contained in the "Field-Notes" provide telling indications of Thoreau's aspiration to use surveying to pursue an eclectic form of scientific inquiry that maintained the dictates of "plain living and high thinking."

At first glance, the "Field-Notes" offer disappointingly little information about Thoreau's personality or psychology. In accordance with the book's narrowly circumscribed purpose, there are no entries of a personal nature, no prose that responds other than objectively to the natural world, no verbal extravagance of any kind, only one reference to the weather—July 3, 1851, was "a cloudy day"—and a perceptible emotional restraint. Nowhere does Thoreau overtly break from the character of hired surveyor to weigh the effects and implications of his work. The notebook is a morally neutral space, objective by design, where calculation, facts and data for the most part not only supersede but exclude sentiment and subjectivity. Given their unswervingly nonliterary focus, the fact that the surveying notes have not been treated as a literary manuscript is not surprising.[25]

Approached from a perspective that pays close attention to the practical details and processes of nineteenth-century surveying, however, the field notebook yields significant insights. A careful look at its residual contents reveals that, on several occasions, Thoreau recorded information connected with surveying but not connected to a specific project for which he received pay. These deviations from the practical recording of surveying data, though infrequent, draw attention to Thoreau's lifelong attempt to invest his surveying with scientific-philosophical meaning and position himself as landscape "inspector" of a higher order.

The first overt indication of an elevated purpose in the "Field-Notes" occurs on page 38, where Thoreau records making an evening observation of the "Pole Star" in order to locate true north or true meridian:

> True Meridian
> Found the direction of the Pole
> Star at its greatest Western
> Elongation (1° 58½')? At 9.h.,
> 26 m. PM! Feb. 7th 1851.
>
> It coincides with a line drawn
> from the SE corner of the stone
> post on the E side of our western
> small front gate, to the S side
> of the first door on the W side
> of the depot.

Between 4 and 5 o'clock the
Next day, I found the above
Line to bear, by my compass,
N 7⅞-E (angle)
1° 58½' (azimuth)
=9⅞°—W
This is the adjustment.

From a procedural standpoint, there is little that could be called unusual about this note or its appearance in Thoreau's notebook. In the mid-nineteenth century, many good surveyors regularly measured the difference or variation between true north (determined by taking a sighting on the North Star or polestar) and magnetic north (determined by means of a magnetic compass). Noting the variation produced more accurate bearings and made it easier to rerun the lines if the land were surveyed in the future.

The use of true north, however, depended on the type of work performed. Guidelines for the plane or flat surveys of primarily domestic property and small woodlands that Thoreau made were very different from the rules governing the more formal Survey of Public Lands in vast unsettled western areas, which stipulated regular use and checking of true meridian along with geodesic adjustments for the curvature of the earth. The type of surveying Thoreau performed was mainly of the metes-and-bounds variety, in which magnetic azimuth and the length of the successive parts of the boundary of a property were measured and used together with supplementary descriptions of landscape features to legally identify a property on a deed.[26] The declination between magnetic and true north was essential in the case of large boundaries, but was often considered inconsequential in the measurement of the smaller plots of land for which Thoreau was usually hired.[27] During this period, even surveyors whose work required true north sometimes did not bother with the intricate and labor-intensive process of finding and checking it on their own. Those who were less precise often simply took another surveyor's word for it and set their declination that way.[28] And Thoreau had been getting along without true north for quite a while. In the work he performed prior to 1851, simple magnetic bearings were the norm, a fact attested to by the sometimes rather crude directional arrows that appear on some of his early surveys. To continue working in and around Concord, Thoreau probably did not have to "shoot Polaris," as modern surveyors term the procedure.

The process of taking a Polaris sighting as Thoreau executed it is a complex two-day operation requiring advance preparation and patient, careful observation. From the astronomical tables in his copy of Davies's *Elements of Surveying and Navigation,* Thoreau saw that the polestar would be at its greatest western elongation at precisely 9:26 p.m. on February 7, 1851. But only if the sky was clear and he was ready with his equipment at the proper moment would the viewing be possible.[29] As a location for the procedure, Thoreau needed a level area with at least fifty or so yards of unobstructed sight line.

He chose the front yard of the Thoreau house on Main Street. In the area just several feet to the west of his front door, Thoreau set up a table from which the observation would be taken by driving two posts firmly into the ground in a line that ran nearly east-west. Assuming that Thoreau did as Davies instructed, the three-foot-high posts were about four feet apart. He then spanned the posts with a board or plank at least a foot wide and smooth on the upper side, nailing the plank to the posts to create a stable surface. When the table was complete, Thoreau took one of the detachable iron sight vanes from his surveyor's compass and tacked it to a piece of board four or five inches square to make a small movable sighting platform. With the small nail only partially driven in, the platform was smooth on the underside and could be moved across the observation table to follow the movement of the North Star.

The next step was to hang a string on the sight line between the observation table and the polestar. About twelve feet in front of the table, and in the direction of the star, Thoreau hung a plummet or plumb bob (a metal weight fastened to a strand of twine) from the top of an inclined staff or range pole. The top of the pole was of such a height that the polestar would appear about six inches below it. The plummet was swung in a bucket of water to prevent it from moving in a breeze.

Thoreau began closely observing the star at about twenty minutes before its elongation. At a little after nine p.m., he placed the sighting board with its attached compass sight on the surface of the horizontal plank. Kneeling behind the table and peering through the sight vane and upward toward the star, Thoreau slid the board east or west until the aperture of the compass sight, the plumb line and the star were brought into alignment. He continued to follow the star as it moved slightly west of the plumb line toward its elongation. When the star stopped moving, it had reached its greatest western elongation, where it remained for several minutes. Thoreau then quickly tacked the sighting board into precise position on the observation table. During the observation, as Davies reminds us, it would have been "necessary to have the plumb-line lighted," which Thoreau probably managed with a lantern placed near it on the ground.

Before the evening's work was finished, a range pole or Jacob staff with a candle attached to it had to be placed at a distance of thirty or forty yards from the plumb line and in the same direction with the compass sight. For this part of the procedure, an assistant crossed over Main Street with the staff and was waved into position in the gently sloping open field as Thoreau continued to look through his sight vane.[30] Once

FIGURE 6.1. Sighting Polaris, February 7, 1851. According to his "Field-Notes," Thoreau had practiced the procedure the night before, "not very successfully." (Myca Hopkins drawing.)

this was done, the plumb line could be removed. Stakes could then be put down where the Jacob staff had stood and at the point of observation through the compass sight. "The line so determined," Thoreau's surveying manual explained, "makes with the true meridian, an angle equal to the azimuth of the pole-star; and, from this line, the variation of the needle is readily determined, even without tracing the true meridian on the ground." [31]

Thoreau had now "found the direction of the Pole Star at its greatest Western Elongation," but it would have been difficult for him to set up his tripod and take the bearing of this line in complete darkness, so he left his stakes in the ground and returned to the spot the next afternoon. "Between 4 and 5 o'clock the next day," as the "Field-Notes" indicate, Thoreau finally got the information he was seeking. The variation of his compass needle from the line he had established the previous evening was 7⅞° east of north. This was a strikingly precise number to arrive at with the naked eye, especially when one considers that the degree graduations of Thoreau's compass were only to the half degree. We can assume that Thoreau took extreme care with his data, probably taking multiple readings of this vital figure and averaging them to get his number.

To get the full declination or adjustment, this angle still had to be added to the polestar's azimuth (the small angle the polestar made with true north when sighted at the star's elongation). Davies's surveying manual included a table of azimuths giving the mean angle for each latitude, calculated for the first of July each year. Thoreau could easily have used Davies's mean figure for 1851, which was 1 degree 59¾ minutes. But he seems to have aspired here to a greater and again unusual level of accuracy. Somehow Thoreau arrived at the figure of one degree, fifty-eight and a half minutes (1°58½') for his azimuth determination. That he wrote a question mark after the figure indicates some uncertainty about the number, but the striking thing is that he bothered to calculate his own adjusted figure. The difference between the azimuth given by Davies and the one Thoreau used is 1.25 minutes. An angular minute is one-sixtieth of a degree. Thoreau changed Davies's azimuth figure—and wondered about the change with a question mark—in order to possibly increase the accuracy of his magnetic declination by two one-hundredths of one degree.

A yearning for precision and a lifelong pursuit of "higher laws" and "higher mathematics" are already part of the Thoreau legend. Thinking about the elaborate steps he undertook to find true meridian, along with the addition of his own azimuth to arrive at a variation from true north of 9⅞°, we sense a desire for perfection, along with the personal satisfaction he took in closing the "Field-Notes" entry entitled "True Meridian" with a decisive-sounding and extremely hard-earned affirmation: "This is the adjustment."

Once Thoreau had found his adjustment, he immediately exploited it in a way that had both practical and theoretical applications. Now able to use his compass to create with confidence a due north-south line, Thoreau marked one out permanently. With his tripod and compass still in place in his front yard, he noted that the north-south line he had determined passed over the corner of a stone post of the western front gate. He sighted the gate corner and then turned his compass exactly 180° to sight another permanent object—a specific part of a door on the Concord railroad depot to his immediate south. Now he had two stationary points on a north-south axis. As his field notebook explains, the direction of true north "coincides with a line drawn from the SE corner of the stone post on the E side of our western small front gate, to the S side of the first door on the W side of the depot." If he wished to check the magnetic variation before or after a day of surveying, he could simply sight a line from the stone post to the depot door, and the compass needle would tell him that day's declination. In other words, Thoreau did not have to conduct further Polaris sightings after February of 1851 because, just outside the front door of his home, he had a permanent Polaris sighting.

With the Walden survey, Thoreau had put his "House" into the geological picture, situating his domestic life at a precise point of contact with symbolic universals. With his determination of true meridian, Thoreau accomplished the same thing another way, bringing a scientifically determined symbolic universal into his domestic sphere. He constructed, instead of a home "as far off as many a region viewed nightly by astronomers," an astronomical attachment to the near-at-hand.[32] There were two gates to the fence in Thoreau's front yard. Each time he passed through the western gate—the one leading away from Concord village—it would have been hard for Thoreau not to be reminded of his precisely determined direction, especially since he verified that direction so often, possibly at the beginning or end of each day he surveyed.

Was finding true meridian then more the act of Thoreau the businessman or Thoreau the scientist and moral philosopher? It seems he
was excited by celestial observation to a degree that contrasts markedly
with the formal and subdued, businesslike demeanor of every previous
entry in the "Field-Notes." The only exclamation points that appear in
the surveying notebook are the one in the "True Meridian" entry and two
that appear as Thoreau rechecked true meridian on July 3 of the same
year.[33] All the more interesting is the first use Thoreau made of his new
and exciting knowledge.[34] His first project after shooting Polaris was not
to subdivide a client's woodlot or lay out a new road in Concord, but to
make a noncommercial survey on his own. On February 17, 1851, Thoreau
spent the day at nearby White Pond doing exactly what he had done
while living in the woods and surveying at Walden Pond five years earlier.
Revisiting a spot he had often praised for its secluded beauty, Thoreau
plotted the White Pond shoreline, mapped its contours and plumbed its
depths with soundings almost as frequent as those made in the Walden
survey. No one hired or paid Thoreau for this work, but his note in the
bottom left-hand corner of the White Pond plan is his first use of true
north determined by his own calculation. The variation of 7⅞°, he noted,
was the "same as when [the] star was observed."[35]

Thoreau's sudden emotion and sudden return to the type of spiritually motivated fieldwork he had performed at Walden support the notion that, while finding true meridian made him a better surveyor, it
also made him something more than a surveyor. As a surveyor, he had
executed complex procedures on a fixed day of the celestial calendar at

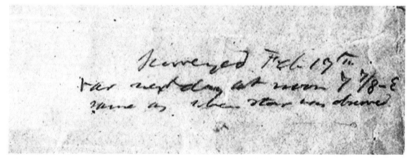

FIGURE 6.2. Detail, survey of White Pond, Feb. 17, 1851. The variation of 7⅞° east,
Thoreau noted, was the "same as when star was observed." Courtesy Concord Free
Public Library.

a preordained time, acting in careful accordance with the rational dictates of science, carrying out precise measurements and calculations that added value to the work that was his livelihood. Described in terms more in keeping with the transcendentalist impulse to transmute observed facts into life-guiding principles, Thoreau had by the same operation accomplished something else. Adding knowledge of longitude to latitudinal coordinates he already knew, Thoreau the scientist-philosopher had literally established his exact place on the earth's surface.[36] Arguably, such knowledge merged productively with the equally centering task of better locating himself amid the chaos of nature, creating new opportunities for perceiving and conveying truths based on the correlation between the rational and the intuitive. In surveying White Pond, it was to the latter results that Thoreau responded first. A journal entry of January 1853 may have explained what he truly sought in first exploring the night sky, then exploring a pond:

> I pine for a new World in the heavens as well as on earth. . . . But it is the stars as not known to science that I would know—the stars which the lonely traveler knows. . . . I see not merely old but new testaments in the skies. . . . The heavens commonly look as dry & meager as our astronomies are. . . . A few good anecdotes is our science—with a few imposing facts regarding distance and size—& little or nothing about the stars as they concern man—teaching how he may survey a country or sail a ship—& not how he may steer his life—Astrology contained the germ of a higher truth than this.[37]

Deemphasizing the practical relevance of stars to surveying or sailing, Thoreau embraces their use in spiritual navigation.

Considering his often-expressed but self-conflicted desires to first carve out an identity separate from surveying as a profession, then to use his surveying less as a business and more as a mode of perception, Thoreau's responsiveness to the philosophical uses and implications of celestial observation is entirely in character. His early essay "The Service," begun in the spring of 1840, had compared the character of the "brave man" to a "fixed star." Thoreau had proposed that if all humanity, like "every star in the nebulae and milky way," should emulate the polestar by "exerting its whole influence," the result would be an equilibrium between the individual and the earth's physical laws. Directly addressing a personified

Nature later in the same essay, Thoreau enlarges his idea: "The stars are thy interpreters to me." [38]

Appreciation of the North Star as a provider of moral direction for man also appeared in Thoreau's 1842 essay "Natural History of Massachusetts." In this early work, composed seven years before Thoreau took up the profession seriously, he is already thinking like a surveyor. The striking claim is that the spirit of adventure that drives the explorer is deepened and improved by connecting terrestrial to extraterrestrial. "And when he has done, he may have to steer his way home through the dark by the north star, and he will feel himself some degrees nearer to it for having lost his way on earth." [39] Here Thoreau presupposes a relation between the compass and the human spirit and asserts that only through a celestial guide is the observer of nature's mission completed. When the actual fugitive slave Henry Williams spent the night with Thoreau's family on his way to Canada in 1851, Thoreau took the opportunity to quiz him about his reliance on Polaris, recording in his journal the next day the information that runaways "steered for the north star even when it had got round and appeared to them to be in the south." [40]

By the time he finished *Walden* in 1854, Thoreau had proposed the North Star as a method of directional negotiation that offered the true course and "sufficient guidance for all our life," observing that "it is by a mathematical point only that we are wise, as the sailor or the fugitive slave keeps the polestar in his eye." [41] In a letter of 1860, Thoreau would equate Polaris with the Great Basin as places representing the furthest limits of mankind's forays into the "unexplored land" and the limits of "the Known and Unknown." [42] Ultimately, Thoreau's formulation of the polestar bespoke sensitivity to a broad array of associations and significations. For a navigator at sea, a slave seeking freedom, or a surveyor seeking corroboration for his own physical and metaphysical course on earth, Polaris could save lives and redeem souls.

Emerson's "Nature" had asserted that "every natural fact is a symbol of some spiritual fact" and that "every natural process is a version of a moral sentence." [43] Thoreau's internalization of this transcendentalist manifesto was one of the formative experiences of his life, and his increasingly profound exploration of its precepts is a recurring topic in Thoreau studies. Perhaps he saw in true meridian a "new weapon" of the type Emerson described in "Nature" as the result of "unconscious truth" miraculously "interpreted and defined in an object."[44] If magnetic north was the real, true north was the ideal, helping to confer moral legitimacy on a surveying profession that Thoreau wanted desperately to transform into more than a source of income. Though some have argued that the younger man took his onetime mentor's axioms overly literally, Emerson's call upon the naturalist-poet to "find something of himself . . . in every fact of astronomy or atmospheric influence which observation or analysis lay open"[45] offers peculiarly apt justification for considering Thoreau's Polaris sighting as motivated by transcendentalist strivings as much as by commercial necessity.

That Thoreau updated his original 1846 survey of Walden Pond to reflect his determination of true north not only suggests his continuing interest in how, as Emerson stated, "the axioms of physics translate the laws of ethics," it also demonstrates how an observation in the surveying field notes literally changed Thoreau's mode of reckoning in both commercial and anticommercial contexts.[46] Plotting by true north was not without purely practical benefits to surveying, benefits that were regularly put to use in Thoreau's subsequent fieldwork, but it also clearly became an integrating principle of the forms of landscape observation and noumenal direction finding espoused in his best prose. By this reasoning, the "Field-Notes" become in part something other than a repository of professional data, instead serving the author's deeply felt nonprofessional urges, changing from a space of purely economic usefulness to a hybridized testing ground for complex speculation.

A second remarkable entry further widens the conceptual scope of the "Field-Notes." This item, located on the bottom half of page 75 below the brief description of a September 30, 1851, survey for the Town of Concord, adds a new subdivision to the numerous forms of landscape appraisal practiced by Thoreau over the course of his career as surveyor and natural historian. With no warning or perceptible transition from the routine entries that surround it, the following sentence appears:

> About the middle of Oct. it
> was 20 ft 6½ inches from the surface
> of Walden Pond to the top of the rail
> of the RR at the western extremity
> of the pond.

As my own measurements confirm, the dimension Thoreau records here is a difference of level rather than of linear distance.[47] The logistics of this differential-leveling procedure are relatively uncomplicated, but neither the information nor the casual tone used to present it is without substantive meaning. To get this data, Thoreau set up his tripod and compass on a turning point, some area of solid ground on the embankment between Walden Pond and the Fitchburg Railroad. He then sent an assistant (perhaps the Irishman helper often mentioned in his journals of this period) directly to the edge of the pond. There the assistant held in place a leveling stave or leveling rod calibrated in feet and inches, making sure that the bottom end of the rod was barely touching the surface of the water. After leveling his compass, Thoreau would have sighted the stave and taken a plus-sight measurement, also termed a back sight, of this starting elevation. He then sent his rodman around behind him to an area on the upward slope, turned his compass 180 degrees, and recorded a minus-sight or fore-sight reading of the stave now held by the assistant at the new location between the compass and the railroad tracks. With his helper remaining in place, Thoreau then climbed the embankment and set up the tripod at a still-higher station closer to the tracks. From here Thoreau took another back sight and fore sight. Depending on the height of the stave, the surveyor would have had to set up his tripod perhaps three times while ascending the steep embankment, finally directing his assistant to the selected bench mark—in this case the rail of the railroad—where he held the stave vertically and in contact with the top of the rail. Once all the measurements were made, the calculation of the vertical distance from the pond to the rail required simply subtracting the sum of the fore sights from the sum of the back sights.

Here as with the Polaris sighting, intriguing inferences stem from a consideration of procedure as metaphor. In surveying terms, the Fitchburg Railroad provided a practicable permanent bench mark, contrasting with the naturally variable level of the pond surface, which Thoreau nevertheless fixes and quantifies through a cipher expressing measurable divergence. The pond level thus becomes a level datum, a surface in interesting ways analogous to mean sea level, which is the generally adopted level datum in standard geographical elevations. Where sea-level data is not available, as in local surveys like Thoreau's, the level datum is often arbitrarily selected. But it would be impossible to argue that either

FIGURE 6.3. Completing the Walden survey. In October 1851, Thoreau measured the difference in level from the "surface of Walden Pond to the top of the rail of the RR at the western extremity of the pond." (Myca Hopkins drawing.)

component of this measurement scheme is arbitrarily selected. Using the train tracks and the pond—the central symbolic icons of *Walden*—as the two stations in an engineering experiment, Thoreau here recorded a physical relation that epitomized in motive and method the organic form of surveying he hinted at in so much of his prose.

By choosing the top of the rail—the precise spot where locomotive meets land—as his bench mark, Thoreau extrapolated his earlier careful soundings of Walden Pond with a new dimension that not only added 20 feet 6½ inches to the pond's legendary depths, but brought its purity into direct contact with its obvious technological antagonist. In a meaningful way, Thoreau knew, the pond began where the railroad left off and vice versa; by spanning the vertical rise from pond surface to railroad, from water to forged iron, he ascertained with improved exactitude the effective limits of his pristine sanctuary. Thoreau seems more interested, however, not in the ways the two opposed entities are separated, but in the ways they are connected. In *Walden*, he emphasized the linkage: "The Fitchburg Railroad touches the pond about a hundred rods south of where I dwell. I . . . am, as it were, related to society by this link."[48] This passage, assigning vital significance to the area where railroad "touches" water, was added to the *Walden* manuscript *after* the leveling experiment recorded in the "Field-Notes."[49] The resulting measurement is arguably the final piece of relevant data in the Walden Pond survey.

Thoreau's interest in this measurement was consistent with the type of environmental research he had been conducting on his visits to Cape Cod. After taking soundings of Massachusetts Bay and commenting on its relative shallowness, Thoreau compared his Cape soundings to other known sea depths, making analogies that placed Walden Pond alongside the proportionately shallow Baltic Sea, the English Channel, and "the Adriatic between Venice and Trieste."[50] Relying on knowledge acquired in the Walden survey, Thoreau was able in *Cape Cod* to formulate thought-provoking evidence for the alleged uniqueness of his Concord environs. Massachusetts Bay, he found, was "not much deeper than a country pond," even at points far from shore, but "a pond in my native town, only half a mile long, is more than one hundred feet deep."[51] These observations of proportional depth effectively tie Thoreau's ocean data from the Cape to his Walden document, associating his Concord environs with the Adriatic and the Baltic, suggesting that a single standard of measure unites them all, and meaningfully including the pond in an environmental analysis with global pretensions.

A good deal of critical speculation has centered on Thoreau's geographical symbolism: how the pond-versus-railroad dichotomy does indeed present "bench mark" measurements of specific philosophical premises in *Walden*. Forty years ago, Leo Marx's groundbreaking *The Machine in the Garden: Technology and the Pastoral Ideal in America* noted that the implacable "man-made power" of the railroad contradicts the "depth and purity" of the waters of the pond, creating a crucial ambiguity in *Walden* as a whole.[52] More recently, Lawrence Buell describes how the railroad and the pond function as opposed foci, the former representing Thoreau's fears about nature's "vulnerability to despoliation," the latter anchoring Thoreau's "pastoralizing impulse" to imagine his environment as an unspoiled place.[53] Both authors note the frequency of Thoreau's references to the railroad embankment along the western reaches of the pond, a landscape anomaly that Marx refers to as a "wound inflicted upon the land."[54]

But the embankment is also the place where, late in *Walden*, the wound is healed, the intrusive commercial-technological drives symbolized by the railroad effectively transcended. The chapter entitled "Spring" describes the forms of "thawing sand and clay" that flow down the incline of the deep cut through which the railroad passes on its way to Concord village. The key deduction in this expressively sketched scene is that the embankment, though it lacerates the land at one point and aggressively curtails the pond at another, is neither insurmountable nor unfathomable, but acquiescent to human understanding: "Not only it, but the institutions upon it are plastic like clay in the hands of the potter."[55] The "living poetry" of this hillside, Thoreau explains, "illustrated the principle of all the operations of Nature."[56] Thoreau undoubtedly made "dozens of visits"[57] to the area where railroad meets water and then cuts onward to Concord; on one of these visits he decided to take surveying data that closed the gap between the "twenty to forty feet high"[58] embankment and the pond itself. Though it has been argued that the self-regeneration achieved at the close of *Walden* is merely "a blatantly, unequivocally *figurative* restoration,"[59] the "Field-Notes" offer quiet countertestimony, adding to Thoreau's epiphany a notably *literal* element—the 20 feet 6½ inches on which the restorative insight is empirically grounded.

A third illustration of varied, shifting and not entirely commercial purposes within Thoreau's field notes involves their likely use in recording environmental statistics and land-use trends that supported Thoreau's legacy as a "pioneer of ecological science."[60] Located in the back matter of the "Field-Notes," five pages from the end of the surveying notebook, is an extensive table entitled "Wood lots When Cut." The three-page group of entries, beginning with "Watts woodlot" in 1849–50 and ending with "John Hosmer—N end of his lot on Factory road" in 1859–60, lists a total of forty-nine deforested areas, some of which Thoreau himself had surveyed for sale and cutting. The entries include descriptions of lots and specific areas of lots cut between the 1830s and 1861, among which "Richardson's Walden Pond Lot" in "1840–1" and "Sam Staples Walden Lot" with a date of "1840(?)" appear to be the earliest, except for "E. wood of Colburn," which was apparently cut in the late 1830s. The dates given for the cuttings are often approximate, such as " '54–5" and " '59–60." All the entries are in pencil rather than the ink that Thoreau normally used for field notes. The location of the table in relation to earlier material and its references to cuttings that took place up to 1860–61 indicate that "Wood lots When Cut" was one of the last uses Thoreau made of his surveying notes.

From its dates and subject matter, it seems fairly certain that the immediate purpose of this table was to provide documentation and a kind of research itinerary for Thoreau's September 1860 address "The Succession of Forest Trees." The impetus for this lecture apparently came in 1856, during a day of surveying along the Marlborough Road, when George Hubbard noted how often oaks came up in the place of pines in recently cut woodlots. Thoreau and Hubbard then confirmed the observation by checking the recently cut white-pine lot of David Loring and finding there large numbers of thriving oak seedlings. Thoreau's journal account of the event ends with the note, "*Mem.*—Let me look at the site of some thick pine woods which I remember, and see what has sprung up."[61] From this point on, Thoreau made extensive observations in his prose journals about the dispersal of seeds by animal, bird, wind or man. Probably because so much of Thoreau's field exploration came in connection with surveying, he kept in his field notes some of the raw data that resulted from his inclination to "look at the site of some thick pine woods" and determine principles of forest regrowth.

Thoreau's strong interest in tree succession predated the 1856 encounter with Hubbard and seems directly traceable to his complex feelings about the costs and consequences of local deforestation, a process that had brought the percentage of wooded land in Concord to its all-time low of just over 10 percent by the mid-1850s.[62] Witnessing to the destruction, Thoreau had lamented in *Walden* that "now for many a year there will be no more rambling through the aisles of the woods," and that the eradication of the forest would reduce his creativity and by implication all human creativity: "How can you expect the birds to sing when their groves are cut down?"[63] After Thoreau's death in 1862, Emerson spoke of his friend's sadness that "the axe was always destroying his forest" and quoted Thoreau's indignation: "Thank God, they cannot cut down the clouds!"[64]

While Thoreau clearly knew that his many surveys "lotting off" wooded areas played a tangential role in deforestation, the documents he produced for business purposes required him to compartmentalize these feelings.[65] No matter how well he did so, however, there might have been a moment of thoughtful compunction as he wrote the following identifying notes on surveys made late in his career for a frequent client:

> Plan of White Pine Woodlot
> Large Growth (very few oaks)
> Belonging to Cyrus Hosmer
> Sold to harvest (the wood)
> & Now Being Cut.
> The lot N of Road (mostly oak)
>   surveyed Jan 21 '58 & Now being cut.[66]

Drawings that Thoreau made to subdivide woodlots around Walden Pond must have required a similar restraint, for they present somewhat unattractive images of arbitrarily geometric boundary distinctions inscribed upon the area he had sanctified in his prose. The undated plan of the Moore and Hosmer "woodlots by Walden," for example, demonstrates the triumph of straight lines over natural curves, showing how Thoreau the surveyor superimposed gridlike right angles onto the Walden woods.[67]

Copying in 1857 a survey originally made by Cyrus Hubbard in 1848, Thoreau preserved the earlier surveyor's angular profanation of the pond's naturally irregular outline. At the same time, however, he reintroduced natural randomness, sketching in wavelike swirls on the pond's surface to achieve the necessary contrast.[68] When Thoreau made his own drawing of this area of the Walden shoreline, he distinguished between the surveyor's man-made lines and the pond's contours with a series of undulating dots.[69] Such were the demands made upon and accepted by the surveyor as he negotiated between numbers and terrain and formed stones and trees into things geometric and cultivated. After looking at these drawings, one wonders whether the surveys of Walden Pond, White Pond, or the detailed and sensitively rendered drawing of B. F. Perham's Concord River survey in 1859–60 might have offered a form of psychological compensation for professional practices that could not but have produced substantial inner tensions.

"The Succession of Forest Trees" is a humorous and engaging text that

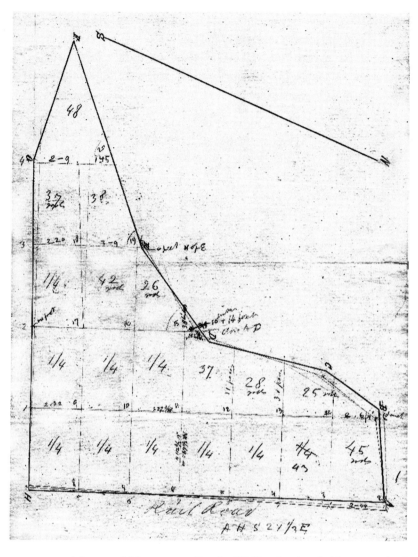

FIGURE 6.4. Moore and Hosmer woodlots by Walden (undated). The triumph of straight lines over natural curves, showing how Thoreau "lotted off" the Walden woods.

accomplishes its didactic purpose informally and without pedantry. It is significant that the speaker—who had at times clearly taken umbrage at being known as a surveyor—now openly presents himself as one, even stating that his "title" or authority to address his audience derived from his paid surveying excursions into their farms and woods. "In my capacity of surveyor," Thoreau explained, "I have often talked with some of you, my employers, at your dinner tables, after having gone round and round behind your farming, and ascertained exactly what its limits were. Moreover, taking a surveyor's and a naturalist's liberty, I have been in the habit of going across your lots much oftener than is usual." Here Thoreau refers pointedly to his commercial relationship with clients, but at the same time he avers that the meaning derived from his profession far exceeds the mundane or mercantile. He also reveals that he was in the habit of mixing his business excursions with the pleasures of both wild experience and scientific inquiry, often exploring an "out-of-the-way nook" of a farm that many of his clients "have seemed not to be aware of." The result of such extracurricular observation, Thoreau asserts, is a better understanding of the character of the landscape: "I have several times shown the proprietor the shortest way out of his wood-lot."[70]

Describing his work in a manner that repeatedly focuses on his unconventional methods and nonacquisitive purposes, Thoreau relates significant discoveries about seed dispersal and tree succession made while surveying. In doing so, he inculcates an argument that emphasizes the benefits of surveying and mitigates its potentially destructive effects. Within Thoreau's assertions that "oaks almost invariably die if the pines are not cut," and that by harvesting of pines "we find ourselves at last doing as Nature does," some critics have detected a somewhat defensive plea for recognition of the ways the speaker's own role in deforestation conforms to an underlying design.[71] Walter Harding, for example, concluded that this lecture "solved the dilemma [Thoreau] had long faced when through his surveying activities he brought about the destruction of Concord's woods."[72]

In fairness to Thoreau, we should note that the dilemma of deforestation as he saw it was certainly far too large and complex to have been solved by the simple argument at the core of "The Succession of Forest Trees." Thoreau was too honest, and too much affected by what he saw happening to trees and woodlands, to have taken permanent comfort in the finding that oaks replaced pines, even though his own surveying had helped make the discovery. When he gave this lecture, Thoreau had been surveying professionally for more than a decade. He had often claimed to do so with goals that differed significantly from those of many of his clients, and with a faith that some good might result, in the form of "cheering and compensatory discovery" within what he described as "otherwise barren work."[73] Having made such a discovery, he apparently delighted in presenting it. Whether or not we choose to find fault with Thoreau for an apparent self-justification in "The Succession of Forest Trees," we might acknowledge that what the address reveals more than anything is a noncomplacent, searching professional intelligence. Rather than illustrating a willingness to accept self-serving solutions to environmental problems, the address seems more indicative of Thoreau's pursuit of the redemptive purpose and "positive values"[74] he believed could follow from his observations. As Emerson once noted, Thoreau "could easily solve the problems of a surveyor, but he was daily beset with graver questions, which he manfully confronted."[75]

Though "The Succession of Forest Trees" is often described as Thoreau's major contribution to scientific knowledge,[76] another point of interest in the address stems less from the authority of its scientific conclusions than from its method of adumbrating Thoreau's surveying principles, including the not irrelevant circumstance of where his preliminary data were recorded. Traditionally, surveyors' field notes have two purposes, both of which are wholly practical. First, they provide raw numerical data along with draft sketches that aid the surveyor in the construction of the formal survey document. Their second purpose (and the reason such notes are kept permanently) is to retain information from which it is possible to reconstruct a survey on the ground. While the greater part of "Field-Notes" satisfies these purposes, there is clearly an alternative, nonutilitarian aesthetic governing the selection of some material.[77] This is readable as a reaction to both the fear expressed in his journals of profaning Walden with "stake and stones," and his faith that the "better part" of his nature could somehow permeate all areas of life and conduct, even an area ostensibly governed by economic necessity and entailing questionable social and environmental outcomes.

In the blank next to *Occupation* on the membership questionnaire he eventually returned to the American Association for the Advancement of Science, Thoreau wrote a response he claimed to have tailored to his audience's limited understanding: "Literary and Scientific, combined with Land-surveying."[78] Apparently Thoreau could say to the scientific community that he was a writer and scientist and surveyor without prompting "ridicule." He could even imply that the three seemingly divergent pursuits were somehow of a piece, "combined with" each other. What he could not express was how the three worked together in support of "the higher law." Explaining this aspect of his varied employments before a conventional forum was indeed a vexing challenge, especially since Thoreau himself was still occasionally uncertain about how they all cooperated. What the "Field-Notes" indicate is that an amalgamation of writing and science with the business of surveying was well under way.

That observations more in character with Thoreau the scientist and ecologist than Thoreau the businessman leach into Thoreau's civil-engineering work is perhaps not surprising. He had maintained in *Walden* that man's "confusion" concerning nature stemmed in part from his "ignorance of essential elements in the calculation," and that geometric patterns and man's individual activities could operate in a manner that rendered personality comprehensible: "Draw lines through the length and breadth of the aggregate of a man's particular daily behaviors," Thoreau wrote, "and where they intersect will be the height or depth of his character."[79] And while Thoreau's entire life displayed "a striking natural skill for mensuration,"[80] he was under no illusions about the inadequacy of mathematical facts alone as a response to the eschatological enigma: "At the same time that we are earnest to explore and learn all things, we require that all things be mysterious and unexplainable, that land and sea be infinitely wild, unsurveyed and unfathomed by us because unfathomable."[81]

In "Life Without Principle," Thoreau offered an intimation of the value of his field notes when he explained his exasperation that "an Irishman, seeing me making a minute [note or memo] in the fields, took it for granted that I was calculating my wages." While Thoreau did in fact make calculations involving work and wages in the fields around Concord, part of him resisted this procedure. In his field notes, Thoreau made a worthy attempt to keep a space of pure business. If he failed at times to do so completely, this is because he could not survey without a conscience.

The evidence of private scientific inquiry and spiritual activity within a space intended as the strictly delimited territory of mundane economics gives these swervings from practical purpose a unique significance. The range of material left by Thoreau in an emphatically nonliterary venue bespeaks the underlying consistency of his outlook, adding up to a sometimes eloquent expression of his long-term aspiration toward a form of surveying ennobled by "spiritual perception."[82]

7

The Concord Surveyor
and the Kansas Surveyor

I went in the spring of last year, with some of my
sons among the Buford men, in the character of a
surveyor, to see and hear from them their business
into the Territory.

—John Brown, "An Idea of Things in Kansas" (1857)

IN MARCH OF 1856, six months after he had arrived in the Kansas Territory to battle proslavery vigilantes and two months before he ordered the killing of five proslavery men at Pottawatomie Creek, John Brown wrote a carefully worded letter to his father, Owen. Mingling personal news with a candid assessment of the political situation, Brown reassured his father that the family was well but expressed only guarded optimism about the abolitionist cause. After a harsh winter during which his children had often gone hungry, spring was coming—"The grass begins to start a little," Brown remarked[1]—but not everything was moving forward. The struggle between Free State and slavery factions was at a standoff, its ultimate outcome impossible to predict.

The Kansas Free State faction had just held elections and submitted a petition to Congress for statehood. Legislators in Washington were bit-

terly divided over it, but President Franklin Pierce was in the pocket of
the Southern bloc, disposed to side with the proslavery legislature that
had been fraudulently elected the previous March. Appraising a tense at-
mosphere in the Territory, Brown divulged that "if Congress do not recognize the action of the Free State people here there is every reason to
expect trouble, as the Missourians will take new courage in that event."
At this stage of the conflict, Brown surely knew that the Southern faction, with its ally in the White House and its willingness to use terror
against Free Staters, might succeed in making Kansas a slave state. Yet
Brown took confidence from what he called the "general disposition . . . to
help one another" among the "Free State people" and noted hopefully that
they were "generally quite firm and determined to persevere even though
Congress do nothing for them." And with the spring thaw had come the
possibility of gainful employment: "We are now able to be about and are
earning something in different ways," he wrote.

If Brown was relieved to be earning bread, he must also have been
especially pleased at his manner of doing so: "Some four of us were out a
few days since tracing out old boundary lines for an Indian tribe." With
his sons Frederick and Oliver and his son-in-law Henry Thompson,
Brown had retraced the southern boundary of land belonging to the
neighboring Ottawas. The Indians, having found that many whites were
settling on their land, had held a tribal council and asked for surveying
help from the Browns, whom they trusted and respected.

In agreeing to survey for the Native Americans, Brown no doubt realized that ridding Kansas of illegal settlers was good for both Ottawas and
abolitionists. Earlier that spring, Major Jefferson Buford of Eufaula, Ala-
bama, had arrived in the Territory with four hundred resolute proslavery conscripts recruited from several Southern states. Buford and other
bands of militants, assuming that the "official" proslavery territorial government would take no action against them, had established their camps
on Indian lands and federally owned tracts surrounding the Free State
settlements of Topeka, Lawrence and Osawatomie. Along with them, a
large number of claim-jumping Missourians had crossed into the Territory not only in order to vote proslavery, but to suppress their neighbors'
votes and seal off the Kansas border, denying entry especially to newcom-
ers from Northern states. They were in effect occupiers, seizing opera-
tional bases on already-owned land to carry on a war of intimidation.

Under these conditions, as John Brown clearly understood, land surveying was a practical and politically useful endeavor. By tracing out old boundaries for dispossessed tribes, Brown and his surveyors were helping to reestablish claims that had been ignored by encroaching vigilantes and nonresident "border ruffian" squatters. Literally, Brown was using his authority as a surveyor to undermine enemy tactics on the main front of the territorial war. Ironically, the proslavery forces in Kansas had called themselves the Law and Order faction, but John Brown's actual imposition of law and order clearly worked against them.[2] As his letter to his father acknowledged, surveying work had substantial effects:

> The Surveying of the government lands seems under Divine Providence to derange the plans of the proSlavery men here much more than of any others. They have been exceeding greedy of the timbered lands; and great numbers of them have intruded upon the Indian reservations. Some Slave holders near us we are informed have become quite discouraged and are about to clear out.

Other members of his party confirmed Brown's assessment. Referring to the results of the survey for the Ottawas, Henry Thompson explained in a letter to his wife, "There is a good many settlers on their lands that will probably have to leave—mostly proslavery." Thompson also indicated that the running of lines for the Ottawas had boosted the morale of the Free Staters, fostering a growing sense of duty and "sacrifice" among Brown's followers.[3]

In retrospect, the elation of Brown's men is not difficult to understand, for in their humble surveying work they had begun to chip away at two of the most pernicious and unyielding racial patterns in U.S. history. Where Native Americans are concerned, the national narrative is a story of almost unbroken triumph by white men over indigenous cultures, with surveyors and measuring technology playing a significant abetting role. Brown's surveying party, however, countermanded the historical paradigm that positions the land measurer as an agent of white cultural incursion. In the hands of Brown and his men, the formerly "land stealing" surveying compass renders compensatory justice, protecting the rights of indigenous peoples and obstructing the rapacity of whites. In Kansas, Brown surveyed not to usurp Indian land but to give it back—not to extend the authority of a slave-owning government, but to curtail it.

John Brown had taught himself surveying in the 1820s, worked intermittently at the profession as necessity dictated for more than two decades, and had taken his surveying equipment to Kansas in part to carry
on the business as a means of subsistence while fighting the abolitionist
cause. Making a living as a surveyor in the Territory was a sound practical plan; wherever settlers flocked and land was available to claim and
own, surveyors were in demand. But this was not the first time Brown
had used the compass and chain for the dual purpose of meeting practical needs and defending a besieged minority. In the summer of 1849,
when abolitionist leader Gerrit Smith purchased land in upstate New
York to provide free blacks with a place to settle and farm, Brown protected the settlers from racially motivated encroachments by surveying
their farms, thereby personally establishing their boundaries and legal
titles.[4] Perhaps recalling this action, Brown called his journey to Kansas
"a surveying tour" and claimed in letters written before setting out for the
Territory that he was going there to direct the operation of a surveying
and exploring party.[5] As he seems to have known, representing himself in
a professional capacity that was normally associated with state authority
would help his chances of getting into Kansas. Once there, the compass
and chain could be made to serve his sacred purpose in essential ways.

Henry Thoreau met John Brown in March of 1857, while the already-
notorious abolitionist, recently returned from Kansas, was in Concord
on a fund-raising tour of New England. Ostensibly, Brown was seeking
money and support to return to the fight in the West, but he was actually
already privately fixated on his plan to strike directly at the South with
a band of armed slave liberators. While visiting Concord, Brown stayed
with Franklin Sanborn at the home owned by Ellery Channing just down
the street from the Thoreau house. Aware that Thoreau wished to meet
the antislavery militant, Sanborn brought Brown with him to his regular
noon meal at Mrs. Thoreau's boarding table. Sanborn recalls that Brown
narrated in detail to Thoreau events from his recent struggles in Kansas, including the battle at Black Jack in which his nine-man force had
captured twenty-six proslavery men. Two hours later, when Sanborn had
to return to his school in Concord, he "left Brown and Thoreau discussing Kansas affairs in Mrs. Thoreau's dining room."[6] Following Brown's
speech the next evening, Thoreau and Brown talked again, apparently for

an even longer period, at an informal gathering hosted by Sanborn at the Channing house. From these extended conversations Thoreau gained what Sanborn, the only witness to parts of both discussions, calls an "intimate knowledge of Brown's character and general purpose."[7]

As the two men got to know each other at their initial meetings, they would surely have discovered that they had much in common—that in addition to their mutual hatred of slavery, they shared a political outlook based on action from principle and the individual right to, as Thoreau once put it, "rebel and revolutionize." In "Resistance to Civil Government," Thoreau spoke of the need "to refuse allegiance to the State." With the War on Mexico and slavery's brutal effects in mind, Thoreau had withheld his poll tax and called on his fellow citizens to break unjust laws. At an early stage of his political thinking, Thoreau enacted peaceful resistance but nodded rhetorically toward the type of direct action Brown later took in Kansas. "Even suppose blood should flow," Thoreau wrote in 1848, "is there not a sort of blood shed when the conscience is wounded? Through this wound a man's real manhood and immortality flow out, and he bleeds to an everlasting death. I see this blood flowing now."[8] By 1854, after a severe Fugitive Slave Law had been passed—its shocking effects made visually apparent in the remanding of fugitives Thomas Simms and Anthony Burns—and the Kansas-Nebraska Act had made possible the extension of slavery into the territories, Thoreau's rhetoric would intensify. "If we would save our lives, we must fight for them," he would announce in his most impassioned antigovernment oration, "Slavery in Massachusetts."[9] In his most important political lectures and essays, Thoreau acknowledged the right of violent resistance; in meeting John Brown, he spoke with the living embodiment of that precept.

While recounting his antislavery exploits in Kansas that afternoon in 1857, John Brown probably could not have avoided making reference to land surveying, especially because "most if not all, of [Brown's] Kansas surveying was to further the abolitionist cause."[10] Thoreau may or may not have been surprised to learn that Brown was a fellow surveyor, but he would surely have reacted to this news by disclosing that he was himself active in the profession. Brown might then have taken the cue to expound on his Kansas surveys, perhaps to the point of acknowledging the many ways his accomplishments there had actually hinged on his surveying background.

Aside from the fact that he had supported himself in Kansas with surveying work,[11] Brown may have explained exactly how the profession had helped him to make it to Kansas in the first place. On his way west in a covered wagon purchased in Chicago, Brown's weapons of war—boxes of rifles, revolvers, knives and broadswords—were concealed beneath his surveying instruments.[12] Brown would also have explained to Thoreau how the surveying instruments were put to tactical use in Kansas. On several occasions leading up to his raid at Pottawatomie, Brown had conducted intelligence-gathering expeditions into the camps of the proslavery men in the guise of a land surveyor.[13] Franklin Sanborn's biography of Brown describes one such foray:

> It was a matter of importance to the Free-State men to know what was the purpose of these bodies of armed men, so that they might shape their action accordingly. Brown, without consulting any one, determined to visit their camp and ascertain their plans. He therefore took his tripod, chain, and other surveying implements, and with one of his younger sons started for the camp. Just before reaching the place he struck his tripod, sighted a line through the center of the camp, and then with his sons began "chaining" the distance. The Southern men supposed him to be a Government surveyor (in those times, of course, proslavery), and were very free in telling him their plans.[14]

If Brown were disposed to speak openly with Thoreau, as it seems he was, he may have confided to his fellow surveyor how the profession had been significant in the lead-up to the notorious killing raid at Pottawatomie Creek. Brown may well have told the story in terms similar to those given by E. A. Coleman, a friend and supporter of Brown's in Kansas, who produced the most detailed version of the covert surveying action. Coleman had asked Brown to explain the execution of the five ruffians at Pottawatomie. Brown answered, "I will tell you all about it, and you can judge whether I did right or wrong" before giving the following account:

> I had heard that these men were coming to the cabin that my son and I were staying in . . . to set fire to it and shoot us as we ran out. Now, that was not proof enough for me; but I thought I would satisfy myself, and if they had committed murder in their hearts, I would be justified in killing them. I was an old surveyor, so I disguised myself, took two men

to carry the chain, and a flagman. The lines not being run, I knew that as soon as they saw me they would come out to find where their lines would come.

According to Coleman, Brown then struck up a political conversation with remarks like, "You have a fine country here; great pity there are so many Abolitionists in it." When the pseudosurveyor remarked, "I hear there are some bad men about here by the name of Brown," one of Major Buford's men replied, "Yes, there are; but next Wednesday night we will kill them." Looking through the sight vanes of his compass, motioning to his flagman and pretending to be taking field notes, Brown was actually writing down "every word" said by each of the ruffians. Having confirmed their violent intent and recorded evidence of it in his field notebook, Brown reasoned that since they planned murder, he was "justified in killing them." The Pottawatomie executions occurred three days later, on May 23, 1856.[15]

Though Coleman or Brown himself may have embellished some elements of the tale, the sharing of some form of this story with Thoreau would not have been out of character for Brown, who disclosed a good deal about his deeds in Kansas—including substantial information about his surveying—during his 1857 tour of New England. In Concord, before an audience that included both Emerson and Thoreau, Brown gave a powerful performance, using as visual props the bowie knife he had taken from a Missouri ruffian and the trace chain used to take his son prisoner near Lecompton.[16] Brown also told his Concord audience of his stratagem for infiltrating the ranks of the vigilantes: "I went in the spring of last year, with some of my sons among the Buford men, in the character of a surveyor, to see and hear from them their business into the Territory."[17] In an appearance before a state legislative committee just prior to meeting Thoreau, Brown was asked if he had had any contact with Buford's men in Kansas. He replied that "he saw a great deal of them at first; that they spoke without hesitation before him, because he employed himself as a surveyor." As Brown explained, "Nearly all surveyors were proslavery men," and Buford's men had thus presumed him to be "sound on the goose"—meaning that his views accorded with the proslavery faction.[18]

After their long talks in Concord in 1857, Thoreau and Brown would meet once more. During Brown's second trip to Concord, in May of 1859, shortly before the militant abolitionist left for Harper's Ferry, Thoreau took a break from a busy week of surveying to visit with Brown. He also attended his lecture on the evening of Sunday, May 8, at the town hall, where Brown regaled listeners with "Kansas affairs and the part taken by him in the late troubles there."[19]

These interactions assured that Thoreau knew quite a lot about Brown's surveying exploits by late October 1859, when he delivered the address "A Plea for Captain John Brown." This lecture, which reached a larger audience than any other work published in Thoreau's lifetime,[20] uses carefully selected elements of Brown's biography to cultivate a supremely heroic ethos for the antislavery militant. In vigorously defending the abolitionist before a largely unsympathetic audience, Thoreau alludes in substantial ways to Brown's surveying experience. It matters to Thoreau, for example, that "for a part of his life [Brown] was a surveyor," and this information is given early, at the opening of the fifth paragraph of the address. To counteract the many post–Harper's Ferry media accounts that had selectively focused on Brown's failures in business and crimes in Kansas,[21] Thoreau points out Brown's surveying skills, along with his earlier wool growing, as evidence that Brown possessed business acumen and discernment—that "he had his eyes about him, and made many original observations."[22] Later, Thoreau establishes Brown's "tact and prudence"—and refutes popular conceptualizations of him as a reckless fanatic—by synthesizing elements of a surveying legend he had probably first heard directly from Brown:

> At a time when scarcely a man from the Free States was able to reach Kansas by any direct route, at least without having his arms taken from him, he, carrying what imperfect guns and other weapons he could collect, openly and slowly drove an ox-cart through Missouri, apparently in the capacity of a surveyor, with his surveying compass exposed in it, and so passed unsuspected, and had ample opportunity to learn the designs of the enemy.[23]

Here Thoreau indicates familiarity with public accounts of Brown's surveying but adds interesting details to the legend, some of which do not square with the historical record. For example, Brown, his son Oliver and Henry Thompson did not travel across northwestern Missouri in an oxcart, as Thoreau writes, but with a horse and covered wagon purchased in Chicago.

More important than this minor solecism is the romantic idea—possibly originating with Thoreau—that Brown actually put his surveyor's compass on display in his wagon as he traveled through Missouri. Making use of the compass in this way—as a signal of sociopolitically legitimate intentions and a tool for defusing the threat Brown actually posed to proslavery forces—is a fascinating maneuver. The tactic—or Thoreau's invention of it—suggests that the status of the surveying profession could be relied upon in specific ways in the 1850s—that tacit associations between the surveyor and conventional institutions were stable and strong. Brown associate James Hanway, a witness to the Kansas war, claimed in an 1860 letter to Brown biographer R. J. Hinton that "the ruffians took it for granted that all surveyors were pro-slavery, and opposed to the 'abolitionists,' believing that the Administration would only employ those faithful to the slavery cause."[24] Surveyors worked for the administration, the thinking went, so their allegiance to the slave power was implicit. In this context, Brown's letting the compass speak for him was more than a clever ruse to outwit the proslavery mind-set; it required a sophisticated understanding of American social and legal thinking at midcentury.

Thoreau was not alone in responding to mythic aspects of the Brown crusade in Kansas. The aptness of Brown's surveying compass as a material icon also captured the imagination of Samuel J. Reader, a member of a Free State task force in Kansas who had met Brown and his men near the Kansas-Nebraska border in 1856. Reader's initial journal description of his meeting with the Brown party does not mention surveying instruments. But his later representation of the scene on canvas embraces a version of events that appears to be derived in part from Thoreau. In the artist's 1906 depiction of himself leading Brown to a Free State camp on Pony Creek, the compass is a major component of the visual narrative, not only put on display by pulling back the cover of the ox-drawn wagon, but positioned on its tripod as if pointing the way. What looks like a surveyor's chain is draped across the front buckboard.

At the center of Reader's and Thoreau's intentions is a message about the symbolic efficacy of Brown's surveying instruments, a message all the more apparent because it is very unlikely that the scene would have taken

FIGURE 7.1. *Directing John Brown to the Free State Camp.* John Brown being led to a camp near Pony Creek in August 1856. Brown's surveying compass and tripod are visible in the oxcart. Painting by Samuel J. Reader, 1906. Courtesy Kansas Museum of History.

place exactly as either Thoreau or Reader rendered it. An experienced surveyor like Brown would never have allowed his delicate compass to be jostled on its tripod in a moving oxcart, and no one knew this better than Thoreau. If Brown's compass were exposed as he traveled, it would still have been kept safely in its wooden compass box. Perhaps in reality the compass box was kept close at hand, with its folded tripod and a Gunter's chain alongside it, so that its contents could be exhibited to approaching parties.

What Thoreau and Reader therefore accomplish by describing the compass as exposed in the cart is a simple, premeditated symbolization—a romanticized acknowledgment of the role the compass played in Brown's activism. Both men emphasize the image of Brown the surveyor in thought-provoking ways, and both centralize the compass as its materialization. In their clearly related interpretations, they confirm that in the case of John Brown, a surveying instrument could and did function—literally or figuratively—as a protective shield, a weapon of war, an emblem in a struggle for social justice.

Knowledge of Brown's actual boundary work in Kansas—performed as a means of gaining a livelihood and as a means of helping the Ottawas—is also hinted at in Thoreau's address. "For some time after his arrival he still followed the same profession," Thoreau remarks. We might ask why a defense of Brown's character—an attempt to establish Brown's credibility among an audience with prejudices against him—would make repeated reference to surveying practices. The logical explanation is that Thoreau was consciously drawing on the ethos of the land surveyor—as it related to both Brown's identity and his own as Brown's advocate—to further his hagiographic purpose. Thoreau's ringing defense of John Brown becomes in part an endorsement of the professional designation he shared with Brown.

The question then concerns the specific qualities that such a rhetorical strategy might confer on its subject. A number of historians have discussed the cultural value of the surveyor's work in the mid-nineteenth-century United States, noting the esteem in which surveyors were commonly held. As Andro Linklater observes, surveyors were trusted, well-compensated technicians, deemed reliable where questions of ownership were concerned. Because Americans have worshipped the right to property as no other nation in history, there were strong associations between the surveying profession and community leadership.[25] In a sense, the surveyor was viewed as a champion of the Constitution, bringing its property-related guarantees, and thus the arm of government itself, to unsettled areas. Into the territories and frontier, "the surveyor carried civilization with him,"[26] putting land into people's hands and enabling economic exploitation of its resources. Linklater observes that "surveyors held the nation together during the first half of the nineteenth century." As a professional class, they were accorded "prestige equivalent to their importance in an economy based on the acquisition of land."[27]

Considering the popular understanding of the profession, it is not surprising that Thoreau drew on his subject's surveying credentials to help confirm his integrity. Mentioning Brown's surveying is in keeping with the characterization of a man of practicality, principle, and the repeatedly emphasized trait of "common sense." As a persuasive tactic, it is in the same category as Thoreau's affirmation that Brown was "an old-fashioned man in his respect for the Constitution" whose grandfather was an officer in the Revolution. Tracing Brown's lineage to the Revolution and then speaking of him as a surveyor might even have prompted analogies among some in Thoreau's audience between the Kansas surveyor and the quintessential statesman-surveyor George Washington, who is mentioned in the address as one of Brown's moral precursors. Since many in Thoreau's Concord audience would have known that the speaker was himself a surveyor, the authority cultivated for Brown would have been transferred to Thoreau.

But capitalizing on the positive ideological connotations of the surveying profession as an ethos-building technique in a defense of a radical abolitionist is not without significant contradictions and paradoxes. First, in the history of American property interests seeking protection, surveyors have been foot soldiers of the status quo and transmitters of Anglo-American imperialism. Second, the ironclad guarantee that the U.S. Constitution gave to property—a guarantee that surveyors embodied—was the very thing that denied slaves any rights. As events in Kansas illustrated, defense of property in land could be understood as a defense of property in men—because the Supreme Law of the Land did not distinguish between the two. The Dred Scott decision of 1857 had clearly asserted that, once defined as property, blacks had no rights the white man was bound to respect. The Scott case also held that "wherever slaveowners went, the United States was required to protect their property."[28] Under the legal syntax that blanketed both land and blacks, the slave's humanity was an anomaly. This dynamic goes far toward explaining why a government surveyor was assumed to be a supporter of the slavocracy until he made the radical, unexpected move of declaring himself an abolitionist. If the crux of the conflict that led to war was that the rights of black Americans were being overridden by unlimited rights to property,[29] engaging in an occupation that supported both of these rights was a complicated act.

As Brown had shown, however, it was also an act with great subversive potential. Demonstrating *how* to charismatically espouse one and not the other could have political impact, as it undoubtedly did for Thoreau, who felt it necessary in making his appeal for the abolitionist to retell the remarkable story that gave Brown the nickname the Spy of Osawatomie:[30]

When for instance, he saw a knot of ruffians on the prairie, discussing, of course, the single topic which then occupied their minds, he would, perhaps, take his compass and one of his sons, and proceed to run an imaginary line right through the very spot on which that conclave was assembled, and when he came up to them, he would naturally pause and have some talk with them, learning their news, and, at last, all their plans perfectly; and having thus completed his real survey, he would resume his imaginary one, and run on his line till he was out of sight.[31]

As Thoreau makes clear, discovering the intentions of the ruffians had been Brown's real survey; the running of a line his imaginary one. The practical and politically conventional purposes of surveying are creatively obliterated in favor of surreptitious, politically dissident functions.

Thoughts recorded in Thoreau's journal in the immediate aftermath of Harper's Ferry imply that these surveying tactics were a factor in Thoreau's ardent devotion to Brown. In an entry of October 22, 1859, eight days before he first delivered "A Plea for Captain John Brown," Thoreau emphasized surveying in order to refute what he considered the single most irksome theme in newspaper accounts of Harper's Ferry: Brown's alleged insanity. After his arrest, many organs of the Southern and Northern press had portrayed Brown as an unstable, delusional fanatic. Even the *Liberator* had called Harper's Ferry "a misguided, wild, and apparently insane" effort. For Thoreau, however, the best and most irrefutable evidence of Brown's keen intellect, mental fitness and *sanity* was the way he used the compass and chain to keep Kansas free. In his journal, Thoreau is fascinated by Brown's "passing for a simple surveyor, who by his very profession, must be neutral" as a means of becoming "thoroughly acquainted with the plans of the Border Ruffians." After recounting the details of this intelligence-gathering ploy, Thoreau reaches a conclusion with profound implications for Brown's entire historical legacy: "This is enough to show that his plans were not crazily laid."[32]

Though this journal excerpt was transposed almost verbatim into the text of "A Plea for Captain John Brown," it is also interesting for the slightly altered language it uses to describe Brown's impersonations. "Passing for a simple surveyor, who by his very profession, must be neutral" is very different from deliberately masquerading as an employee of the Pierce administration, as Brown had actually done. When Brown surveyed in Kansas, he was not assumed to be neutral—he was assumed to be proslavery. Brown's guise was deeply politically involved, but Thoreau records a less-political connotation in the surveyor's work, one closer to the ideal he had at times personally pursued—a seeker of pure facts who modeled the "most correct" and thus nonpartisan methods of measurement. Just as telling is Thoreau's use of the phrase "simple surveyor." Simplicity and surveying had been key words at Walden, where Thoreau had embodied uncomplicated life while mapping a pond. Though neither of these phrases appears in the final text of the address, they may nevertheless be read as indications of how the Concord surveyor viewed himself in relation to Kansas surveyor, their basic suggestion being that Thoreau did consider the meaning of the employment they held in common. Both he and Brown, after all, had at one time or another recorded facts in their field notebooks that had nothing to do with surveying and everything to do with their convictions. In thinking about Brown's shaping of the profession into positive outcomes, Thoreau contemplated comparisons with his own creative uses of fieldwork. Absent from Thoreau's journal and his final lecture text, however, is any sense of what had actually enabled Brown's access to the ruffian camp: his presumed sympathy with the proslavery cause. Since it is not likely that Thoreau lacked awareness of the connotations of surveying in Kansas, this omission seems important. One explanation for Thoreau's reticence may be the circumstances under which the address was delivered. In making his case for Brown, the rhetorical challenge or problem Thoreau confronted, as Robert Albrecht once argued, was "to defend a notorious man before an unfriendly audience."[33] In this climate, it was perhaps not useful to broach the actuality that the faction Brown did battle with in Kansas had believed him to be a government employee. Describing his subject as a simple surveyor rather than a Pierce administration impersonator may have allowed for a more sympathetic characterization of the abolitionist.

It is also possible that Thoreau was privately ill at ease with the notion that a land surveyor simply going about his business was welcomed among Buford's men—that surveyors, as hirelings of the state, were assumed to be "sound on the goose" where slavery was concerned. Coming from the man soon to be referred to by Bronson Alcott as the "resident Surveyor-general" of his locality, an acknowledgment of affinities between his chosen livelihood and an outlook amenable to proslavery vigilantes might have had dubious implications. Obviously, Southerners in Kansas perceived analogies between surveying for the government and supporting slavery, and there is no better evidence of the profession's widely understood institutional loyalties. Perhaps for these reasons, the invocation of surveying within "A Plea for Captain John Brown" somewhat elides its Kansas-specific meaning as a proslavery practice.

While Thoreau in his address does not overtly identify the surveyor's work as necessarily "neutral," as he did in his journal, his audience would certainly have come away with this impression, and not only because surveyors were generally trusted. In Concord, where the address was first delivered, it certainly mattered that the speaker himself was a respected professional, that his skill and integrity were known commodities—that the word "surveyor," coming from Thoreau, could be counted on to call up favorable associations. The address thus makes use of not only the general cultural repute of surveyors but an experienced meaning the profession had acquired for a Concord audience, many of whom knew Thoreau to be a fair arbiter. The standing Thoreau had acquired through meticulous fieldwork was paying political dividends for him in his role as social activist.

Viewed in terms of its function as oratory, the essay's somewhat simplified version of Brown's surveying escapades has clear merits. As Thoreau renders the situation, it is not Brown's assumed political designation but his legitimate professional designation that allows him to pass unmolested through Missouri and to freely converse with Buford's ruffians. The effect is to elevate the ethics of the profession in a general moral sense, strip it of the proslavery associations that were actually crucial to Brown's uses of it, and heighten personal resemblances between Thoreau and the subject of his plea.

Reading Thoreau's address today, one might wonder what it was about land surveyors—if not their reputation for fairness—that allowed them to pass freely through dangerous, contested areas. Better than we do now, Thoreau's audience would have known that surveyors enjoyed a securely established legal right of necessary access to properties adjoining their work. Twenty years before the Fugitive Slave Law of 1850 guaranteed universal protections and instituted severe penalties for interfering with the property of slave owners, the nation's legislators instituted severe penalties for obstructing the work of land surveyors. The U.S. Land Law of 1830 guaranteed the "sufficient force" of local and federal agencies to protect the surveyor in the execution of his duty.[34] Brown in Kansas—and to a certain extent Thoreau in his persona as Brown's advo-cate—aptly exploited the protections afforded by one form of property law as a means of attacking another.

For Brown and Thoreau, however, the real privileges of the profession were less a matter of legal precedent than of moral necessity. This is why both men also put faith in the compass, seeing in its northern-pointing directional arrow an indicator of incontestable universals—the ethical truths that were forgotten in the country's acceptance of slavery. Perhaps somewhere among the underlying explanations Thoreau accepted for Brown's near-miraculous reliance on surveying instruments was his long-held notion of the compass needle as a metaphysical guide. If this is so, it indicates another philosophical tenet that Thoreau and Brown shared. During a February 1857 interview with abolitionist Wendell Phillips, Brown was eager to determine the character of various Free State leaders and asked "many questions" about the soundness of the men's personal commitments to end slavery. As Phillips later recalled, Brown

> was very apprehensive that many of the free-state leaders would jeopar-dize the principles of the party in order to get power. . . . One very good man he criticized for several things he had done, and in response to my assurances about him he used one of his striking comparisons. He took out a large pocket compass, and unscrewing its brass lid laid it down on the table before me, while he said—"You see that needle; it wobbles about and is mighty unsteady, but it wants to point to the north. Is he like that needle?"[35]

For a nation corrupted by a great evil, a direction had been indicated. Of course, Brown and Thoreau had personally determined that direction and heeded its mandates for their own physical guidance in the woods and fields. To the extent that both men also recognized the correspond-ing moral guidance suggested by the compass needle, the bond they shared as surveyors cannot be dismissed as insignificant or merely coin-cidental. When Thoreau called Brown "a Transcendentalist above all" in his public defense of the abolitionist, he bestowed a high tribute that was based on his friend's ability to intuitively derive ethics from physics and plot a life course accordingly.

Certainly, Thoreau had always known that it was possible to conduct both "real" and "imaginary" surveys, to ostensibly cooperate with the state but actually pursue ends antithetical to it. A surveyor, Thoreau hoped, need not acquiesce to the institutions he served. Even "government surveyor"—a title Brown simulated and Thoreau actually held—could be a guise, a cover for a purer form of righteousness, just as the survey of Walden was a cover and metaphor for vital contact with the natural world, and just as nearly all of Thoreau's surveys could in some way become "imaginary" pretexts for one or another surrogate objective. If Thoreau had any lingering doubt at this stage of his career that the complicated self-positioning of a poet-naturalist-abolitionist-surveyor was negotiable and tenable, Brown likely helped to relieve those doubts. Brown's use of surveying as more than a livelihood—his exploitation of the profession as a pretext for radical activism—was an inspired, imaginative and wholly ingenious strategy. Effectively, it converted a negative political meaning associated with the profession into a positive one, infusing the work with transcendentalist values. Though Brown had outwardly conformed to professional-political mores, he was in principle responding to the dictates of character and conscience. Thoreau's expressed view was that these illustrations of surveying potentialities were "enough to show" the soundness of his intellect.

Thoreau would also have recognized in the heroic abolitionist and Kansas surveyor the outline of professional dilemmas he had himself confronted. Like Concord's surveyor, Brown seems to have understood the ethical tensions of getting paid to turn fields and forests into pelf and power. While working as a surveyor, Brown had on at least one well-publicized occasion condemned "the sale of land as a chattel" and called attention to private property in land as one of the country's "infinite number of wrongs."[36] If Thoreau had loathed himself for establishing civic boundaries, as it seems he did after his first paid perambulation for the Concord selectmen in 1851, he could look to Brown as a reminder that there still existed ways to "go north," to turn his skills to purer purposes. If he worried about taming the Walden woods with stake and stones, or furnishing deeds and creating property lines, or helping landowners squeeze profit from their dwindling forests, he could weigh Brown's example as he sought conciliating solutions.

Equally compelling to Thoreau may have been Brown's work on behalf of Native Americans. In the same journal entry that discussed Brown's surveying, Thoreau recalled conversations with the abolitionist about the Ottawas, whose land Brown had protected. Brown had remarked to Thoreau that "the Indians with whom he dealt in Kansas were perhaps the richest people in a pecuniary sense on the earth" and that "they were, moreover, more intelligent than the mass of the Border Ruffians." In Kansas, Thoreau noted evocatively, Brown had been "befriended only by Indians and few white men," a fact that probably further elevated the abolitionist in his eyes.[37]

Thoreau had long been intrigued by Native American history and customs, but it seems possible that Brown's advocacy of Indian rights and camaraderie with the Ottawas pushed him toward further direct contact with indigenous culture. During the summer after meeting Brown, in July of 1857, he embarked on his third trip to the Maine woods—the excursion described in his lecture "The Allegash and East Branch"—for the purpose of actively seeking cultural knowledge and exchange. From his Penobscot Indian guide, Joe Polis, Thoreau learned important lessons about the aboriginal worldview and discerned a kind of genius in Polis's response to the wilderness. Thoreau asked to learn the Penobscot language but also paid close attention to the way nature spoke to the Indian, eventually coaxing Polis to share literally all he knew with him.

It is also significant that Thoreau seeks fresh perspectives on the art of measuring from Polis, who, if Thoreau's character sketch is accurate, deserves to be called a surveyor in his own right. Polis finds his way in the woods by instinct, but Thoreau learns that he has also been part of a white surveying party and given advice "respecting the eastern boundary of Maine." He had even been "employed with the surveyors on the line."[38] Like a white surveyor, Polis marked his woodland dwelling places with axe blazes and inscriptions on trees. While exploring the wilderness through a surveyor's eyes, Thoreau strives to empathize with Native culture in a way that replicates a known aspect of Brown's surveying in Kansas. "I wished to learn all I could before I got out of the woods," he avers, and measuring methods are a predominant issue.[39] Through Polis, Thoreau seems to be looking for—and finding—the spiritually infused "different ways of surveying" that are referred to in "Life Without Principle." Accordingly, the trip produces an overt commentary on the cultural limitations that predispose white Americans to land acquisition and environmental destruction while limiting our awareness of the consequences of such devastation:

The Anglo-American can indeed cut down, and grub all this waving forest, and make a stump speech, and vote for Buchanan on its ruins, but he cannot converse with the spirit of the tree he fells, he cannot read the poetry and mythology which retire as he advances.[40]

Observing especially Polis's reactions to mapping, measuring, direction finding and land-ownership customs, Thoreau broadened his perceptions of the "white men's institutions" and formed a cross-cultural friendship that had profound influence on the final stage of his life.[41] He also, it seems, took another step forward in his long-term pursuit of a form of landscape measurement that, like Brown's, did not simply encourage the reproduction of the dominant culture's epistemology.

After Thoreau's death in 1862, Emerson asserted that John Brown and the "Indian guide, Joe Polis" were two of the three men who had become his primary role models, the other being Walt Whitman. Brown was Thoreau's political hero, Polis a cultural ideal, Whitman an artistic paradigm. Emerson may not have realized that land surveying was a compelling connection between the political and cultural figures in this pantheon. Through Brown's surveying work for the Ottawas, abolition of slavery and respect for Native cultures had been brought together in a mutually productive relation. While Thoreau's great admiration for Brown was surely a multifaceted and complex sentiment, one of its root motives may be simply stated: no man in American history before Brown had employed the compass and chain with such humanitarian creativity, fighting simultaneously for both African Americans and Native Americans.

When he delivered "A Plea for Captain John Brown" on October 30, 1859, Thoreau almost certainly did not know that during preparations for the raid on Harper's Ferry, the symbol of land surveying had been resurrected. At the "constitutional convention" held by Brown and his allies at the Canadian settlement of Chatham in 1858, the men in Brown's company referred to themselves as a "surveying party."[42] They did so, undoubtedly, because they wished to commemorate their daring subversion of the state under the guise of state authority. Conceiving of a new American nation that would fulfill its original promise, Brown's delegates adopted a provisional constitution that abolished property in human beings and gave voting rights to "all persons of mature age, whether Proscribed, oppressed, or enslaved." Speaking among themselves as they trained for their direct attack on the South, they called the radical insurgency that would institute the new American order "the surveying expedition." In doing so, they expressed the bond that joined them in terms the Concord surveyor had comprehended and presaged. As Thoreau undoubtedly realized and historian Evan Carton's research has more recently noted, "Brown's surveyors signified freedom."[43]

We might then ask how Brown's example manifested itself from the time Thoreau met him to the end of his paid surveying fieldwork in 1861. Whether Brown had a form of tangible impact on Thoreau's business is hard to determine. There are, however, some interesting observations to be made relating to Thoreau's professional output from 1857 onward. During the nine months following Brown's visit to Concord, Thoreau made twenty-four surveys, many of which took several full days of work, and he made a total of thirty surveys in the calendar year after he met Brown. In terms of jobs completed, this was by far the most active stretch of his surveying career. In 1859, Thoreau would dedicate himself to surveying in an unprecedented way, undertaking hundreds of hours of fieldwork in his largest single engineering project, the survey of the Concord River, and composing the most extensive surveying-based journal entries he had ever written.

Overall, the final stages of Thoreau's active life evince not less but more commitment to land surveying, along with a qualitative difference in his feelings about his work. As we might then expect, fieldwork and the lessons taken from it are a strong thematic thread in several of Thoreau's important late essays. "Walking" and "Life Without Principle" display the author's heightened attention to the ordering of his literary legacy, but they are far from silent about his legacy as a measurer of land. Thoreau died before he could undertake the book-length biography of Brown he had apparently intended, a work that some thought him the most suited of all Brown's admirers to write.[44] If Thoreau had written this book, he would have extolled Brown's heroic example, explained the philosophical bonds they shared, and almost certainly enhanced his treatment of the abolitionist's famous deeds and famous words with a carefully written chapter about land surveying.

8

"I am a surveyor"

I have a commonplace-book for facts and another
for poetry—but I find it difficult always to preserve
the vague distinction which I had in my mind . . . I
see that if my facts were sufficiently vital and significant—perhaps transmuted more into the substance
of the human mind,—I should need but one book
of poetry to contain them all.

—Thoreau, *Journal*, February 18, 1852

My practicalness is not to be trusted to the last.

—Thoreau, *Journal*, June 6, 1851

From the late 1850s to his final paid surveying job in January of 1861, the
documentation of measuring projects in Thoreau's "Field-Notes" gets noticeably smaller and the handwriting less legible. Earlier in his career, a
typical field-notes entry might include a page to several pages of well-or-
ganized compass bearings, distances and calculations, but later there are
seven to eight short entries per notebook page, with no supporting data.
The attenuation of surveying descriptions in the "Field-Notes" does not

mean that Thoreau was professionally inactive—his eleven jobs in 1859 and thirteen in 1860 are about average for his career—but it does indicate that he was making notes and calculations on other sheets and kept the notebook simply as a nominal record of work performed. Thus near the end of the "Field-Notes" appears the laconic one-line datum "Aug 20 1860 surveyed N. Hawthorne's land."

As the formal documentation of surveys in his field notes shrinks, the recording of surveying data in Thoreau's journal increases exponentially. The sudden proliferation of facts and statistics in a space that had been reserved primarily for personal and philosophical prose occurs in connection with Thoreau's long-term study of the Concord River, a project that engaged him on an almost daily basis for extended periods in 1859 and 1860. Referring to this project, Emerson exaggerated only slightly when he wrote in August of 1859 that "Henry T. occupies himself with the history of the river, measures it, weighs it, and strains it through a colander to all eternity."[1] That summer, Thoreau took literally thousands of rivers soundings, sometimes returning to the same spot hourly to check on barely measurable fluctuations of the water level. He determined the height and width of bridges, physically measured and charted distances between bridges, sketched and theorized the causes of riverbed irregularities, analyzed the river's current, checked moisture levels in its floodplains, described water temperatures and turbidity, and noted the location and condition of dozens of plant species in the river valley ecosystem. From June through August of 1859 and 1860, the "river survey" was often an all-consuming, more-than-full-time labor.

Emerson's bemused, somewhat condescending tone toward Thoreau's work on the river exemplifies a misconception that has skewed the priorities of some Thoreau scholars over the years. The implication that Thoreau was wasting time in arcane nonliterary pursuits—for example merely "occupying himself" by carefully surveying the river—persisted into the twentieth century. When Bradford Torrey and F. H. Allen published Thoreau's edited *Journal* in 1906, they excised large amounts of river-survey material, explaining that such environmental facts were mere details that were without scientific value and "could be of no interest to the general reader."[2]

Even with Torrey's excisions, the *Journal* entries covering the period of the river survey are saturated with observations about the physical state of the river. It seems that a good deal of environmental data evades the editorial censor only because the surveyor had begun to transform his data into sentences, to render numerical "facts" into formal prose: "From upper end of Sudbury Canal to Sherman's Bridge is 558 rods (1 mile 238 rods); by thread of river, 1000 (3 miles 40 rods), or nearly twice as far," Thoreau wrote in July of 1859. In August he noted, "The river began to fall perhaps yesterday, after rising perhaps fourteen or fifteen inches. It is now about one foot higher than before the rain of the 25th."[3] The rationale for these observations and many others was both work related and philosophical; in essence, Thoreau's surveying field notes and his prose journal had finally become one document.

Torrey's decision to expurgate the *Journal* is all the more ill advised because the data produced by Thoreau's close monitoring of the river's characteristics and biodiversity were politically important. These were the points of contention in the ongoing legal dispute between farmers and industrialists in the Concord River ecosystem. What became known as the Concord River flowage controversy began in the late eighteenth century with the construction of the Middlesex Canal Dam in Billerica. In a series of lawsuits against the dam owners that began in 1811, the farmers owning meadows along the Concord River claimed repeatedly that because the dam slowed drainage, the river flooded more frequently and retained moisture longer following summer rains. They argued that their meadows had grown softer and wetter, making access to them more difficult and spoiling the valuable crops of meadow hay or "pipes" that were used as winter fodder for their livestock. When the river level fell and the meadow hay began to dry out every July and August, the mill owners opened their supply reservoirs, flooding the meadows and spoiling farmers' hay before it could be harvested. The farmers lost several court cases in the 1810s and '20s. By Thoreau's day the problem had been worsened by dozens of textile and powder mills that had proliferated on the river and its tributaries. This "explosion of water-powered industry" put the flow rate of the Concord River under the control of emerging industrial interests, much to the detriment of the farmers who had worked the area for generations.[4]

At the peak of the legal controversy in 1859, Thoreau was hired by the River Meadow Association to help survey the river in preparing their case against the dam. He was asked to monitor depths and flow rates at numerous points, including all of the river's bridges from East Sudbury to Billerica, a distance of over twenty-two miles. Thoreau's observations, measurements and soundings were supplemented by research into the river's history and the history of settlement along the Concord watershed. To obtain information he could not gather on his own, he interviewed or corresponded with many longtime residents of farms adjoining the river and its tributaries, asking them to remember when bridges were constructed or altered and how the geography of adjoining meadows had been changed by economic development over several decades. He recorded these recollections alongside the numerical data in his journal.[5]

While Thoreau brought an almost obsessive energy to this project, he seems not to have become a formal participant in the legal side of the controversy. Almost certainly due to his recognized need to carry out "neutral" surveying work, Thoreau's signature does not appear on any legal petitions submitted by the River Meadow Association. There are, however, ample indications that he basically sympathized with the farmers against the corporate interests that had damaged the meadows and tamed the river. In June of 1859, he noted that "the testimony of the farmers, etc., is that the river thirty to fifty years ago was much lower in the summer than now."[6] After discussing the case with Abel Hosmer and several other plaintiffs a month later, Thoreau caustically assessed the environmental consequences of commercial expansion, referring to the Concord River as "completely emasculated & demoralized" by the shutting of mill gates by industrial "operatives" above Concord.[7] In early 1860, Thoreau echoed the testimony of Colonel David Heard of Wayland, who said that the farmers' valley was now "dammed at both ends and cursed in the middle."[8] Ultimately, it was the more-politically-connected mill owners who prevailed in the case. They successfully argued before a legislative committee that the state had no right to appropriate their property for the benefit of a few farmers. As the Massachusetts legislature declared, reopening the river would "disturb and unsettle the existing manufacturing interests of the Commonwealth."[9]

The flowage controversy was a classic case of pitting the nation's emerging commercial-industrial power against the agrarian traditions of the past, but this was not the only reason Thoreau took a strong interest in it. Before he was hired by the meadow owners, he had expressed a desire to survey the river, not for its importance in a legal battle but for what it would show about the laws of nature. A journal entry of March 17, 1859, records his amazement at the "unexpected water-lines" of the Concord River at flood stage, along with his inclination toward a herculean measuring task that would reveal the earth's "unseen shores" and the integrating principles of its geography:

> Even if the highest water-mark were indicated at one point, the surveyor could not, with any labor short of infinite, draw these lines for us which wind about every elevation of earth or rock. Yet, though this slight difference of level which water so simply and effectually points out, is so unobservable by us ordinarily, no doubt Nature never forgets it for a moment, but plants grow and insects, etc., breed in conformity to it. Many a kingdom of nature has its boundaries parallel with this waving line. By these freshets, the relation of some field, usually far from the stream, to future or past deluge is suggested.[10]

Thoreau judges that it would take an extreme, "infinite" form of surveying labor to reveal "that part of the earth whose geography has never been mapped." He is intrigued by the insights that might be derived from locating the often-invisible boundaries between marine and dry-land environments, thereby "revealing the relation of this surface to the flood ordinarily far from it." One explanation for the extraordinary energy with which Thoreau formally surveyed the river beginning a few months later is that he already realized the project's great natural-science potential.

When the meadow owners engaged Thoreau for the river survey, he likely saw the project as an opportunity to put engineering principles into practice in a way that fortuitously merged purposes. Aside from aiding a creditable political cause, the survey was a chance to confront the challenging task of learning and internalizing the river's physiography while directly assessing the environmental impact of industrial development around his Concord home. His implacable efforts on the project were no doubt further legitimized by the unknown pay he received for the work, but it seems safe to say that his main motivations were far from financial, if only because the long hours he spent at the river were almost certainly out of all proportion to whatever wages he received.

The extensive statistics Thoreau gathered about the Concord River are not the only example of a surveying project that was integrated into his journal in the final stages of his life. On his fourth trip to Mount

Monadnock, in August of 1860, he made a detailed—though according to his personal standards "rudely measured"—topographical study of the vicinity, pacing distances on foot and taking directional bearings with a pocket compass, producing a survey map of the Monadnock peak and its immediate environs to a scale of sixty rods to an inch. In his entry of August 9, he combined his drawing with rapt verbal descriptions of the area, even using a compass to determine the direction of the grooves in stone formations on the mountain surface. A reference study that Thoreau consulted on the mountain had found that the diluvial grooves ran nearly north and south. Thoreau looked carefully at the topography, sketched the grooves, and concluded that their direction actually varied between five and twenty compass degrees, "or, by the true meridian, more yet." Thoreau's apparent hypothesis asserted an analogy between the direction of the formations and the variable influence of terrestrial magnetism.[11]

Though the Monadnock experiment was certainly something Thoreau enjoyed in the short term, the Concord River undertaking was a long-standing passion. What it ensured was that Thoreau's last major survey project was, in relation to his literary ambitions, very much like his first. Like his survey of Walden Pond made thirteen years earlier, the river survey had been incorporated into a coproduced literary text. Once there, both surveys were to some degree misunderstood by readers—the Walden map as a "capital satire and joke" by Emerson's classmate, the river data as superfluous enough to be expunged by an editor. Both surveys linked and analyzed relationships between natural and man-made environmental bench marks and therefore carried implicit sociopolitical relevance. Finally, both surveys not only merged physics and philosophy but clearly asserted a coresponsiveness between the two. In sounding the Concord, for example, Thoreau had found that "the deep places in the river are not so obvious as the shallow ones and can only be found by carefully probing it. So perhaps it is with human nature"—an insight clearly of a kind with his discoveries about the anthropomorphically reflective dimensions of Walden Pond.[12]

Thoreau's psychological management of the river survey—his unflinching acceptance of its physical demands and extensive translation of the project into literary subject matter through his journal—indicates that he had in part overcome his fears about the negative spiritual influences of hired engineering. Between the Walden Pond survey and the river survey—crucial examples of spiritually motivated fieldwork—more than 150 paid jobs, performed by Thoreau the businessman, had intervened. Though he was still surveying for money and still writing about the natural world, he no longer felt a desperate need to separate these processes, finding instead that his surveyor and naturalist incarnations could coexist and jointly serve the purposes to which his life was dedicated. Early in his surveying career, Thoreau had wondered if his "Field-Notes" and his journal could be the same book. By the summer of 1860, the merger was complete; poetry and facts were united in a single location, in one category, under a one-word title. And in the Concord census of 1860 undertaken by Samuel H. Rhoades, assistant marshal, Henry D. Thoreau, age 42, was for the first time listed as "Surveyor."

Thoreau's feelings about this aspect of his legacy are addressed in two of his final essays, the posthumously published "Life Without Principle" and "Walking," both of which bravely confront paradoxes in the author's economic life. A working title for "Life Without Principle" during its development as a lecture in the 1850s was "The Connection Between Man's Employment and His Higher Life." This may have been a more cumbersome designation than the one the author eventually agreed to, but it better conveys the essay's final content. In February of 1862, as Thoreau's health rapidly declined and he struggled to bring lecture notes together into a unified essay, his employment as a surveyor, along with his long-term attempt to align it with higher law, was a focal point of his thoughts.[13]

"Life Without Principle," which Thoreau composed in full knowledge of his imminent death, draws attention to the important gap between the perceptions of surveying and Thoreau's personal surveying rationale. Meaningfully embracing an identity he had earlier rejected, Thoreau unflinchingly describes land surveying as "my own business" and affirms with candor and finality, "I am a surveyor."[14] Throughout the essay, he uses a series of implicit contrasts to explain and define his labor. By describing lives lived without principle, he adumbrates a life with principle; by relating to his audience how *not* to get one's living, he illustrates through opposition how he has gotten his. When Thoreau states, "To have done anything by which you earned money *merely* is to have been truly idle or worse,"[15] he stresses differences between thoughtless drudgery and more elevated exertions, implying that his own hired work has transcended pecuniary motives.

Nevertheless, the author is troubled because his contemporaries remain blind to the value of labor generally and his labor specifically. "Commonly, if men want anything of me, it is only to know how many acres I make of their land."[16] Differentiating his professional standards from those of "most" of his townsmen, he asserts his refusal to work for a "coarse and boisterous money-making fellow" who plans to "build a bank-wall under the hill on the edge of his meadow."[17] Accepting surveying as his business but stating also that he has chosen to pursue "certain labors which yield more real profit, though but little money," he realizes that he has been looked on as "an idler." It is only because his work has *not* been meaningless that he can declare with confidence, "I do not need the police of meaningless labor to regulate me." Many of his contemporaries "are no more worthily employed" than "in throwing stones over a wall, and then in throwing them back."[18]

Since Thoreau, on the other hand, had been running a surveying business, the question then becomes one of how this occupation is redeemed—how it is inherently different from the allegedly pointless exertions of so many of his countrymen. Among Thoreau's implicit rejoinders is the satisfaction he has derived from his work. The "slight labors" which afford him his livelihood and by which he is "to some extent serviceable" to his contemporaries, "are as yet commonly a pleasure" to him, and he is therefore "not often reminded that they are a necessity." While this thinly veiled admission that he enjoys fieldwork contradicts statements made in other moods, it is not the only hint in "Life Without Principle" that Thoreau had on some level accepted surveying, had reconciled it with his manner of living. After announcing his profession, he tells readers, "I am not without employment at this present stage of the voyage."[19]

Another stipulation made in the essay is that earning one's living should not be a full-time enterprise. Half a day's work, or irregular work, was plenty for Thoreau. His purposeful reduction of wants had reduced his need for self-sustaining labor, thereby partially preserving his autonomy. Full-time work would become "a drudgery," a selling of his birthright for a mess of pottage: "If I should sell both my forenoons and afternoons to society . . . for me, there would be nothing left worth living for."[20] While Thoreau put in many a full day of surveying fieldwork, the intermittent nature of his business suited him well, as did the ability to use his time in the field creatively. Simply through temperamental self-adjustment in the field, Thoreau could observe nature, a skill that was after all undoubtedly enhanced by the long hours of perceptual practice he had while locating boundaries, and by the bodily knowledge of the land he had acquired while chaining, blazing and running line.

Finally, in this his most searching public analysis of the dangers of "getting a living," Thoreau is careful to contrast the predominantly economic motives of his clients to his own objectives. In doing so, he outlines a type of occupational integrity that is unique to land surveying but applicable in principle to all professions that partake of the profit motive:

> That kind of surveying which I could do with most satisfaction my employers do not want. They would prefer that I should do my work coarsely and not too well, ay, not well enough. When I observe that there are different ways of surveying, my employer commonly asks which will give him the most land, not which is the most correct.[21]

In a striking reversal of capitalist paradigms, Thoreau avers that, to the extent that profit-greedy clients are satisfied, he is dissatisfied. His initial advertising claims of exactness in his work had assumed an overlap between the desires of his clients and the surveyor's desire for precision. Having discovered antagonisms between truth and profit, he severs the relation but retains the "satisfaction" derived from correct measurement. Referring to the copious engineering he had performed only for the sake of pure discovery or for what he calls "scientific, or even moral ends," Thoreau concludes that "the aim of the laborer should be, not to get his living ... but to perform well a certain work."[22]

While Thoreau implicitly shifts the burden of environmental destruction to his surveying clients who have cut down the Concord woods, "making the earth bald before her time," he is acutely conscious of the ways he has abetted them. Perhaps in expressing these thoughts about his work, he remembers his advertising broadside, which had explicitly offered to lot off wooded property "distinctly and according to a regular plan." Now he is contemplating what he considers a failure in his actions—the living of an "unsatisfactory life, doing as others do"—but he reiterates a desire to follow the higher way—a route described as a "solitary path across-lots."[23]

The cross-lot route is nothing new for Thoreau—it is in essence the way taken by the Walden surveyor, who ignored established boundaries and instead used the compass to pursue an ideal. By choosing this route, Thoreau remains consistent in embracing surveying itself, but denying conventional surveying, as a metaphor for his life. Closing out a long series of allusions to professional matters, he warns that "there is no more fatal blunderer than he who consumes the greater part of his life getting his living. . . . You must get your living by loving."[24] While Thoreau did work for money, he also proved his love for that type of surveying undertaken in a spirit of truth seeking rather than financial gain seeking, striving in clear ways to offset his professional role by embodying the more vital personae of philosopher and natural historian.

After submitting "Life Without Principle" to the *Atlantic* on February 28, Thoreau began at once to revise what he referred to as his "paper on Walking." Often too weak to write in pen, Thoreau scribbled textual emendations in pencil for Sophia's transcription, dictated others, and was eventually able to send the manuscript to James T. Fields on March 11. The resulting essay, which contains a remarkable number of survey-themed passages, explores the frame of mind with which the saunterer of fields and woods undertakes his forays. "We should go forth," Thoreau explains, "in the spirit of undying adventure, never to return."[25] Such an attitude is important because, as Thoreau had determined through a lifetime studying the problem, it is only through issues of intent and spirit that the work of the surveyor transcends the boundaries he has himself created. Setting his compass needle toward land that "is not private property" and "is not owned," Thoreau eschews complicity in processes which "deform the landscape, and make it more and more tame and cheap."[26]

But the intended escape into wildness is profoundly troubled in this essay, parts of which are among Thoreau's darkest treatments of surveying as a profession. Early in the address, Thoreau positions the conventional surveyor in the decidedly unattractive role of foolish and misguided helpmeet to a land-greedy employer. Drawing from a journal entry of 1850, Thoreau describes a scene extremely common to the profession: the land surveyor "lost in the middle of the prairie" accompanied by a "worldly miser" landowner. Desensitized to beauty, temporarily only semiconscious because he is focused on finding a lot corner, the surveyor is blind to the miraculous: "While heaven had taken place around him, he did not see the angels going to and fro, but was looking for an old post-hole in the midst of paradise." When the bewildered surveyor actually finds his reference point and lot-corner monumentation, the boundary-making work begins. At this point, Thoreau's self-portrayal gains in intensity, shifting from images of disorientation to those of horrific damnation:

> I looked again, and saw him [the landowner] standing
> in the middle of a boggy, stygian fen, surrounded by
> devils, and he had found his bounds without a doubt,
> three little stones, where a stake had been driven,
> and looking nearer, I saw that the Prince of Darkness
> was his surveyor.[27]

What this image clearly projects is its author's awareness of how his chosen profession could serve the very purposes he had dedicated himself to resisting and rejecting body and soul. To the extent that he furthers the economic purposes of land commodification, giving sanction to the spiritual debasement of both man and nature, the land surveyor incarnates an ultimate form of evil. Harrowing images of the inherent dangers of surveying processes and purposes mark this essay as Thoreau's public act of contrition for complicity in his society's transgressions against the natural order.

Preoccupied with the process of looking after superficial land boundaries, the surveyor succumbs to a perilous state of mind: that of being physically present in the wild but absent in a spiritual sense, focused on the business that occupies him in the woods rather than the "great happiness" offered by its wildness. "It sometimes happens that I cannot easily shake off the village," Thoreau states. By adding that "the thought of some work will run in my head, and I am not where my body is," he reveals that he has fallen into this trap because of his surveying.[28] In "Slavery in Massachusetts," it is the state that ruins Thoreau's walk; here it is surveying work, but the two are simply different expressions of the identical institutional authority from which the saunterer seeks refuge. He struggles to preserve the pleasure of sauntering against a recurring sense that such uninhibited journeys will someday be impossible, and that he will be partly to blame for it.

Later in "Walking," Thoreau begins a severe questioning of his culture's network of legally expressed property rights. While many have

He did it ← (handwritten marginalia)

read this essay as a paean to Manifest Destiny, there is undeniably an acknowledged downside to westward expansion and continental conquest. In seeming recognition of a historical progression revealed to him in the fields with compass and chain—the process of "improvement" which tends to convert the country into the town—Thoreau foresees the coming of "evil days" to his culture and nation, days when the landscape will be fully partitioned off and technologies of exclusion completely entrenched. The dystopia he briefly envisions is one in which surveyed boundaries become impassable barriers, no longer serving merely to establish ownership but to alienate man from man, and man from himself. As sketched by Thoreau, the future is one "in which a few will take a narrow and exclusive pleasure only,—when fences shall be man-trapped and other engines invented to confine man to the *public* road, and walking over the surface of God's earth shall be construed to mean trespassing on some gentleman's grounds."[29]

Arguably, what Thoreau has in mind is the constitutionally established concept of unrestricted autonomous proprietorship, a concept that was under siege in the 1850s when it came to property in human beings, but generally accepted when it came to property in land. The question seemingly asked here concerns what would happen when the Public Land Survey, going on in the West as Thoreau wrote, was completed, with all lines run, all land owned, all fences built. Thoreau's advocacy of wildness in the essay is thus a call for "a people who would begin by burning the fences and let the forest stand!"[30] The inner debate the author permits himself goes beyond immediate syntactical arguments about what constitutes property, instead raising the question of whether men can or should achieve contentment under the characteristically American system of owners' rights. "To enjoy a thing exclusively is commonly to exclude yourself from the true enjoyment of it," Thoreau observes.[31]

As Thoreau had made clear, a surveyor may embody evil, but he may also choose a better direction. In "Walking," he is certain that "it is not indifferent to us which way we walk" and that "there is a right way."[32] Set against the figure of the satanic surveyor is he who ignores worldly boundaries to follow the "perfectly symbolical" path. The saunterer's proper course thus tends away from boundaries, but he is still guided as the land surveyor is guided, by the directional needle of a compass, and his perceptions are subject to the principles of earthly magnetism. "I believe that there is a subtile magnetism in Nature," Thoreau states, "which, if we unconsciously yield to it, will direct us aright." In the case given, the invisible attraction is toward the southwest, "toward some particular wood or meadow or deserted pasture or hill," a place where the solitary walker is least likely to encounter civilization, a land "where no settler has squatted." Relying on the compass, Thoreau is nevertheless aware of the difference between true and magnetic direction finding: "My needle is slow to settle," he observes, and though it "varies a few degrees, and does not always point due southwest," he can confidently state that "it has good authority for this variation."[33]

As the dying writer worked on these lines from his bed in the parlor of the family home on Main Street, he could look out the window to his front yard and see clearly the spot where he had found the direction of the polestar eleven years earlier. He could see the stone post on his "western small front gate"—a spot from which east led toward town and west away from town, and over which, as he knew quite well, ran the true meridian. His remark "Eastward I go only by force; but westward I go free. Thither no business leads me"[34] has both a national and a personal application. By mastering surveying principles, Thoreau established his claim of "good authority" for his life's course. In "Walking," he indexes his visible, self-created directional matrix to the invisible forces then leading the country westward. The surveyor's ontogeny recapitulates cultural phylogeny, and both are guided by the stars and the compass.

Just as significantly, Thoreau indicates a desire to traverse fields and woods not in a straight line or closed circle, as an ordinary surveyor must, but in a parabola or plane curve. "The outline which would bound my walks would be, not a circle, but a parabola, or rather like one of those cometary orbits which have been thought to be non-returning curves, in this case opening westward, in which my house occupies the place of the sun."[35] Considering Thoreau's often-repeated convictions about the symbolic value of facts, it seems worthwhile to pursue the implications of the parabola, a U-shaped curve with interesting specific properties. By definition, all points on a parabola are equidistant from a fixed line and a fixed point not on the line. Proposing the parabola as his desired and proper course, Thoreau expresses a desire to limn out an open arc rather than a closed border. In geometrical terms, the fixed, previously surveyed line or boundary becomes Thoreau's directrix, while the fixed point not on the line is his focus. A parabola is the curved figure created by stringing together a set of points such that the distance to the focus always equals the distance to the directrix. Aesthetically, parabolas soften the rigidity of intersecting lines. When surveyors use parabolas it is not to establish a boundary but to aesthetically tailor it by producing decorative curves rather than severely angled corners.

Proposing the parabola as an alternative life course means that Thoreau is positioning himself in an unvaryingly mediary space with his "house" as the focus. Moving not along but between known points, he inscribes a line that does not close, an open curve more beautiful than a square or angular figure, and made so by its creator's establishment of a measurable relation to his known point. Producing a parabola requires the surveyor to *use* a line to *make* a curve, effectively transforming the linear to the contoured. It also reintroduces open-endedness as a means of counteracting the implacably delimited profiles surveyors usually create.

It seems extraordinarily significant that the parabola is not a closed figure. *Closure* is a surveying term referring to the need to fully traverse each line at the outer boundaries of a land parcel, take back sights and reverse bearings from each station, and thereby arrive at a mathematically balanced or "exactly closed" surveying document. A fully closed plat was a product that separated better surveyors from the less-precise ones. In tracing the arc of a parabola, the precise knowledge that determines the surveyor's position is present, but the courses and bearings that enclose the parcel are absent. Since the colonial era, land enclosure had been a task of primary national importance, transforming wilderness into property while validating the surveyor's work and the profit-based economic order that made it necessary. Surveyors took an oath in which they swore to close the survey by taking readings at every station and traversing the full perimeter of a land parcel.

Even in Thoreau's day, the exigencies of full closure could present substantial challenges—entering into marshes, penetrating thickets, wading streams and rivers were routine occupational hazards. Meeting these physical challenges made possible the mathematical balancing of the survey document, achieving a form of completeness unattainable if bearings had not been taken from all stations. It was therefore hardly necessary for Davies's surveying textbook—the one Thoreau owned and a standard text of its day—to remind surveyors of the need to "go entirely around the land, measuring the lengths of the bounding lines with the chain, and taking their bearings with the compass" in order to exactly close the drafted plan.[36] Through his adoption of the parabola as his sauntering objective, Thoreau metaphorically refuses to close his survey.[37]

The word *parabola*, from the Greek, means a "comparison" or literally "a throwing beside." Pythagoras afforded it significance as a fundamental operation in his method of application of areas in plane geometry. But its root meaning, as Thoreau would certainly have known, is the same as *parable*, a simple story with a moral lesson. Sauntering by the compass and polestar but not toward civilized or owned land, running curves instead of running line, Thoreau adapts Pythagorean geometry creatively and transformatively to the conventional surveyor's role. His parabola expresses a merger of geometry and morality by seizing a meaning already available but rarely developed in the term's etymology. Thoreau had once wrongly believed that a surveyor's *perambulation* could fill his need for a term that reconciled his employment with his ideals; here in his last essay, he embraces the saunterer's parabola as his redemptive alternative.

Acknowledging this aspect of "Walking" heightens the essay's political implications. It is apparent that in going west, Thoreau conforms to "the prevailing tendency of my countrymen . . . we go westward as into the future."[38] Thoreau does so, however, at some variance with his countrymen's desire to settle, civilize and tame. "Hope and the future" for this particular surveyor lie "not in lawns and cultivated fields, not in towns and cities, but in impervious and quaking swamps." The West of which Thoreau speaks is "but another name for the Wild," an unequivocally internal rather than external state. The country is guided by one moral compass, one ideology, the Concord surveyor by another. Though the majority is "very liable from heedlessness and stupidity" to misread nature's compass, we are called on by Thoreau to realize that the path through the "actual" or worldly domain is "perfectly symbolical of the path . . . in the interior and ideal world."[39]

Exemplifying a frequent thought pattern in his works, the saunterer cannot for long discuss wildness without having recourse to a cache of anecdotes relating to the tools and skills of his trade. The great counterpoint to his earlier nightmarish formulation of the satanic surveyor, for example, comes late in "Walking," when he establishes his divergence with the purposes of his employers. Surveying a single straight line one hundred and thirty-two rods long through a nearly impassable swamp, Thoreau is amazed at the landowner's determination to complete the line and extract gain from his holdings. "I saw my employer actually up to his neck and swimming for his life in his property," Thoreau wryly comments, echoing sentiments he often expressed about the dangers to body and soul of material attachments. Thoreau worked for many such clients, so he feels justified in portraying the swamp developer as "the type of a class," a category of farmer who "displaces the Indian because he redeems the meadow."[40] It is interesting that the proprietor in question effectively embodies the meadow owners who brought suit against the mill owners in the Concord River flowage controversy. They were outraged over the flooding of their meadows, but in many cases their acreage had in fact been created by draining wetlands that were naturally inundated. In this passage, the author reacts to his employer's ocular demonstration of incipient environmental exploitation with a mix of both wonder and repulsion, but the latter feeling wins out: "I would not have every man nor every part of a man cultivated," Thoreau asserts, "any more than I would have every acre of earth cultivated."[41]

In "Walking," Thoreau seems clearly conscious of his professional legacy. Aware of the ways he has been defined by surveying, he sifts it openly and purposefully, first admitting his own sins, then appraising the rapacity of owners, but finally finding a perspective to sum up the business that had often dictated his relation to his Concord neighbors. When Thoreau declares late in the essay, "I feel that with regard to Nature I live a sort of border life," he has in mind his intermittent compromises with the cultural and institutional status quo. Forever divided by what society makes him do, he exists "on the confines" of a world into which he makes "occasional and transient forays only," and his "patriotism and allegiance to the state" into whose "territories" of institutional relationships he retreats are "those of a moss-trooper [border marauder]," carrying more potential subversion than meets the eye.[42]

Returning to an idea he had first treated over a decade earlier in "Resistance to Civil Government," Thoreau finds common ground between his youthful, iconoclastic civil disobedience and his supposedly law-bound civil engineering. In the earlier essay, the limits of authority were exposed when Thoreau emerged from prison to first complete his shoe-mending errand and then join a huckleberry party. A short time later, finding himself in a field on a hill two miles away, he observes that "the State was nowhere to be seen." In "Walking," this lawbreaker's insight is recast as a surveyor's insight:

> The walker in the familiar fields which stretch around my native town sometimes finds himself in another land than is described in their own-ers' deeds, as it were in some faraway field on the confines of the actual Concord, where her jurisdiction ceases, and the idea which the word Concord suggests ceases to be suggested.[43]

Simply by differentiating between the fields he knows through percep-tual experience and those described in "their owners' deeds," the surveyor transcends conventional confines and escapes the grasp of the commu-nity's erstwhile pervasive reach. Subverting conventional definitions of material reality, he creates and metaphysically inhabits a space wherein the state's presence has been superseded. He may still be carrying his employer's deed, may even still be referring to it as he labors in the fields. But to the extent that he supplants legal descriptions with his own per-ceptions, mediating between paper property and its real counterpart, the state is absent, insubstantial, nowhere to be seen.

One day in August of 1860, near the end of his surveying career and at the end of a summer that found him deeply engaged in the river survey, Thoreau was prompted to think about berries. "Going a-berrying implies more things than eating the berries," he observed. At other times in his life, Thoreau might have gone almost anywhere with this thought. He could have continued with a consideration of the taste, smell, shape or color of berries, perhaps also noting where he had found them, their sea-son of ripeness, the species of flora that grew near them or the species of birds that fed on them. On this day, he instead considered the question of who owned them. "It is true," he went on, "that we have as good a right to make berries private property as to make grass and trees such." Not a very radical sentiment politically, but what other conclusion was defen-sible after a decade of land surveying? Still, Thoreau reflects, there was a meaningful price to be paid for such a right: "What I chiefly regret is the, in effect, dog-in-the-manger result, for at the same time we exclude man-kind from gathering berries in our field, we exclude them from gathering health and happiness and inspiration and a hundred other far finer and nobler fruits than berries, which yet we shall not gather ourselves there, nor even carry to market."[44]

Here was richer material, more in character for the author of *Walden*. In Aesop's fable, a dog had slept in a hay manger and then prevented the returning cattle from eating the hay he now considered his own, though it was useless to the dog and needed by the cattle. Possession—especially when it is beyond basic needs or when it denies what is more necessary to others than to the possessor—is a dubious concept driven by base instincts. Clearly, Thoreau was thinking about more than blueberries. Perhaps his metaphor also comprised the valuable hay in the Concord River meadows, or the rights to the flow of the river that were appropriated by mill owners, or the timber in the woods he had lotted off for sale, or any and all of the commercial products of the landscape. By exerting the rights of possession, he realized, "we strike only one more blow at a simple and wholesome relation to nature."

From this platform, it is only a short distance to a rejection of all things owned, a moral that Thoreau does not overlook: "As long as the berries are free to all comers they are beautiful . . . but tell me that is a blueberry swamp which somebody has hired, and I shall not want even to look at it." The philosophical rub therefore lies in the act of laying claim to the produce of the land, in commodifying the "spontaneous fruit of our pastures." Setting up boundaries garners profit, but in keeping others out we hem ourselves in, inevitably lowering ourselves in the eyes of the community. "The berry party whom we turn away," Thoreau notes, "naturally look down on and despise us." The tally of negatives associated with the process of land enclosure culminates with the realization that a more natural ethics would have ignored such limitations: "If it were left to the berries to say who should have them, is it not likely that they would prefer to be gathered by the party of children in the hay-rigging, who have come to have a good time merely?"

Thoreau had made a living marking boundaries and transferring onto survey plats the lines dictated by man's law and ignored by nature's law. Having agonized over these processes for a decade, he knew what he was talking about when he lamented, "I do not see that these successive losses are ever quite made up to us. This is one of the taxes we pay for having a railroad." He had also learned, however, that property rights were ineluctable in the American sociopolitical order, that dissociation from all forms of ownership and possession was a Sisyphean task, and that he was himself an economically constructed being. Looking on these truths dispassionately, he concedes that his fable of property rights in berries "suggests what origin and foundation many of our laws and institutions have" and ends his discourse with a poignant sense of resignation: "I do not say this by way of complaining of this particular custom. Not that I love Caesar less, but Rome more."[45]

Thinking of himself as Shakespeare's Brutus, whose conspiracy to murder Caesar exhibited a preeminent dilemma of divided political loyalties, Thoreau casts his own circumstances, and his self-positioning against them, as a soul-splitting problem of allegiance. Brutus's words to the Roman populace in Shakespeare's play had crucially addressed a question of loyalty, arguing fundamentally that violence toward Caesar was enacted in obedience to higher principles. Rather than diminishing his seditious deed, Brutus affirmed the more complicated verity that subversion of the state on one level, and adherence to it on another, could be contained in the same act. In the context of Thoreau's parable of property rights in berries, the plea underscores a similar duality in Thoreau's work and outlook.

The story of Thoreau the land surveyor is itself a kind of parable, a didactic narrative with strong contemporary relevance. In the winter of 1846, an emerging writer living in a cabin near Walden Pond carefully sounded the pond's depths and surveyed its frozen surface for the purpose of drafting onto paper a sublime three-dimensional microcosm. Realizing how well this image expressed his ethics and aspirations, he later inserted the unusual illustration in lithograph form into the text of his literary masterpiece. Processes of measuring and the data they generated were ultimately more than stages in the development of a lithograph— they were the genesis of his great book.

The author's initial decision to measure and plot the pond did not take place in a cultural vacuum. It was motivated in part by the Coastal Survey and its public descriptions of surveying as a national duty. A fascination with national surveying science was apparent in his book, where tropes for pond discovery both reflected and rewrote the justifications of the national survey as articulated by its charismatic superintendent and echoed in journalism of the period.

When the literary auteur's need to earn a living became an acute concern, he logically turned to surveying, something for which he had a natural talent and that put him where he wanted to be. But there were perils to hired work. Perambulating the petty boundaries of towns for money was not the same as sauntering in the woods and fields. A strict psychological separation of naturalist and businessman functions proved unworkable. Taming and changing the landscape, the surveyor feared, destroyed his perceptions of its wildness and vigor. Awakening to the purposes he had lent himself to, he inwardly rebelled. Clinging to a faith that measuring the natural world increased his understanding of it, he committed himself to a deeper-than-was-necessary knowledge of surveying, using his field notes to record environmental data and bringing astronomical science and compass bearings into his daily life as indicators of material and moral direction.

For years he wrestled with the consequences of serving Admetus, striving to atone for his subservience to an economic order he mistrusted. Uneasy with his compromises, he found inspiration in John Brown, who used surveying to fight evil. In making a public plea for the Kansas surveyor, the Concord surveyor extolled politically creative uses of the compass and chain, drawing on this aspect of Brown's identity—and his own—to further a discourse of revolution.

Not long after his declaration of support for the abolitionist surveyor, the man of Concord stood again before an audience, this time as a scientist and environmentalist-surveyor. Sharing his discoveries about the succession of forest trees, he displayed his own version of professional creativity, enabling him to take increased pride in his work. In the public eye and in the official census of his community, he no longer shunned self-identification as a surveyor. Simultaneously, he was becoming a surveyor where it mattered most—in the record of his inner life. When surveying notes became an important part of his journal, it signaled that a discord among professional, political and private identities had been addressed. His last large measuring project, the Concord River survey, was as enthusiastically performed and spiritually motivated as his first, that of Walden Pond.

Just before he died, the surveyor composed documents that further defined the nature of his attachment to the compass and chain. "Life Without Principle" and "Walking" were conscience-driven commentaries on the economically motivated persona he had assumed for over a decade. In these works, he drew clear distinctions between types of surveying and attested to his protracted struggle against his work's negative potential. His long-term inquiry into the meaning of his profession bore philosophical fruit that displayed a discernible reciprocity between the man and his measures. Woven inextricably into the fabric of his literary works is a deftly crafted, socially and politically significant, countercultural surveying treatise.

In "Resistance to Civil Government," Thoreau envisioned the result of undue respect for authority: the sight of men marching off to fight in wars they did not believe in. On a less lethal plane, Thoreau himself showed a form of "undue" respect for authority by making bounds and lending himself to environmental harm. He was aware that surveying potentially contradicted his ideals, and this knowledge disturbed him. "This process by which we get our coats is not what it should be," he wrote near the end of his life.[46]

In eulogizing Thoreau, Emerson expressed some regret that instead of "engineering for all America," his friend had chosen to be "the captain of a huckleberry party."[47] Thoreau's extensive surveying-related documents and commentaries argue that he did both. If he was often divided and ambivalent about how he made a living, it was because he had a muscular conscience and did not want to waste any part of his life. He tried hard to resist the almost ineluctable process of being spiritually reduced by the need to earn money. While he did not "transcend" the conditions of existence within his specific historical context, he did something inspirational by confronting and channeling the tension between getting a living and living by values—a tension we all encounter in some form.

How we respond to the dictates of conscience in our professional lives says a lot about us. Certainly, not all of us are able to choose jobs or follow lifestyles whose requirements are at every moment in perfect alignment with our deepest-held convictions. To the extent that we are divided about what society or the state makes us do, we are well equipped to understand Thoreau's surveying dilemmas. To the extent that our consciences are troubled by our tacit participation in environmental destruction, we recognize ourselves in Concord's surveyor.

Paradoxically, the "permanent" markers Thoreau left while surveying in the Walden woods have disappeared,[48] while the literary legacy only partially comprehended at the time of his death endures. Early in his experience with surveying, Thoreau sensed the transitory nature of man-made boundaries, composing in his journal a passage that later became one of the culminating insights of "Walking": "These farms I have myself surveyed; these lines I have run; these bounds which I have set-up; appear dimly still as through a mist; but they have no chemistry to fix them; they fade from the surface of the glass."[49] As Thoreau seems to have predicted, the mounds of stone he left to mark lot corners in the Walden woods are gone, scattered back into the geology from which they were extricated. In surveying terms, Thoreau's "monumentation" is all but eradicated. Near the cabin site at Walden, however, there is another mound of stones, the memorial cairn that pilgrims to the pond have made into a monument that has lasted since 1872 and is still being added to.[50] There is undeniably a thought-provoking symmetry in the fact that some of the very stones Thoreau handled while surveying, stones which he knew to have profaned the wildness of Walden, have now found a more permanent home in the cairn memorial, venerating the writer and surveyor who counseled, "Enjoy the land, but own it not."[51]

Notes

The standard text of Thoreau's journal is the Princeton University Press edition, abbreviated as *PJournal* below. Publication of the Princeton edition is in process and currently covers the years from 1837 to 1854.

Journal citations after 1854 appear below under the title *Journal* and refer to the 1906 edition edited by Bradford Torrey and Francis H. Allen.

Preface

1. Thoreau, *Journal*, 10: 232 (31 December 1857).
2. Thoreau, *Journal*, 8: 319 (30 April 1856).
3. Thoreau, *Journal*, 10: 362 (7 April 1858).
4. Thoreau, *Journal*, 10: 232 (31 December 1857).

CHAPTER I. The Surveyor and the State

1. Smith, 47.
2. Love, A2-A3.
3. Daniel, 53.
4. Linklater, *Measuring America*, 211.
5. Philander Chase, 179.
6. Ibid., 161.
7. Even after his presidency, Washington continued to survey his own lands in a variety of ownership disputes. Five weeks before his death in 1799 he was rerunning the lines of his land in northern Fairfax County (Philander Chase, 181).
8. Washington to Jonathan Boucher, July 9, 1771, in *Washington Papers*, Colonial Series, ed. W. W. Abbot et al. (Charlottesville: University Press of Virginia, 1983–95), 8: 494–98, quoted in Philander Chase, 180.
9. Longmore, 108.
10. Cooper, 20, 21.
11. Ibid., 288, 306.

12. Reeve Huston's "Land and Freedom" provides an overview of the social implications of the Anti-Rent Wars. Thoreau may have had information about the conflict through his friend and supporter Horace Greeley, an outspoken ally of the Anti-Rent cause. See also Newman, 28–33.

13. Cooper, iv. In his preface to *The Chainbearer,* Cooper frankly underscores his intent to assess current political questions, to make the Littlepage trilogy "more and more relevant to the times in which we live."

14. Cooper, 332, 284, 341.

15. Ibid., 160, 90.

16. Ibid., 123, 250, 122 (italics in original).

17. Ibid., 214, 223. 119.

18. Ibid., 18, 29, 440, 19.

19. Ibid., 222.

20. More than a decade after the Civil War, Henry George's 1879 treatise *Progress and Poverty* would famously propose a similar linkage: "If chattel slavery be unjust, then is private property in land unjust" (347). In assessing the ultimate results of private property in land, George saw a relation between slavery and individual land ownership, concluding that the former was merely a "different form of the law of rent," and that private ownership of land would always produce the ownership of men (347).

21. Cooper, 312, 401, 473.

22. Thoreau, *Walden,* 79.

23. Emerson, *Essays and Lectures,* 560. Richard Drinnon credits Emerson's "Politics" with having more direct influence over Thoreau's political views than was exerted by other contemporaries such as Alcott, Channing, or Theodore Parker. See Drinnon, 155. See also Sattelmeyer, 51.

24. Emerson, *Essays and Lectures,* 560, 561.

25. Ibid., 561, 566.

26. Ibid., 560, 561.

27. Ibid., 563, 570.

28. Thoreau, *Reform Papers,* 84.

29. For a focused treatment of Thoreau's varied scientific interests, see Deevey. Deevey tested Thoreau's observations about the biological composition and geological characteristics of Walden Pond, concluding that Thoreau was a genuine scientist and pointing out "the neglect of Thoreau's writings by the scientific world" (8).

30. Thoreau, *A Week,* 295.

31. Thoreau, *Journal,* 10: 221 (7 December 1857).

32. Stoller, 54.

33. Thoreau, *Essays,* 191.

34. Thoreau, *Reform Papers,* 79, 84.

35. Ibid., 74.

36. Town of Concord, *Reports of the Selectmen,* 1851–52, quoted in Hoeltje, 354.

37. Thoreau, *PJournal 4*, 77 (12 September 1851).

38. Ibid., 101 (26 September 1851).

39. Thoreau, *Reform Papers*, 158.

40. Hoeltje, 355–56.

41. See, for example, the *Town Records*, vol. 8 (March 1834 to September 1851), 493, quoted in Hoeltje, 355.

42. Thoreau, *A Week*, 787.

43. Wilson, 159, 170. Concerning the court appearances, Wilson probably has in mind an 1853 case in the Court of Common Pleas in which Thoreau was called to Cambridge to testify. The case was a dispute over water rights. Suit was brought against William O. Benjamin, whose land Thoreau had surveyed. Thoreau's testimony has been lost, but the jury found for the plaintiff. See Cameron, "Thoreau in the Court."

44. Wilson compared Thoreau to New England surveyors Park Holland and Ira Allen.

45. Harry B. Chase, 220, 221, 218.

46. Ibid., 219, 222.

47. Hoy, 64, 63, 64.

48. Ibid., 61, 62, 65.

49. Howard, 31, 32; Thoreau, *PJournal 7*, 201 (22 December 1853).

50. Savage, 44.

51. Interview with Barry Savage by the author. November 12, 2007.

52. Savage, 42, 44.

53. Ibid., 43.

54. Ibid., 44.

55. Ibid.

56. Emerson, "Thoreau," 480.

57. In 1968, Albert F. McLean explored the significance of Thoreau's 1851 sighting of Polaris to determine the variation of his compass from true meridian. More recently, Rick Van Noy's study *Surveying the Interior* addresses Thoreau's anxiety over surveying in the specific context of his relationship with his Indian friend Joe Polis. Several of Van Noy's insights have been of value to this study, especially his exploration of Thoreau's "uneasiness" about the many signs of human presence left in the landscape by both surveyors and cartographers. And Leslie Perrin Wilson's article in the 2007 *Concord Saunterer* provides a useful look at several of Thoreau's more interesting engineering documents.

CHAPTER 2. Material to Mythology

1. Thoreau, *Walden*, 276.

2. Ibid., 284.

3. Ibid., 283.

4. "An action is the perfection and publication of thought," Emerson stated in "Nature" in 1836. Emerson also noted the distinction, later developed by Tho-

reau, between experiential and legal ownership of the physical world: "There is a property in the horizon which no man has but he whose eye can integrate all the parts, that is, the poet. This is the best part of men's farms, yet to this their warranty deeds give no title" (*Essays and Lectures*, 30, 9).

5. Thoreau, *Walden*, 283.

6. Ibid., 281.

7. Thoreau did not need to measure all the way around the pond in order to establish its circumference of 1.7 miles. He determined circumference by measuring the total length of his lines on his drawing and then converting this figure to rods using the scale of ten rods to an inch he had established with his baseline.

8. Thoreau accurately chained the pond's width and "greatest length" of 175½ rods but took no useful bearings from these lines.

9. Thoreau, *Walden*, 283.

10. Ibid., 280.

11. Ibid., 281.

12. Ibid., 85.

13. Ibid.

14. Marchitello, 18.

15. Ibid., 32.

16. Stowell, 9.

17. Ibid., 5–7.

18. McLean, 577.

19. Huntington Library images, accessed January 5, 2009, http://www.huntington.org/LibraryDiv/WaldenPict.html. For a microform version of the manuscript, see *Walden and other manuscripts of Henry David Thoreau (1817–1862) from the Huntington Library* (Marlborough, Wildshire: Adam Matthew Publications, 1998).

20. McLean, 577.

21. In "Bartleby, the Scrivener" (1853), Melville's narrator, a complacent corporate lawyer, is befuddled by the passive nonconformity of Bartleby, who ignores the "standard usage" of the business world and thereby challenges the "doctrine of assumptions" of the prevailing socioeconomic order (Melville, *Great Short Works of Herman Melville*, 63).

22. "Early Massachusetts Records, Concord Vol. 7–11, Selectmen's meetings, and Lincoln Records, Vol. 2 p. 270," cited by Steve Ells.

23. With a thick blanket of snow on the ground, a surveyor might have had difficulty finding the monumentation for the town line, but Thoreau had no doubt noted its location during his many explorations of the area. Between the pond survey and the 1854 publication of *Walden*, Thoreau himself surveyed this line where it crossed the pond and referred to the location in his journal.

24. Thoreau, *PJournal 4*, 85 (20 September 1851).

25. The numbers in Table 2.1 are close approximations of the mathematics of the Walden map, gathered from the surviving preliminary draft of the survey.

26. In *The Making of Walden: With the Text of the First Version*, J. Lyndon Shanley establishes that the first manuscript version of *Walden* was begun in 1846–47. Shanley's ordered and transcribed "First Version" of *Walden* suggests that the pond survey, and thus the field notes produced in early 1846, predated the initial draft version of *Walden*.

CHAPTER 3. *Walden, Cape Cod,* and the Duty of the Coast Survey

1. Although the Coast Survey was authorized by the Jefferson administration in 1807, actual work did not begin until 1816. For background on the formative years of the survey, see Slotten, *Patronage*, 42–60.

2. Hassler's only allegiance was to an ideal of mathematical precision. He spent the first forty-three days of his tenure as survey superintendent measuring and remeasuring an initial baseline less than nine miles long. Linklater, *Measuring*, 194.

3. Slotten, *Patronage*, 101.

4. Letter, Bache to George Back, May 7, 1858, quoted in Slotten, *Patronage*, 99.

5. Slotten, *Patronage*, 90.

6. Robert M. Patterson to Robert J. Walker, December 4, 1843. Bache Papers, Smithsonian Institution Archives, quoted in Slotten, *Patronage*, 73.

7. "Miscellanies," *American Journal of Science and Arts* 46: 1 (April 1844): 213.

8. "The Coast Survey of the United States." *American Journal of Science and Arts* 49: 2 (July/September 1845): 229–49.

9. *The Biblical Repertory and Princeton Review* 17: 2 (April 1845): 321–55.

10. Slotten, "Dilemmas," 37.

11. Bache to R. W. Brown, November 20, 1851, A. D. Bache Papers, Library of Congress, quoted in Slotten, "Dilemmas," 40.

12. Pamphlet, *Tides and Currents*, roll 60, Bache Correspondence. Quoted in Slotten, "Dilemmas," 41.

13. Letter, Benjamin Peirce to Bache, April 7, 1850, quoted in Slotten, "Dilemmas," 34.

14. Thoreau's manuscript entitled "Lovering & Bond on Mag. Observations at Cambridge," located in the Henry David Thoreau Papers, 1836–[1862], Series II: "Survey-Related Notes, Mss., Etc., 1840–1861," Concord Free Public Library, quotes directly from accounts of the Coast Survey's geodetic work.

15. All of which Thoreau owned and read. See Sattelmeyer, 48.

16. C. F. Hoffman. "The United States Coast Survey." *Literary World* 2: 32 (September 11, 1847): 125–29.

17. Slotten, *Patronage*, 99.

18. Louis Agassiz accompanied several Coast Survey expeditions in the shoal areas where dredging and bottom sampling operations were carried out, during which he made numerous scientific discoveries including "the first viviparous scale-fish known to naturalists" (Ammen, 161–62). Beginning in 1847, the renowned professor Louis Agassiz of Harvard had regularly accompanied the hydrographical-survey parties engaged in deep-sea soundings and mappings of underwater topographical formations. A "Review of the Annual Report on the U.S. Coast Survey" appearing in the May 1848 *American Journal of Science and the Arts* noted that Agassiz had "reaped a rich harvest of discovery relative to the animals which inhabit the different depths of water. Every few feet of increase in the depth give changes in the character of organized beings which inhabit the ocean." In allying himself with the Coast Survey, Agassiz saw "an opportunity of examining the animals inhabiting the depths that are rarely accessible" (Davis, 318), and he later detailed his findings in the prefatory material of the Coast Survey reports subscribed to by Thoreau in the 1850s.

19. Thoreau, *A Week*, 954.

20. Ibid.

21. Ibid. (italics in the original).

22. The Highland Light now stands 450 feet back from its original location. See the Truro website: http://lighthouse.cc/highland/history.html.

23. Thoreau, *A Week*, 955.

24. The distance Thoreau estimated from the lighthouse to edge of the bank—twenty rods or 330 feet—suggests a loss of about 170 feet of coastline in the fifty years from the building of the lighthouse in 1797 to Thoreau's 1849 survey.

25. Thoreau, *A Week*, 957. See also Thoreau, *Journal*, 2: 45 (after 16 July 1850).

26. Thoreau, *A Week*, 956.

27. Thoreau, *Journal*, 7: 439 (11 July 1855).

28. Thoreau, *A Week*, 891.

29. Ibid., 904.

30. Ibid., 909–10.

31. Ibid., 910. While there were, before and after the mid-nineteenth century, many documented cases of such woefully inadequate compensation for the slope of land by inexperienced chain men, evidenced by a much-exaggerated acreage total in the surveyor's plat as compared to the land encompassed in the physical tract, surveyors' manuals from the eighteenth century onward insist on the chain being held level regardless of terrain. "If the terrain was so steep that the chain could not be held level, it was to be measured in sub-chain increments, which would be totaled at the completion of the survey" (Daniel, 22).

32. Thoreau, *A Week*, 910.

33. As Moss notes, "The earliest record which we have of [Thoreau's] woodlot

surveying is a signed receipt from the Misses Hosmer for surveying their wood-lot and making a plan of the same dated Dec. 18, 1845" (3).

34. Thoreau, *A Week*, 910.

35. Ibid. This passage is based on an entry in Thoreau's journal of 1850:

"I met with a man on the beach who told me that when he wanted to jump over a brook he held up one leg a certain height, and then, if a line from his eye through his toe touched the opposite bank, he knew that he could jump it. I asked him how he knew when he held his leg at the right angle, and he said he knew the hitch very well. An Irishman told me that he held up one leg and if he could bring his toe in a range with his eye and the opposite bank he knew that he could jump it. Why, I told him, I can blot out a star with my toe, but I would not engage to jump the distance. It then appeared that he knew when he had got his leg at the right height by a certain hitch there was in it. I suggested that he should connect his two ankles with a string. (*Journal*, 2: 51–52, after 16 July 1850)

36. Thoreau, *A Week*, 911.

37. Ibid., 877.

38. Schneider, 93, 107.

39. Davis, 82.

40. Davis, 65. For a sampling of critical attitudes toward the Coast Survey, see the editorial "Survey of the Coast of the United States," *Hunt's Merchants' Magazine*, February 1849, 131–49.

41. Davis, 65, 67, 73.

42. Thoreau, *PJournal 3*, 96 (16 July 1850):

"According to Lieutenant Davis, the forms, extent, and distribution of sand-bars and banks are principally determined by tides, not by winds and waves. On sand-bars recently elevated above the level of the ocean, fresh water is obtained by digging a foot or two. It is very common for wells near the shore to rise & fall with the tide—It is an interesting fact that the low sand-bars in the midst of the ocean, even those which are laid bare only at low tide, are reservoirs of fresh water at which the thirsty mariner can supply himself. Perchance like huge sponges, they hold the rain and dew which falls on them, and which, by capillary attraction, is prevented from mingling with the sur-rounding brine."

43. Thoreau to Ralph Waldo Emerson, November 14, 1847, in *Correspondence*, 190.

44. Thoreau's journal reports the encounter. "Conversed with John Downes, who is connected with the Coast Survey" (*PJournal 3*, 241, June 1851). That same year Downes's report, titled *Occulations Visible in the United States during the Year 1851*, was published by the Smithsonian Institution. Downes had been a

friend and colleague of the Coast Survey superintendent's from Bache's days at the University of Pennsylvania.

45. Among Thoreau's surveying-related documents is a page of data entitled "Diurnal Magnetic Variations in Declination deduced from five days' continuous observation at Cambridge, Mass." Thoreau's penciled note at the bottom of the document states, "This sheet written for me by Wm. C. Bond June 9, 1851." Henry David Thoreau Papers, 1836–[1862], Series II: "Survey-Related Notes, Mss., Etc., 1840–1861," Concord Free Public Library.

46. In 1845, the *Biblical Repository and Princeton Review* had noted the appointment of Bond, who would "make a series of astronomical observations at Cambridge" that would have "beneficial effects on the science of the country." "Review of The Coast *Survey,*" *The Biblical Repository and Princeton Review* 17: 2 (April 1845), 321; retrieved January 3, 2009, from American Periodicals Series Online database.

47. Bond is especially prominent in Bache's 1851 *Annual Report of the Superintendent of the Coast Survey,* which praises his work on what came to be known as the "American method" of determining longitude. Bache's summary of Coast Survey activities for that year underscores that Bond's "determination of difference in longitude by the telegraph" was an important innovation accomplished "for the first time, as part of a geodetic work" (6).

48. "Lovering & Bond on Mag. Observations at Cambridge," Henry David Thoreau Papers, 1836–[1862], Series II: "Survey-Related Notes, Mss., Etc., 1840–1861," Concord Free Public Library. In Bronson Alcott's *Superintendent's Report of the Concord Schools to the School Committee,* for the year 1860–61, Thoreau recommended maps produced by the Coast Survey as among "the best he knows" (50).

49. As indicated in his "Field-Notes," Thoreau conducted experiments in terrestrial magnetism and became interested in the phenomenon of diurnal magnetic variation in his surveying work during the same summer he discussed these topics with Bond. McLean speculates that Bond had "likely" been the inspiration for the experiments (McLean, 571).

50. Thoreau, *PJournal 3,* 297 (9 July 1851).

51. Ibid.

52. Thoreau's chapter "The Highland Light" epitomizes his focus on commercial shipping—"'If the history of this beach could be written from beginning to end, it would be a thrilling page in the history of commerce" (*A Week,* 960)—but not at the expense of extensive botanical observation or patriotic pride in the Cape region: "I saw this was a place of wonder. . . ." (971).

53. Thoreau, *Walden,* 19.

54. Ibid.

55. Ibid., 279–280.

56. *Annual Report of the Superintendent of the Coast Survey, 1853* (Washington: Robert Armstrong, 1854), 10.

57. Thoreau, *Walden*, 281.

58. Bache, *Annual Report of the Superintendent of the Coast Survey, 1853*, 10; Davis, 68.

59. Saunders, 4.

60. Thoreau, *Walden*, 19.

61. Ibid. When Thoreau espouses his entrepreneurial desire "to be your own telegraph, unweariedly sweeping the horizon, speaking all passing vessels bound coastwise" (19), he refers specifically to a noted scientific innovation adopted by Bond for the Coast Survey: the use of the signals of the magnetic telegraph to calculate meridian differences and determine accurate longitudes.

62. Thoreau, *Walden*, 310.

63. Davis, 69.

64. Ibid., 70, 68, 81.

65. Thoreau, *Walden*, 20.

66. Ibid.

67. Ibid., 89.

68. Ibid., 20. As Jeffrey Cramer notes in his excellent annotated edition of *Walden*, tare and *tret* are "measures used in calculating the net weight of goods. Tare is a deduction for the wrapping or receptacle containing the goods; tret is a 'good measure' allowance of 4 pounds in every 104 pounds for waste or damage" (20).

69. Thoreau, *Walden*, 282.

70. Ibid.

71. Ibid.

72. Ibid.

73. Ibid., 49.

74. "What is Talked About," *Literary World* 3: 98 (December 16, 1848), American Periodicals Series Online, 925; accessed January 5, 2009.

75. Henry, 195. Quoted also in Slotten, "Dilemmas," 29.

76. Linklater, *Measuring*, 163.

77. Thoreau, *Walden*, 83.

78. Ibid., 160.

79. Ibid., 161.

80. Ibid., 19.

CHAPTER 4. The Skillful Engineer

1. James, 56.

2. Thoreau, *PJournal* 1, 197 (11 November 1840).

3. Ibid., 198. The Princeton University Press *Journal* restores calculations for the Cliff Hill leveling exercise that had been excised from Torrey's 1906 edition.

4. Stoller, 53. Stoller speculates that this survey took place in September 5, 1845, but acknowledges that the date is possibly erroneous.

5. Thoreau, *Walden*, 17.

6. Moss, 3. Moss describes a "signed receipt from the Misses Hosmer for surveying their woodlot and making a plan of the same dated Dec. 18, 1845" (3). The survey itself is no longer extant.

7. Stoller, 53. Emerson's account book records his payment to Thoreau on April 27, 1847.

8. Harding, 197; Emerson, *Letters*, 3: 397.

9. Harding, 220. In his letter to the secretary of his class at Harvard, Thoreau wrote, "I am a Schoolmaster—a Private Tutor, a Surveyor—a Gardener, a Farmer—a Painter, a Carpenter, a Mason, a Day-Laborer, a Pencil-maker, a Glass-paper Maker, and sometimes a Poetaster" (Thoreau, *Correspondence*, 186).

10. Stoller, 50–51. Stoller estimates that the cost of printing *A Week* was "not very much less than $450 . . . for one thousand copies, half to remain unbound."

11. For a detailed accounting of Thoreau's finances during this period, see Stoller 51–52. Stoller argues persuasively for a direct link between the debt incurred for *A Week* and Thoreau's serious pursuit of surveying jobs beginning about 1850.

12. Borst, 139.

13. Wetherbee, 192. For information about Cyrus Hubbard, see Wetherbee's *Memoirs*, 192–94.

14. The first page of Thoreau's "Field-Notes" includes the following notation made in connection with the November 1849 survey of Isaac Watts's woodlot: "With Hubbard's compass & chain."

15. Borst 144. The Concord Town Board, using Henry's survey, approved John Thoreau's proposed road on April 2, 1849.

16. Surveying historian Silvio Bedini describes the King family as "among the earliest and most distinguished dynasties of mathematical instrument makers in New England" (256). Benjamin King established the shop in Salem in 1764. Under the direction of Charles Gedney King, the company moved to Boston in 1839. King showed his compasses at Massachusetts fairs in the 1840s and 1850s and won several awards for his instruments, "the performance of which," he boasted, "cannot be surpassed" (Bedini, 257).

17. Thoreau, "Field-Notes," 2.

18. Located in the Special Collections of the Concord Free Public Library.

19. When Thoreau died in 1862, he left a sizable body of his working papers—including surveying field notes and draft surveys—in the care of his sister Sophia. At her death in 1876, Sophia Thoreau formally bequeathed the trunk containing the surveys to the Concord Free Public Library, where the collection is still located. The library's holdings comprise over 190 of Thoreau's surveys made between 1846 and 1860, along with the aforementioned volume of surveying field notes made between 1849 and 1861. In 2003, the surveys were scanned and made available for public Internet access: http://www.concordnet.org/library/scollect/Thoreau_surveys/Thoreau_surveys.htm.

20. See Davies, 53–54. Thoreau's annotated copy of this book is in The Concord Free Public Library's Special Collections. Davies notes the use of marking pins "made of iron, about ten inches in length and an eighth of an inch in thickness." The pins were strung on an iron ring that was attached to a surveyor's belt. Two six-foot-long staves were also standard. These were passed through the rings at the end of the chain and secured in the ground to hold the chain in place while it was stretched or pulled for measurements (54).

21. See Kenneth Walter Cameron, "Emerson's Fight," 90–95.

22. See Robbins, 2. Describing techniques and equipment used also by Thoreau, Robbins notes that "with ordinary skill in chaining," an error of "one part in three or four hundred" might be expected when running line "through tangled undergrowth or some forest lands."

23. Thoreau often went back and made later emendations to his notes, but these were mainly concerned with linking the notes to the plan they were used to produce, not with improving the accuracy of his measurements.

24. For a detailed account of the Concord River flowage controversy and Thoreau's role in it, see Donohue, 46–67. See also Hoy, 63.

25. Alcott, *Essays on Education*, 174.

26. Thoreau, *PJournal 3*, 273 (22 June 1851).

27. Wood, 74. Wood includes a photograph and description of this chain. See also his chapter on Thoreau's surveying equipment (74–83).

28. The advantage of the Gunter's chain lies in the easy conversion of its measurements into acreage. Ten square chains equals an acre. The 100 links of the chain also provide decimalization. For example, 5 chains and 22 links equals 5.22 chains, facilitating the calculation of acreage data.

29. Though some smaller house-lot surveys made by Thoreau include distances in feet and decimals of feet, these were usually given for the property owner's convenience.

30. There are numerous instances in both the "Field-Notes" and on copies of draft surveys that show measurements made with a standard chain. On a draft, for example, of his 1853 survey of a new road to Bedford (located in the Thoreau Survey Collection of the Concord Free Public Library), Thoreau converts 25.07 chains into a measure of 100 rods and 7 links—to get the measure in rods, he multiplies the number of chains by four (not three, as he would if he had been using the three-rod chain owned by the museum).

31. After I shared my concerns about the chain, Concord Museum curator David Wood and Concord Free Public Library curator of Special Collections Leslie Perrin Wilson were helpful in determining a gap in its provenance. The three-rod engineer's chain was among the items bequeathed to Sophia Thoreau and donated to the museum "before 1909 by Cummings Davis or George Tolman" (Wood, 75). Between 1862 and the time when the chain found its way to the museum, however, Sophia Thoreau had sold Henry's surveying equipment at auction to Sampson Mason Jr., a surveyor and collector of surveying instru-

ments. Wood speculated that the nonstandard chain currently in the museum did not go to auction and was instead left behind at the Thoreau Main Street house because it was known to be without value.

32. Thoreau, *Walden*, 79.

33. Handbill announcing Thoreau's availability as a surveyor, Berg Collection, New York Public Library.

34. Harding, 84.

35. Alcott, *Journals*, 1: 239 (January 22, 1851).

36. Thoreau, *Familiar Letters*, 251 (February 27, 1853).

37. Town of Concord, *Reports of the Selectmen, 1874–1875* (also referred to as Concord's Annual Report), 42. Quoted in Hoeltje, 359, and in Leslie Wilson's "Concord Library Scans Thoreau Surveys for Internet Access," *Concord Magazine*, January/February 2000, http://www.concordma.com/magazine/janfeboo/thoreausurvey.html.

38. See Ells, "Upernavik." Steve Ells first noticed this small but thought-provoking memo on the Hunt survey, which he analyzes in his brief article.

39. Ells, "Upernavik." Ells argues eloquently that Upernavik may have become for Thoreau "a metaphor to connect Concord with the world of physical danger and human aspiration."

40. Thoreau, *Essays*, 35.

41. Thoreau, *Reform Papers*, 46.

42. Thoreau, *PJournal 6*, 20 (21 March 1853).

CHAPTER 5. Serving Admetus

1. Thoreau, *Familiar Letters*, 118 (August 6, 1843).

2. Ibid., 340 (November 18, 1856).

3. Respective dates of these journal entries are February 11, 1853 (*PJournal 5*, 466), January 1, 1857 (*Journal*, 9: 205) and December 7, 1857 (*Journal*, 10: 221).

4. "This my life in nature . . . is lamentably incomplete. The whole civilized country is to some extent turned into a city, and I am that citizen whom I pity. . . . All the great trees and beasts, fishes and fowl are gone . . . I see that a shopkeeper advertises among his perfumes 'meadow flowers' and 'new-mown hay.'" Thoreau, *Journal*, 8: 221 (22 March 1856).

5. Thoreau, *PJournal 5*, 135 (9 November 1850).

6. Thoreau, *Journal*, 10: 219 (3 December 1857).

7. Thoreau, *Journal*, 8: 319 (30 April 1856).

8. Ibid.; Thoreau, *Journal*, 8: 315 (28 April 1856).

9. Thoreau, *Journal*, 9: 207 (7 January 1857).

10. Thoreau, *Journal*, 8: 363 (3 June 1856).

11. Thoreau, *PJournal 4*, 153 (19 October 1851).

12. Thoreau, *Walden*, 186–187.

13. Thoreau, *Essays*, 162.

14. Stoller, 69.

15. Thoreau, *PJournal 5*, 465–466 (11 February 1853).

16. Harding, 276.

17. Thoreau, *PJournal 4*, 77 (12 September 1851).

18. Ibid.

19. Thoreau, *Writings*, 5: 98.

20. Thoreau, *Journal*, 14: 305–6 (3 January 1861).

21. Thoreau, *PJournal 4*, 77 (12 September 1851).

22. Ibid.

23. *Johnson's and Walker's English Dictionaries*. Boston: Perkins and Marvin, 1830.

24. Thoreau, *PJournal 4*, 101 (26 September 1851).

25. Thoreau, *PJournal 4*, 100–101 (26 September 1851);Ibid., 85 (20 September 1851).

26. Ibid., 85 (20 September 1851).

27. Horace Hosmer, "Reminiscences of Thoreau," *Concord Enterprise*, April 15, 1893, quoted in Cameron, *Contemporary Dimension*, 103.

28. The variation problem is briefly described in Thoreau's "Field-Notes." See also Harding, 276, and McLean 569–70.

29. Horace Hosmer, quoted in Cameron, *Contemporary Dimension*, 103.

30. *Oxford English Dictionary*, 2nd. ed. (Oxford: Oxford University Press, 1989), 11: 518.

31. Thoreau, *PJournal 4*, 83 (16 September 1851).

32. Ibid., 85 (20 September 1851).

33. Thoreau, *PJournal 3*, 150 (25 November 1850).

34. Thoreau, *PJournal 4*, 201–2 (12 December 1851).

35. Ibid., 203–4 (13 December 1851).

36. Ibid., 204 (13 December 1851).

37. Thoreau *PJournal 8*, 59–60 (8 April 1854). Deriving from surveying an experiential and thus literary benefit "equal to a journey" is a particularly apt trope for Thoreau. His expeditions to the Maine woods and Cape Cod, ostensibly retreats from commitments in Concord, were also in large part surveying expeditions, saturated with observations fully intelligible only from a perspective informed by land-measuring technology.

38. Thoreau, *Journal*, 8: 314, (28 April 1856).

39. Thoreau, *PJournal 8*, 55 (5 April 1854).

40. Thoreau, *Journal*, 8: 7 (5 November 1855).

41. Ibid., 330 (11 May 1856).

42. Thoreau, *PJournal 3*, 321 (21 July 1851); Thoreau, *Journal*, 10: 146–47 (29 October 1857).

43. Thoreau, *PJournal 4*, 85 (20 September 1851).

CHAPTER 6. The Science of the Field Notes

1. According to its original "Rules and Objects," a document available on the current AAAS website, the organization sought to establish a cohesive organization that would "aid in bringing together and combining the labours of individuals who are widely scattered, into an institution that will represent the whole." This quest began under the leadership of Alexander Dallas Bache and founding members Louis Agassiz, Joseph Henry, Benjamin Peirce, Henry Darwin Rogers and his brother William Barton Rogers, James Dwight Dana, Oliver Wolcott Gibbs, Benjamin A. Gould, William Redfield and Benjamin Silliman Jr.: http://archives.aaas.org/exhibit/origins2.php.

2. Thoreau, *PJournal 5*, 469 (5 March 1853).

3. Ibid., 470 (5 March 1853).

4. Thoreau, *Correspondence*, 309–10.

5. Thoreau, *PJournal 5*, 469–70 (5 March 1853).

6. Despite turning down the offer, Thoreau was added to the AAAS organization roll for 1853 only. Thoreau is touted on the current AAAS website.

7. See Morton, Samuel G., *Crania Americana* (Philadelphia: J. Dobson, Chestnut Street; London: Simkin, Marshall, 1839.) See also Schoolcraft, Henry Rowe, *Historical and Statistical Information Respecting the History, Condition and Prospects of the Indian Tribes of the United States*, 6 vols. (Philadelphia: Lipincott, Grambo, 1851–1857) and Agassiz, Louis, *Contributions to the Natural History of the United States of America*, 2 vols. (Boston: Little, Brown, 1857).

8. Harding, 429.

9. Joshua D. Bellin's article "In the Company of Savagists" argues that Thoreau largely accepted the framework of ethnologic racism espoused by his scientific contemporaries. Jessie Bray takes an opposing position, calling for a chronological reading of the Indian notebooks and arguing that Thoreau "refuses to reify oppressive, Western models for assessment" of Indian culture (Bray, 4).

10. Bray, 4.

11. After a close study of the Indian notebooks, Bray suggests that Thoreau's failure to directly "advocate on behalf of Indian philanthropies—Indian schools, reservations and missions, etc.—was a function of his acceptance of *real* Indians" (9). Bray also notes Thoreau's surprise at Joe Aitteon's anglicized manners.

12. Thoreau, *A Week*, 696–97.

13. Sattelmeyer, 108. For another useful treatment of the development of Thoreau's interest in Native Americans, see ibid., 99–109.

14. Ibid., 107–8.

15. Thoreau, *Walden*, 204. See also the journal entry of August 18, 1854: "I have just been through the process of killing the cistudo for the sake of science; but I cannot excuse myself for this murder, and see that such actions are inconsistent with the poetic perception, however they may serve science, and will affect the quality of my observations" (*PJournal 8*, 278).

16. The preface to the 1833 edition of White's *Selborne* offers this brief biographical sketch:

Being of an unambitious temper, and strongly attached to the charms of rural scenery, he early fixed his residence in his native village, where he spent the greater part of his life in literary occupations, and especially in the study of Nature. This he followed with patient assiduity, and a mind ever open to the lessons of piety and benevolence, which such a study is so well calculated to afford. Though several occasions offered of settling upon a college living, he could never persuade himself to quit the beloved spot, which was indeed a peculiarly happy situation for an observer. Thus his days passed tranquil and serene, with scarcely any vicissitudes other than those of the seasons . . . till they closed at a mature age, on June 26, 1793. (iii–iv)

17. Ralph Waldo Emerson may have been the first to discern likenesses between White and Thoreau: in a preliminary note to Thoreau's "Natural History of Massachusetts" in the July 1842 *Dial*, Emerson referred to his friend as a possible successor to "White of Selborne." See Hyde's edition of Thoreau, *The Essays*, 2.

18. White, *Selborne*, 26.

19. Humboldt, "Author's Preface to First Edition," vi.

20. Humboldt, "Author's Preface to the Second and Third Editions," viii.

21. Ibid., vii.

22. Ibid., viii.

23. Thoreau, *PJournal* 5, 469 (5 March 1853).

24. Dassow Walls, 138.

25. A possible exception is the Albert F. McLean article, which looked closely at the "Field-Notes" entry describing Thoreau's sighting of the polestar.

26. Hoy, 62.

27. Wilford, 175.

28. George Dunbar, LS, "Following in Sometimes Faulty Footsteps," *Professional Surveyor* 16: 6 (September 1996).

29. Perhaps for this reason, Thoreau made a practice observation. As the field notebook indicates, he had "not very successfully" determined a variation of 9⅝° on the evening of February 6.

30. As Concord historian Jayne Gordon clarified for me in July 2009, the house that currently stands across from the Thoreau house on Main Street would not have obstructed his view of the polestar—it was not built until 1859.

31. Davies, 131–32.

32. Thoreau, *Walden*, 85.

33. On page 63 of his notes, Thoreau used two exclamation points in noting the discrepancy between his own variation and that used on a previous map: "Var. named on map 5°54'!! It should be 9¼+." The next day, July 3, he made nine observations between 7 a.m. and 7 p.m. to check the true north/magnetic

north variation, following these with seven more readings between 7 a.m. and 1 p.m. on July 5, four more on July 12, and two more on July 14.

34. McLean notes that the simple fact of variance between magnetic and true north had been known to Thoreau "at least as early as his college years" (568). Thoreau had probably even carried out an observation of the polestar for the benefit of his students at the Concord Academy in the winter of 1840–41. At this time, however, Thoreau appears not to have pursued larger meanings in the process of celestial observation. He did not make celestial readings for his 1846 survey of Walden Pond or in connection with his surveying work prior to the Polaris sighting described in the field notes of 1851.

35. Thoreau Survey Collection, Concord Free Public Library website, survey 148—"White Pond Feb. 17 [1851]," http://www.concordnet.org/library/scollect /Thoreau_surveys/148/148-d.jpg.

36. Robbins, 34. Finding true meridian, Robbins observes, enables the surveyor or the navigator "to determine his position on the surface of the earth" (34).

37. Thoreau, *PJournal 5*, 446–47 (21 January 1853).

38. Thoreau, *Reform Papers*, 3–17.

39. Thoreau, *Essays*, 17.

40. Thoreau, *PJournal 4*, 114 (1 October 1851).

41. Thoreau, *Walden*, 68.

42. Thoreau to Harrison Blake, May 20, 1860, in *Familiar Letters*, 418–19.

43. Thoreau, *Essays and Lectures*, 20.

44. Ibid., 25.

45. Ibid., 44.

46. McLean has also acknowledged the ways this updating of Thoreau's Walden survey was "no accident, but a carefully selected and suggestive gleaning from the *Field Notes* of February 1851" (577).

47. It seems certain that Thoreau's figure represents a difference of vertical level and not horizontal distance, first because Thoreau's diction in indicating the "top of the rail" and the "surface" (not the edge or bank) of the pond suggests a vertical measurement. In July of 2006, I measured the horizontal distance between the bank of Walden Pond and the top of the rail of the railroad tracks at three separate points along the pond's westernmost extremity. With the water level of Walden Pond unusually high, the distances were 39 feet 9 inches, 40 feet 6 inches, and 41 feet 2 inches. In March 2008, Andy Kis and I returned to the same area and remeasured, recording a distance of 38 feet 9 inches. Separate readings of the difference in level between the pond surface and the top of the rail—also taken in 2006 and 2008—yielded results of 20 feet 5 inches, 20 feet 6 inches, and 21 feet 11 inches, which are all close to the measurement given in Thoreau's field notes. Thoreau's measurement is given in feet and inches, normal for recording differences of level and used in recording the water depths of Thoreau's pond surveys. He recorded his linear distances in rod-chain-link units.

48. Thoreau, *Walden*, 109.

49. Marx, 250. Credit goes to Marx for pointing out that Thoreau added this statement to "The Iron Horse," an earlier-published description of the locomotive at Walden Pond that appeared in volume 11 of *Sartain's Union Magazine of Literature and Art* (July 1852), 66–68.

50. Thoreau, *A Week*, 936.

51. Ibid., 935–36.

52. Marx, 251.

53. Buell, 120.

54. Marx, 251.

55. Thoreau, *Walden*, 290.

56. Ibid., 289.

57. Buell, 134.

58. Thoreau, *Walden* 287.

59. Marx, 262 (my italics).

60. Worster, 57. For a discussion of this aspect of Thoreau's legacy, see also Buell, 136 and 477n55.

61. Thoreau, *Journal*, 8: 315–16 (28 April 1856). This account of the lecture's origin is derived in part from Harding, 438–40.

62. Gordon G. Whitney and William Davis, "From Primitive Woods to Cultivated Woodlots: Thoreau and the Forest History of Concord, Massachusetts," *Journal of Forest History* 30 (April 1986): 70–81.

63. Thoreau, *Walden*, 182.

64. Emerson, "Thoreau," 482.

65. The online collection of Thoreau surveys of the Concord Free Public Library includes thirty-five of Thoreau's woodlot plans.

66. Thoreau Survey Collection, Concord Free Public Library website, survey 59—"Plan of a White Pine Woodlot, Large Growth, Dec. 28, [18]57," http://www.concordnet.org/library/scollect/Thoreau_surveys/59/59-a.jpg.

67. Thoreau Survey Collection, Concord Free Public Library website, survey 63c—"Moore & Hosmer Woodlots by Walden," http://www.concordnet.org/library/scollect/Thoreau_surveys/63c/63c-a.jpg.

68. Thoreau Survey Collection, Concord Free Public Library website, survey 31a—"RWE [Ralph Waldo Emerson] Lot by Walden . . . Dec. 1857," http://www.concordnet.org/library/scollect/Thoreau_surveys/31a/31a-a.jpg.

69. Thoreau Survey Collection, Concord Free Public Library website, survey 104—"J. Richardson's Heirs Walden Pond Lot Dec. 2 & 3, 1857," http://www.concordnet.org/library/scollect/Thoreau_surveys/104/104-a.jpg.

70. Thoreau, *Excursions*, 165 66. "The Succession of Forest Trees" was originally delivered to the Middlesex Agricultural Society in Concord on September 20, 1860, and printed in the *New York Tribune* for October 6, 1860.

71. Among these views, Lawrence Buell's recent discussion provides a frank assessment of Thoreau's oppositional voice in this address, which does not de-

tract from Thoreau's "ability to package nature usefully" in an argument whose underlying aim is "less to disorder the status quo than to strengthen it, and by implication prove the author's value to society." See Buell, 136–39.

72. Harding, 439.

73. Thoreau, *Journal*, 10: 221 (7 December 1857).

74. Ibid.

75. Emerson, "Thoreau," 453–54.

76. Harding, 438–39.

77. Another noteworthy example of the nonstandard uses of the "Field-Notes" is a detailed table in the back of the notebook describing the etymologies, historical origins and equivalencies for weights and measures in France and England during several historical periods. Thoreau discusses measuring terms from the "Paris Perch" and "Acre de Normandie" to English feet and furlongs.

78. Thoreau to Spencer F. Baird, December 19, 1853, in *Correspondence*, 309–10.

79. Thoreau, *Walden*, 273.

80. Emerson, "Thoreau," 453–54.

81. Thoreau, *Walden*, 298.

82. Emerson, "Thoreau," 474.

CHAPTER 7. The Concord Surveyor and the Kansas Surveyor

1. John Brown to Owen Brown, March 26, 1856. John Brown Collection, Hudson Library and Historical Society, Hudson, Ohio.

2. Evan Carton's *Patriotic Treason* gives a brief but useful account of the motives of Brown's surveying activities in Kansas (179–80).

3. Henry Thompson to Ruth Thompson, April 16, 1856, quoted in Villard, 133.

4. Carton notes that Brown "surveyed each grantee's property" (120) in Smith's New York settlement and "[made] sure that the tracts were properly delineated" (116). See also "Former Land Surveyor Hanged," 3.

5. "Former Land Surveyor Hanged," 4.

6. Sanborn, *Recollections*, 103.

7. Ibid.

8. Thoreau, *Reform Papers*, 77.

9. Ibid., 108.

10. "Former Land Surveyor Hanged," 4. The full quote reads, "It is obvious that most, if not all, of [Brown's] Kansas surveying was to further the abolitionist cause in 'Bleeding' Kansas where John and his sons had dedicated themselves to the irrepressible conflict."

11. Villard notes that "surveying was to give [Brown] a livelihood while he remained" in Kansas (93). The famed abolitionist is said to have used this equipment mostly in Anderson, Linn and Bourbon counties. He formed a partnership with Simon B. McGrew, who settled southwest of Mound City and had been

trained as a surveyor. Brown and McGrew often worked together on survey projects. Like Brown, McGrew was an outspoken Free State advocate. Known as the Fighting Quaker, he was opposed to war and violence but kept a pair of Colt Navy revolvers on hand for protection. It is likely that both men used their surveying skills as a pretense for tracking proslavery men. Two of Brown's sons usually accompanied their father on surveying outings. Territorial Kansas Online features a collection of primary sources relating to Brown's activities in Kansas, http://www.territorialkansasonline.org/cgiwrap/imlskto/index.php.

12. Carton, 165.

13. "It was in the early part of May that John Brown executed a maneuver which has often been related, not always in the same manner, and which he may have repeated when necessary—his visit to the camp of the proslavery men in the guise of a land-surveyor" (Sanborn, *John Brown*, 229).

14. Sanborn, *John Brown*, 230.

15. E. A. Coleman, quoted in Sanborn, *John Brown*, 259. According to Coleman's account, Brown later showed him and his wife the field notebook in which the conversations were recorded. In interviews conducted in the 1880s, John Brown Jr. confirmed that "the running of that line occurred a few days before our second call to assist Lawrence, May 20, 1856" (Sanborn, *John Brown*, 260).

16. Ruth Wheeler, "John Brown in Concord," *Concord Journal*, October 15, 1959, 1, 4.

17. Brown, "An Idea of Things in Kansas" (notes prepared for his addresses in Concord and other New England meetings on Kansas affairs early in 1857). Quoted in Sanborn, *John Brown*, 243–46 and Hinton, 611–14.

18. Sanborn, *John Brown*, 243. Numerous sources confirm the idea that Kansans and Missourians would have taken Brown for a government surveyor who was in the employ of President Pierce and Kansas governor Shannon and therefore likely to be proslavery in his views. See especially Carton, 180.

19. Alcott, *Journals*, 2:315. The date of Brown's lecture is established by Sandra Harbert Petrulionis in her excellent recent study, *To Set This World Right* (128). In January of 1859, Thoreau had also conversed at length with George L. Stearns, one of Brown's most important financial supporters, who spent an afternoon at Walden Pond with Thoreau and Emerson and "devoted a good part of his time extolling Brown's virtues," reportedly convincing Thoreau of Brown's heroism (Harding, 416).

20. "A Plea for Captain John Brown" drew extensive commentary in the daily press and was reported or summarized in the Boston *Traveler*, the Boston *Journal*, the *Boston Atlas and Daily Bee*, the *New-York Daily Tribune* and the *Liberator*. It was reprinted in full in James Redpath's *Echoes of Harper's Ferry* in 1860.

21. Petrulionis, 136.

22. Thoreau, *Reform Papers*, 112.

23. Ibid., 115–16.

24. Letter, James Hanway to R. J Hinton, December 5, 1859. Territorial Kan-

sas Online; accessed January 3, 2009, http://www.territorialkansasonline.org/cgiwrap/imlskto/index.php.

25. Hughes, *Surveyors and Statesmen*, 156.

26. Linklater, *Fabric*, 124.

27. Ibid., 128.

28. Ibid., 226.

29. Ibid., 187.

30. A fascinating fictional treatment of Brown's heroic surveying is Mary E. Jackson's *The Spy of Osawatomie; or, The Mysterious Companions of Old John Brown* (St. Louis: W. S. Bryan, 1881). Jackson's novel dramatizes Brown and his men running their line as surveyors through the camp of proslavery "invaders" in the Kansas territory (255). To a lesser degree, Russell Banks' more recent *The Cloudsplitter* (New York: HarperCollins, 1999) acknowledges Brown's use of surveying tactics in Kansas.

31. Thoreau, *Reform Papers*, 116.

32. Thoreau, *Journal*, 12: 428 (22 October 1859).

33. Albrecht, 393.

34. Stewart, 30. In addition to access rights, the U.S. Land Law of 1830 explicitly gave legal protections to surveyors of public lands, stipulating that "any person who shall . . . interrupt, hinder, or prevent the surveying of the public land of the United States . . . shall be fined a sum not leas than fifty dollars nor more than three hundred dollars, and be imprisoned for a period of time not less than three years" (Stewart, 30). Persons interfering in the enforcement of the Fugitive Slave Law could be jailed for up to six months and fined up to one thousand dollars.

35. Phillips, 741–42.

36. Ibid., 741.

37. Thoreau, *Journal*, 12: 433 (22 October 1859). Walter Harding observed that Thoreau's intended but never completed book about Native Americans might have influenced American history by advancing recognition of Indian rights and cultural contributions. See Harding, 428–29.

38. Thoreau, *A Week*, 744.

39. Ibid., 815.

40. Ibid., 745–46, 769.

41. Ibid., 726.

42. Anderson, 45.

43. Carton, 260.

44. Sandra Petrulionis attributes this sentiment to Mary Stearns, wife of abolitionist and Brown-supporter George Stearns (155).

CHAPTER 8. "I am a surveyor"

1. Ralph Waldo Emerson letter to Elizabeth Hoar, August 3, 1859, quoted in Harding, 411.

2. Thoreau, *Journal*, 12: 219 (5 July 1859). Torrey's explanation was given in footnote form to this journal entry. The full text of Thoreau's journal, including the excised material from the period of the river survey, is now available online at the website of The Thoreau Edition, in conjunction with Princeton University Press and the Davidson Library at the University of California, Santa Barbara, http://www.library.ucsb.edu/thoreau/project_main.html.

3. Thoreau, *Journal*, 12: 225 (7 July 1859); Thoreau, *Journal*, 12: 303 (30 August 1859).

4. Donohue, 52. Donohue provides an overview of the Concord River flowage controversy, on which my summary of the case relies.

5. One product of Thoreau's work for the River Meadow Association is a chart he compiled showing the type of material and date of construction for the bridges between East Sudbury and Billerica. Located in the Henry David Thoreau Papers, 1836–[1862], Series II: "Survey-Related Notes, Mss., Etc., 1840–1861" of the Concord Free Public Library, the chart includes such information as which bridges were the oldest, newest, shortest and longest; the average height of the bridges; the greatest, least and average width of the river at these points; areas of "swiftest water" and "narrowest width"; and the average water depths at summer level.

6. Thoreau, *Journal*, 12: 211 (22 June 1859).

7. Ibid., 247 (20 July 1859).

8. Thoreau, *Journal*, 13: 149 (16 February 1860).

9. Massachusetts General Court, *Report of the Joint Committee of the Legislature, March 27, 1862* (Boston, 1862), 10. Quoted also in Donahue, 57.

10. Thoreau, *Journal*, 12: 53–54 (17 March 1859).

11. Thoreau, Journal, 14: 37–39 and 43–44, (9 August 1860). The reference work Thoreau consulted is geologist Edward Hitchcock's *Final Report on the Geology of Massachusetts* (Boston: J.H. Butler, 1841).

12. Thoreau, *Journal*, 13: 219, (5 July 1859).

13. As Glick explains, the title "Life Without Principle" was suggested by *Atlantic Monthly* editor James T. Fields. In a letter to Fields of March 4, Thoreau appears to have accepted the change (*Reform Papers*, 369).

14. Thoreau, *Reform Papers*, 158, 155.

15. Ibid., 158.

16. Ibid., 155.

17. Ibid., 156.

18. Ibid., 156–57.

19. Ibid., 160, 159.

20. Ibid., 160.

21. Ibid., 158.

22. Ibid., 159.

23. Ibid., 157, 164.

24. Ibid., 160.

25. Thoreau, *Essays*, 150.

26. Ibid., 153.

27. Ibid., 153–54. The source of the passage is a fragmented journal entry (*Journal*, 2: 94–95, 11 November 1850).

28. Thoreau, *Essays*, 163.

29. Ibid., 157.

30. Ibid., 153.

31. Ibid., 157.

32. Ibid.

33. Ibid.

34. Ibid., 158.

35. Ibid., 157–158.

36. Davies, 95.

37. By avoiding closure, Thoreau's parabola also counteracts the intersecting grid lines made famous by the ongoing U.S. Public Land Survey, which parceled out the entire western United States into thirty-six-square-mile sections that were subdivisible only to smaller and smaller squares.

38. Thoreau, *Essays*, 158.

39. Ibid., 164.

40. Ibid., 165–166.

41. Ibid., 171.

42. Ibid., 173.

43. Thoreau, *Reform Papers*, 84; Thoreau, *Essays*, 173–74.

44. Thoreau, *Journal*, 14: 56–57 (22 August 1860).

45. Ibid.

46. Undated manuscript, Thoreau Surveying Papers, Concord Free Public Library, Box 1, Folder 10.

47. Emerson, "Thoreau," 480.

48. In 2003, a group of university surveying students and their instructor attempted to retrace several Thoreau surveys near Walden Pond. Looking for the points of reference described in the surveys, they apparently located two split stones that Thoreau had used to mark a line on Emerson's property. The group attested to the accuracy of Thoreau's measurements, but in their careful search of the area around Walden Pond, no more monumentation was found. See Savage, 43.

49. Thoreau, *Essays*, 174. A draft version of this passage appears in Thoreau's journal of October 31, 1850 (*PJournal* 3, 125).

50. With the exception of the years 1975 to 1978. The State of Massachusetts removed the cairn in 1975 and replaced it in 1978 (see James Dawson, "A History of the Cairn," *Thoreau Society Bulletin* 232 (Summer 2000): 1–3).

51. Thoreau, *Walden*, 196.

Bibliography

Albrecht, Robert. "Thoreau and His Audience: 'A Plea for Captain John Brown.'" *American Literature* 32: 1 (January 1961): 393–402.

Alcott, Amos Bronson. *Essays on Education*. Edited by Walter Harding. Gainesville, Fla.: Scholars' Facsimiles, 1960.

———. *The Journals of Bronson Alcott*. 2 vols. Edited by Odell Shepard. Port Washington, N.Y.: Kennikat Press, 1966.

Ammen, Daniel. *The Old Navy and the New*. Philadelphia: J. B. Lippincott Company, 1891.

Anderson, Osborne. *A Voice From Harper's Ferry: A Narrative of Events at Harper's Ferry*. Boston, 1861.

Bedini, Silvio. *With Compass and Chain: Early American Surveyors and Their Instruments*. Frederick, Md.: Professional Surveyors Publishing, 2001.

Bellin, Joshua. "In the Company of Savagists: Thoreau's Indian Books and Antebellum Ethnology." *Concord Saunterer: A Journal of Thoreau Studies*, n.s., 16 (2008): 1–32.

Borst, Raymond R. *The Thoreau Log: A Documentary of the Life of Henry David Thoreau, 1817–1862*. New York: G. K. Hall, 1992.

Bray, Jessie. "'A so-called savage tribe': Defying the Culture of Imperialism in Thoreau's Indian Writings." Lecture, Thoreau Society Annual Gathering, Concord, Mass., July 9, 2009.

Buell, Lawrence. *The Environmental Imagination: Thoreau, Nature Writing, and the Formation of American Culture*. Cambridge, Mass: Harvard University Press, 1995.

Cameron, Kenneth Walter. *Contemporary Dimension: An American Renaissance Literary Notebook of Newspaper Clippings on Alcott, Emerson, Whitman, Thoreau, Hawthorne, Longfellow, Lowell, Holmes, Poe, Bryant, Irving, Whittier, and Others*. Hartford: Transcendental Books, 1970.

———. "Emerson's Fight for His Walden Wood-lots." *Emerson Society Quarterly* 22 (1961): 90–95.

———. "Thoreau in the Court of Common Pleas (1854)." *Emerson Society Quarterly* 14 (1959): 86–89.

Carton, Evan. *Patriotic Treason: John Brown and the Soul of America.* New York: Simon & Schuster, 2006.

Chase, Harry B. "Henry Thoreau, Land Surveyor." *Journal of Surveying and Mapping* 25: 2 (June 1965): 219–22.

Chase, Philander D. "A Stake in the West: George Washington as Backcountry Surveyor and Landholder." In *George Washington and the Virginia Backcountry,* edited by Warren R. Hofstra, 159–94. Madison, Wis.: Madison House, 1998.

Chura, Patrick. "Economic and Environmental Perspectives in the Surveying 'Field-Notes' of Henry David Thoreau." *The Concord Saunterer: A Journal of Thoreau Studies,* n.s., 15 (2007): 37–64.

Cooper, James Fenimore. *The Chainbearer; or, The Littlepage Manuscripts.* 1845. New York: Appleton, 1873.

Daniel, Jim. *Historic Surveying: A Guidebook for Historic Sites.* Greensboro, N.C.: Tudor Publishers, 2002.

Davies, Charles. *Elements of Surveying and Navigation.* Rev. ed. New York: 1847.

Davis, Charles H. "The Coast Survey of the United States." *American Almanac and Repository of Useful Knowledge (1830–1861),* January 1, 1849: 65. American Periodicals Series Online. ProQuest. University of Akron. http://www .proquest.com.proxy.ohiolink.edu:9099/; accessed January 3, 2009.

Deevey, Edward S. "A Re-Examination of Thoreau's *Walden.*" *Quarterly Review of Biology* 17: 1 (March 1942): 1–11.

Donohue, Brian. "'Dammed at Both Ends and Cursed in the Middle': The 'Flowage' of the Concord River Meadows, 1798–1862." *Environmental Review,* Fall/Winter 1989: 46–67.

Drinnon, Richard. "Thoreau's Politics of the Upright Man." In *Thoreau in Our Season,* edited by John Hicks. Amherst: University of Massachusetts Press, 1962.

Ells, Steve. "The Lost Lincoln-Concord Town Boundary in Walden Pond." Steve Ells' Thoreau Research Page, rev. April 8, 2005. http://homepage.mac.com/ sfe/henry/index.html; accessed January 6, 2009.

———. "Upernavik, the most northerly inhabited spot on the globe." Steve Ells' Thoreau Research Page. http://homepage.mac.com/sfe/henry/index.html; accessed July 16, 2009.

Emerson, Ralph Waldo. *Essays and Lectures.* Edited by Joel Porte. New York: Library of America, 1983.

———. *The Letters of Ralph Waldo Emerson.* Edited by Eleanor Marguerite Tilton. New York: Columbia University Press, 1995.

———. "Thoreau." In *The Complete Works of Ralph Waldo Emerson.* 12 Boston: Houghton, Mifflin, 1904. Vol. 10: 449–85.

"Former Land Surveyor Hanged at Charlestown, Virginia—December 2, 1859." *Empire State Surveyor* 5: 2 (March-April 1969): 3–6.

George, Henry. *Progress and Poverty.* New York, 1879.

Harding, Walter. *The Days of Henry Thoreau*. New York: Knopf, 1966.

Henry, Joseph. 'Biographical Memoir of Alexander Dallas Bache." In *Biographical Memoirs, National Academy of Sciences, 1877*. Vol. 1: 181–212d.

Hinton, Richard J. *John Brown and His Men*. Rev. ed. London: Funk & Wagnalls Company, 1894.

Hoeltje, Hubert. H. "Thoreau in Concord Church and Town Records," *New England* Quarterly 12 (June 1939): 349–59.

Howard, Richard. "A New Look at Henry Thoreau the Surveyor." *Professional Surveyor* 3: 1 (January/February 1983): 30–33.

Hoy, Thorkild. "Thoreau as a Surveyor." *Journal of Surveying and Mapping* 36: 1 (March 1976): 59–65.

Hughes, Sarah S. *Surveyors and Statesmen: Land Measuring in Colonial Virginia*. Richmond: The Virginia Surveyors Foundation, 1979.

Humboldt, Alexander von. *Aspects of Nature, In Different Lands and Different Climates, With Scientific Elucidations*. Translated by Mrs. Sabine. Philadelphia: Lea and Blanchard, 1849. Second and Third Editions, London: John Murray, 1850.

Huston, Reeve. "Land and Freedom: The New York Anti-Rent Wars and the Construction of Free Labor in the Antebellum North." In *Labor Histories: Class Politics and the Working-Class Experience*, edited by Eric Arneson, Julie Greene, and Bruce Laurie, 19–43. Urbana: University of Illinois Press, 1998.

James, Mary Ann. "Engineering an Environment for Change: Bigelow, Peirce, and Early Nineteenth-Century Practical Education at Harvard." In *Science at Harvard University: Historical Perspectives*, edited by Clark A. Elliott and Margaret W. Rossiter, 55–75. Bethlehem, Penn.: Lehigh University Press, 1992.

Linklater, Andro. *The Fabric of America: How Our Borders and Boundaries Shaped the Country and Forged Our National Identity*. New York: Walker, 2007.

———. *Measuring America: How the United States Was Shaped by the Greatest Land Sale in History*. New York: Penguin Group, 2003.

Longmore, Paul. *The Invention of George Washington*. Berkeley: University of California Press, 1988.

Love, John. *Geodaesia; or, The Art of Surveying and Measuring of Land Made Easie*. London, 1688.

Marchitello, Howard. "Political Maps: The Production of Cartography and Chorography in Early Modern England." In *Cultural Artifacts and the Production of Meaning*, edited by Margaret M. Exell and Katherine O'Brian O'Keeffe, 13–40. Ann Arbor: University of Michigan Press, 1994.

Marx, Leo. *The Machine in the Garden: Technology and the Pastoral Ideal in America*. New York: Oxford University Press, 1967.

McLean, Albert F., Jr. "Thoreau's True Meridian: Natural Fact and Metaphor." *American Quarterly* 20: 3 (Autumn 1968): 567–79.

Melville, Herman. *Tales, Poems and Other Writings*. Edited by John Bryant. New York: The Modern Library, 2001.

Moss, Marcia. *A Catalog of Thoreau's Surveys in the Concord Free Public Library.* Thoreau Society Booklet 28. Geneseo, N.Y.: The Thoreau Society, 1976.

Newman, Russell T. *The Gentleman in the Garden: The Influential Landscape in the Works of James Fenimore Cooper.* Lanham, Md.: Lexington Books, 2003.

Petrulionis, Sandra Harbert. *To Set This World Right: The Antislavery Movement in Thoreau's Concord.* Ithaca, N.Y.: Cornell University Press, 2006.

Phillips, Wendell A. "Three Interviews with Old John Brown." *Harper's Monthly,* December 1979, 738–44.

Robbins, Arthur G., S.B. *An Elementary Treatise on Surveying and Navigation.* Boston: D. C. Heath, 1909.

Sanborn, Franklin B. *The Life and Letters of John Brown; Liberator of Kansas, and Martyr of Virginia.* Concord, Mass.: F. B. Sanborn, 1910.

———. *Recollections of Seventy Years.* Boston: The Gorham Press, 1909.

Sattelmeyer, Robert. *Thoreau's Reading: A Study in Intellectual History.* Princeton, N.J.: Princeton University Press, 1988.

Saunders, Judith. "Economic Metaphor Redefined: The Transcendental Capitalist at Walden." *American Transcendentalist Quarterly* 36 (Fall 1977): 4–7.

Savage, Barry. "The Quintessential Surveyor." *Point of Beginning* (April 2003): 42–45.

Schneider, Richard J. *Henry David Thoreau.* Boston: Twayne Publishers, 1987.

Shanley, J. Lyndon. *The Making of Walden: With the Text of the First Version.* Chicago: University of Chicago Press, 1957.

Slotten, Hugh Richard. "The Dilemmas of Science in the United States: Alexander Dallas Bache and the U.S. Coast Survey." *Isis* 84(1993): 26–49.

———. *Patronage, Practice, and the Culture of American Science: Alexander Dallas Bache and the U.S. Coast Survey.* Cambridge, Eng.: Cambridge University Press, 1994.

Smith, John. *The General History of Virginia, New England, and the Summer Isles.* London: 1624.

Stewart, Lowell O. *Public Land Surveys: History, Instructions, Methods.* Ames, Iowa: Collegiate Press, 1935.

Stoller, Leo. *After Walden: Thoreau's Changing Views on Economic Man.* Stanford, Cal.: Stanford University Press, 1957.

Stowell, Robert F. *A Thoreau Gazetteer.* Edited by William L. Howarth. Princeton, N.J.: Princeton University Press, 1970.

Thoreau, Henry David. *The Correspondence of Henry David Thoreau.* Edited by Walter Harding and Carl Bode. New York: New York University Press, 1958.

———. *The Essays of Henry David Thoreau.* Edited by Lewis Hyde. New York: Farrar, Straus and Giroux, 2002.

———. *Excursions.* Edited by Joseph J. Moldenhauer. Princeton, N.J.: Princeton University Press, 2007.

———. *Familiar Letters of Henry David Thoreau.* Edited by F. B. Sanborn. Cambridge, Mass.: Riverside, 1894.

———. "Field-Notes of Surveys Made by Henry D. Thoreau Since November 1849." Special Collections. Concord Free Public Library, Concord, Mass.

———. *Journal, Volume 1:1837–1844.* Edited by Elizabeth Hall Witherell, William L. Howarth, Robert Sattelmeyer and Thomas Blanding. Princeton, N.J.: Princeton University Press, 1981.

———. *Journal, Volume 2: 1842–1848.* Edited by Robert Sattelmeyer. Princeton, N.J.: Princeton University Press, 1984.

———. *Journal, Volume 3: 1848–1851.* Edited by Robert Sattelmeyer and Mark R. Patterson, William Rossi. Princeton, N.J.: Princeton University Press, 1990.

———. *Journal, Volume 4: 1851–1852.* Edited by Leonard N. Neufeldt and Nancy Craig Simmons. Princeton, N.J.: Princeton University Press, 1992.

———. *Journal, Volume 5: 1852–1853.* Edited by Patrick F. O'Connell. Princeton, N.J.: Princeton University Press, 1997.

———. *Journal, Volume 6: 1853.* Edited by William Rossi and Heather Kirk Thomas. Princeton, N.J.: Princeton University Press, 2000.

———. *Journal, Volume 7: 1853–1854.* Edited by Nancy Craig Simmons and Ron Thomas. Princeton, N.J.: Princeton University Press, 2009.

———. *Journal, Volume 8: 1854.* Edited by Sandra Harbert Petrulionis. Princeton, N.J.: Princeton University Press, 2002.

———. *The Journal of Henry David Thoreau.* Edited by Bradford Torrey and Francis H. Allen. 14 vols. Boston: Houghton Mifflin, 1906; New York: Dover, 1962.

———. *Reform Papers.* Edited by Wendell Glick. Princeton, N.J.: Princeton University Press, 1973.

———. *Walden.* Edited by Jeffrey S. Cramer. New Haven: Yale University Press, 2004.

———. *A Week, Walden, The Maine Woods, Cape Cod.* New York: Library of America, 1985.

———. *The Writings of Henry David Thoreau.* 20 vols. Boston: Houghton Mifflin, 1906.

Van Noy, Rick. *Surveying the Interior: Literary Cartographers and the Sense of Place.* Reno: University of Nevada Press, 2003.

Villard, Oswald Garrison. *John Brown: 1800–1859, A Biography Fifty Years Later.* 1910. New York:. Knopf, 1943.

Walls, Laura Dassow. *Seeing New Worlds: Henry David Thoreau and Nineteenth-Century Natural Science.* Madison: University of Wisconsin Press, 1995.

Wetherbee, Rebecca. "Memoir of Cyrus Hubbard." In *Memoirs of Members of the Social Circle in Concord,* From 1795 to 1840, 2nd ser., 192–94. Cambridge, Mass., 1888.

White, Gilbert. *The Natural History of Selborne.* 1789. Oxford: Oxford University Press, 1993.

Wilford, John Noble. *The Mapmakers.* New York: Knopf, 1981.

Wilson, Donald A. "Early Land Surveyors in New England." In *Plotters and*

Planners of American Land Surveying: A Collection of Articles from the Archives of the American Congress on Surveying and Mapping, edited by Roy Minnick. Rancho Cordova, Cal.: Landmark Enterprises, 1985.

Wilson, Leslie Perrin. "Concord Library Scans Thoreau Surveys for Internet Access." *Concord Magazine,* January/February 2000.

———. "Thoreau's Manuscript Surveys: Getting Beyond the Surface." *Concord Saunterer: A Journal of Thoreau Studies,* n.s., 15 (2007): 24–35.

Wood, David F. *An Observant Eye: The Thoreau Collection at the Concord Museum.* Concord, Mass.: Concord Museum, 2006.

Worster, Donald. "The Subversive Science: Thoreau's Romantic Ecology." Part 2 in *Nature's Economy: A History of Ecological Ideas.* 1977. 2nd ed. Cambridge, Eng.: Cambridge University Press, 1994.

Index